IMAGES
of America

CLARKE COUNTY

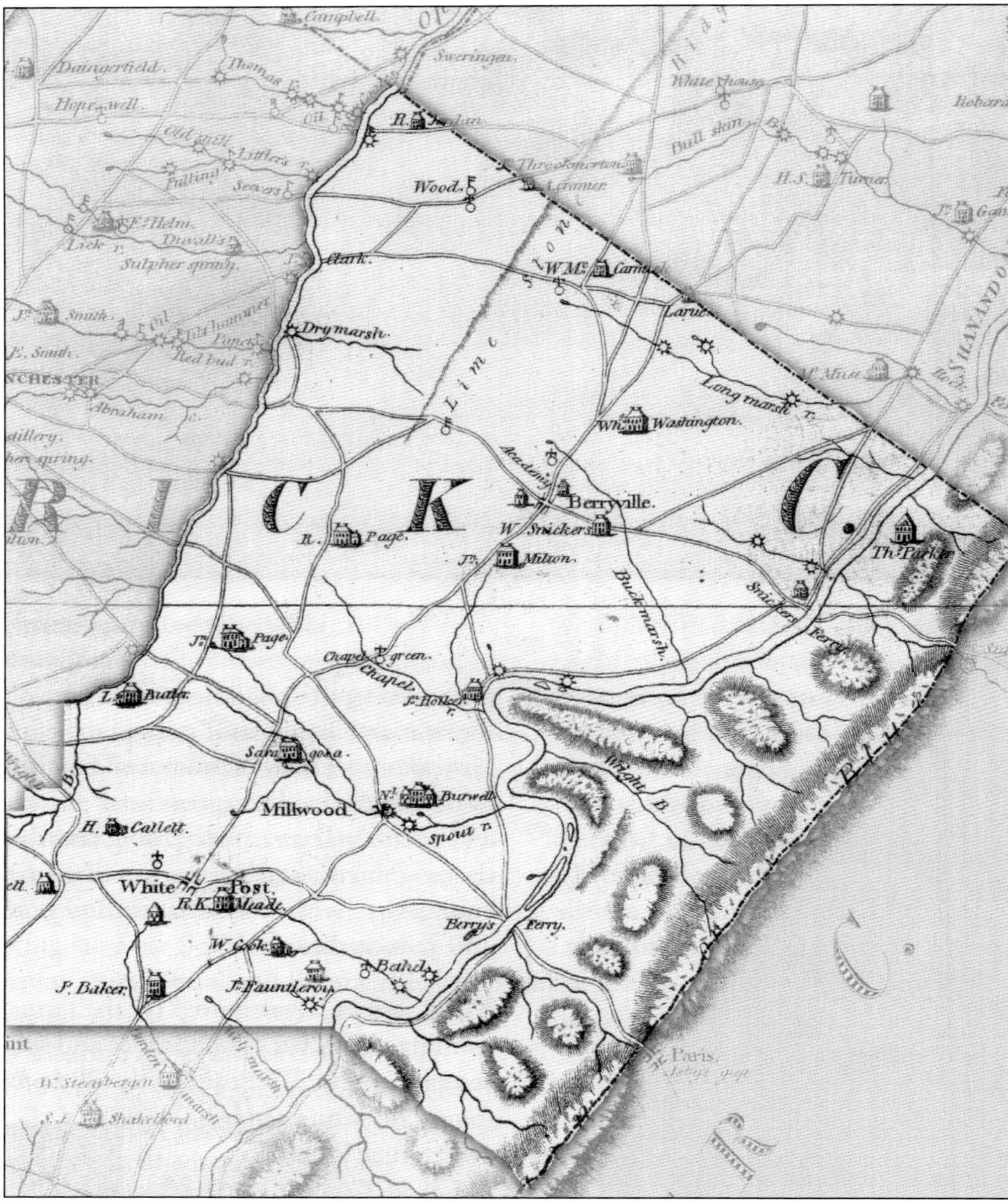

This 1809 Charles Varle map of Frederick, Berkeley, and Jefferson Counties in the state of Virginia appeared in an advertisement designed to attract settlers from Maryland and Pennsylvania to the area. Clarke was part of Frederick County at the time the map was made, but its future boundaries are shown. Early communities, including White Post, Millwood, and Berryville, are depicted along with mills, churches, roads, and some of the larger estates. (Library of Congress.)

On the Cover: Taken in the 1920s, this image of J.L. "Foley" Carper driving a cart of corn pulled by two mules embodies the agricultural tradition of Clarke County that continues today. Carper, who lived west of Boyce, often stored his wheat in tall mounds until it was threshed. (Herman Lloyd.)

IMAGES of America

CLARKE COUNTY

Maral S. Kalbian

ARCADIA PUBLISHING

ISBN 978-0-7385-8249-8

Published by Arcadia Publishing
Charleston, South Carolina

Printed in the United States of America

Library of Congress Control Number: 2010942069

For all general information, please contact Arcadia Publishing:
Telephone 843-853-2070
Fax 843-853-0044
E-mail sales@arcadiapublishing.com
For customer service and orders:
Toll-Free 1-888-313-2665

Visit us on the Internet at www.arcadiapublishing.com

To the extended Clarke County community, past and present, whose appreciation of history provided the inspiration for this project, these are your stories.

Contents

ACKNOWLEDGMENTS

Many people helped in bringing this long-overdue book to publication. I wish to particularly thank Doug Bartley, vice-president of the Clarke County Historical Association (CCHA), who scanned all the images; CCHA president and author Howard Means and historian Margaret Peters, who generously reviewed the text; and archivist Mary Morris, who always provided valuable information. CCHA director Jennifer Lee and Simon McKay also gave immensely helpful comments.

The majority of images in this publication come from the Clarke County Historical Association archives photograph collection in Berryville. I thank all those who have donated their private photographs to the CCHA and made the images of Clarke County's past so accessible. Since 2002, CCHA has been digitizing many of these photographs, making it easier than ever to conduct research. The photograph collection at the Stewart Bell Archives at Handley Regional Library in Winchester (SBA/HRL) also contains images used in this publication.

I heartily thank those who provided access to their private collections: Herman Lloyd, Billy Thompson, Shirley McKay, Gin Mitchell, Barbara Clagett, Tracee Wink, Louise McLaughry, Les Querry, Blandy Experimental Farm, Bonnie Jacobs, Geraldine Keifer, and Fred Alger. I feel privileged that you shared your images with me. Appreciation also goes to the many people who answered questions and provided insight into the county's history, including Dorothy Davis, Houston Wedlock, Chuck Johnston, Frank Scheer, Billy Thompson, Jack Hardesty, Robin Greenhalgh, Nancy Talley, Mary Robare, and Harry Jones.

My husband, Branson, and sons, Simon and Evan, provided moral support for this project. My parents, Ada and Vicken Kalbian, have always shown me through example that anything is possible.

I also wish to thank any and all who I may have forgotten to list but who so kindly offered ideas and searched through their private collections for old images of the county. I appreciate your patience and encouragement. Although I have worked on historical projects in Clarke County for 24 years, this publication allowed me to step back and look at the county as a whole. The richness of its history continues to astound me.

INTRODUCTION

Located only 60 miles northwest of Washington, DC, in the northern Shenandoah Valley, Clarke County has been able to maintain rural and agricultural traditions begun in colonial times. Within this still-pristine setting are an unusually large number of well-preserved historic sites and structures. Modern development has generally been limited to residential construction at the edges of existing communities, with little sprawl outside the established town centers.

Misspelled at the outset, Clarke County was named for Revolutionary War hero George Rogers Clark (without an E) when it was formed in 1836 from Frederick County. Clarke is small in population (about 15,000 residents) and size (174 square miles). Only eight of the commonwealth's 95 counties occupy less space. The Shenandoah River, a State Scenic River, runs south to north through the county, dividing the primarily forested and mountainous land in the east from the rolling agricultural lands in the west. The county's two incorporated towns, Berryville (the county seat) and Boyce, and two villages, White Post and Millwood, are all located west of the Shenandoah. In addition to being part of the John Singleton Mosby Heritage Area, Clarke County also falls within six National Register Historic Districts. Permanent conservation easements protect approximately 20 percent of the county from future development. The county is bounded by the crest of the Blue Ridge Mountains to the east, Warren County to the south, Jefferson County, West Virginia, to the north, and Frederick County and the Opequon Creek to the west.

By the time European explorers entered the Shenandoah Valley in the 1710s, Native Americans had inhabited the region for centuries. Although few Native American groups were still resident, archaeological sites discovered along the banks of the Shenandoah River confirm the limited presence of settlements and hunting activity when Europeans arrived. Today, the Native American habitation survives in the names of Clarke County's principal bodies of water: the Shenandoah River ("Daughter of the Stars") and the Opequon Creek.

All of present-day Clarke County was once part of the five-million-acre Northern Neck Proprietary, which embraced the lands within the heads of the Rappahannock and Potomac Rivers—most of what is now Northern Virginia and eastern West Virginia. Inherited by Thomas Fairfax, Sixth Baron Fairfax of Cameron (1693–1781), through his mother, the proprietary had uncertain boundaries, leading to lengthy disputes between the Virginia colony and Fairfax as to who had the power to assign rights to his land. Regardless, in 1730, Robert "King" Carter—among the wealthiest and most prominent landholders in Tidewater Virginia and one of Lord Fairfax's land agents—granted 50,212 acres of the Northern Neck Proprietary to 10 of his own heirs. The largest portion of this grant encompassed what was later to become Clarke County, and Carter's descendants moved from Tidewater Virginia to settle here in the late 18th century. The remaining parts of the county were distributed in smaller grants, either by Lord Fairfax or the Council of Virginia, or retained by Fairfax as the Manor of Greenway Court (near White Post and his home after 1752) and as the Manor of Leeds.

The rest of the Shenandoah Valley, including Frederick County, was settled primarily by Scots-Irish, English Quakers, and Germans who migrated south from Pennsylvania. The descendants of Carter who eventually moved into the area of Clarke imported their wealth, lifestyle, and slave-based plantation system, all of which are reflected in the structures they built and their land-use patterns. The deep contrast in the economic and cultural differences between the Tidewater settlers and those of the rest of Frederick County contributed to the formation of Clarke County in 1836. The town of Berryville was chosen as the county seat.

Lord Fairfax is only one of the county's many notable historical figures. Bishop William Meade, who led the 19th-century revival of the Episcopal Church in Virginia, was born in White Post. Revolutionary War soldier Daniel Morgan lived in Clarke County and began construction of his home Saratoga while on leave from the war. Brothers and noted mid-19th-century authors John Esten and Philip Pendleton Cooke lived and wrote in Clarke. Other significant figures who hailed from or resided in the county include Warner Washington, cousin of George Washington; "Wild Bill" Donovan, director of the OSS (which later became the CIA); and the Byrd family, led by governor and eventual US senator Harry Flood Byrd, the most influential political leader in 20th-century Virginia.

The early to mid-19th century was very prosperous in Clarke County. Several new mills reflected the emergence of wheat as the primary cash crop of the period. Slaves brought from eastern Virginia made the settlement and production of large plantations possible in Clarke. Beautiful homes echoing popular architectural styles of the day were constructed along with large barns and other ancillary buildings that supported farm operations.

The Civil War brought an abrupt halt to any new construction and growth in Clarke. Troops were constantly passing through the area, and several engagements occurred in Clarke. The most notable was the Battle of Cool Spring, which took place on July 18, 1864, along the banks of the Shenandoah River north of the present-day Route 7 crossing. Although a number of houses, barns, and mills were damaged or lost during the period, Clarke County's buildings suffered little of the widespread destruction that characterized other parts of Northern Virginia and the Shenandoah Valley.

Clarke County experienced much change during the Reconstruction era and late 19th century. Before the Civil War, more than half of the population had been enslaved African Americans. After the war, many freedmen remained in the area and built their own communities, often centered on their schools and churches. The construction of the Shenandoah Valley Railroad in 1880 led to the creation of the town of Boyce as well as several other small hamlets along the line. Bridges carrying traffic on Routes 7 and 50 across the Shenandoah River replaced ferries that had plied the river's waters for a century or more.

The early 20th century saw an influx of wealthy residents from the North, drawn to the county by affordable land, a milder climate, and the presence of fox hunting, first initiated by Lord Fairfax. Many remodeled existing houses, while others chose to construct new ones along with massive horse-related outbuildings. Some built summer homes along the Blue Ridge, attracted by the mountain's cooler climate.

Clarke's economy has always been agriculturally based, beginning with wheat planted and harvested by slaves and shipped to eastern markets along the Shenandoah River. By 1900, apples replaced wheat as the mainstay of the local agricultural community, as they did in other regions of the Shenandoah Valley. Competition from western and foreign markets made orchards unprofitable by the close of the 20th century. Although farming is no longer the primary economic force in the county, Clarke has maintained its picturesque rural quality through innovative land-use policies.

One

Early History and Settlement

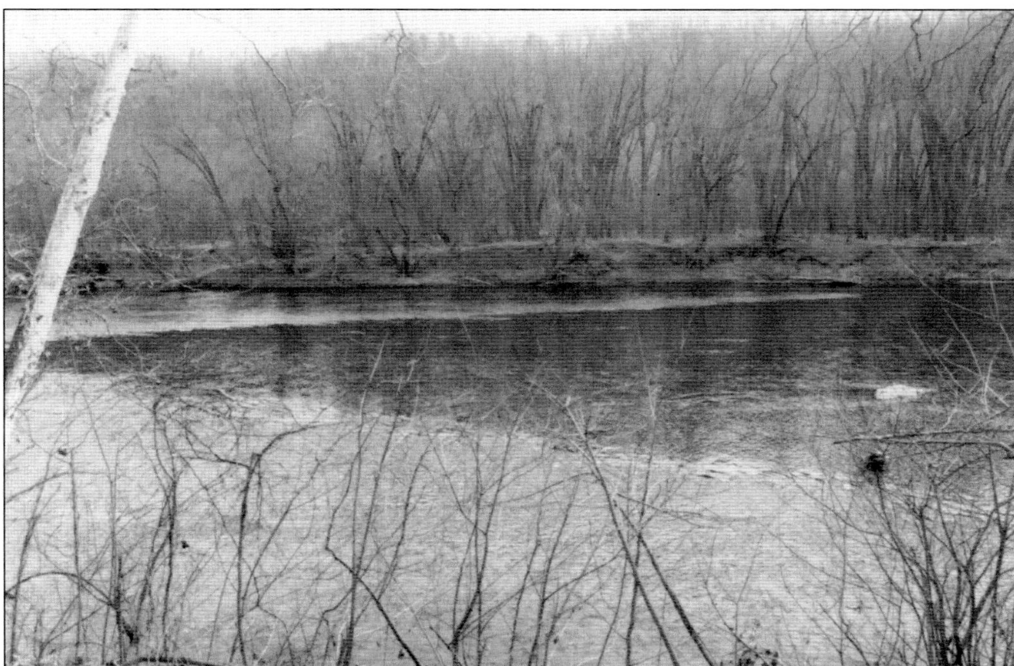

Three V-shaped stone structures exist in the Shenandoah River in Clarke. Generally believed to have been constructed by Native Americans, these weirs originally had taller walls and would have forced fish to the central opening at the point of the V, where nets waited. Although Native Americans had left the area by the early 18th century, it is known that they came back for hunting purposes. (Author.)

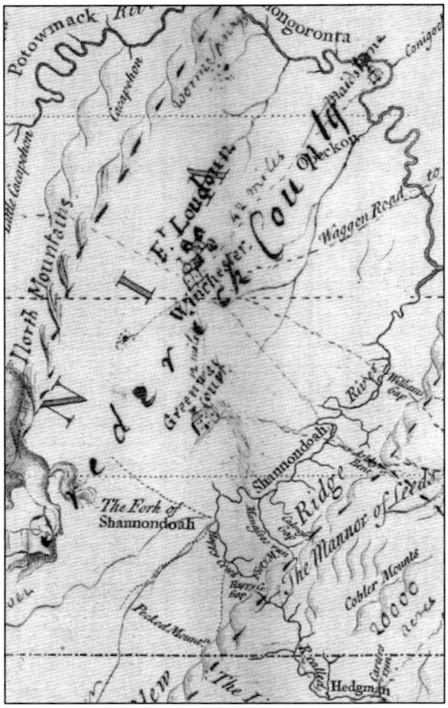

This 1737 map was undertaken by John Warner to establish the westernmost boundary of lands that belonged to Lord Fairfax. Known as the Northern Neck Proprietary, this 5,282,000-acre tract was situated between the headwaters of the Rappahannock and the Potomac Rivers. The location of Greenway Court, Winchester, and some of the old roads west of the "Shannondoah River" were later added, probably in the 1750s. (Library of Congress.)

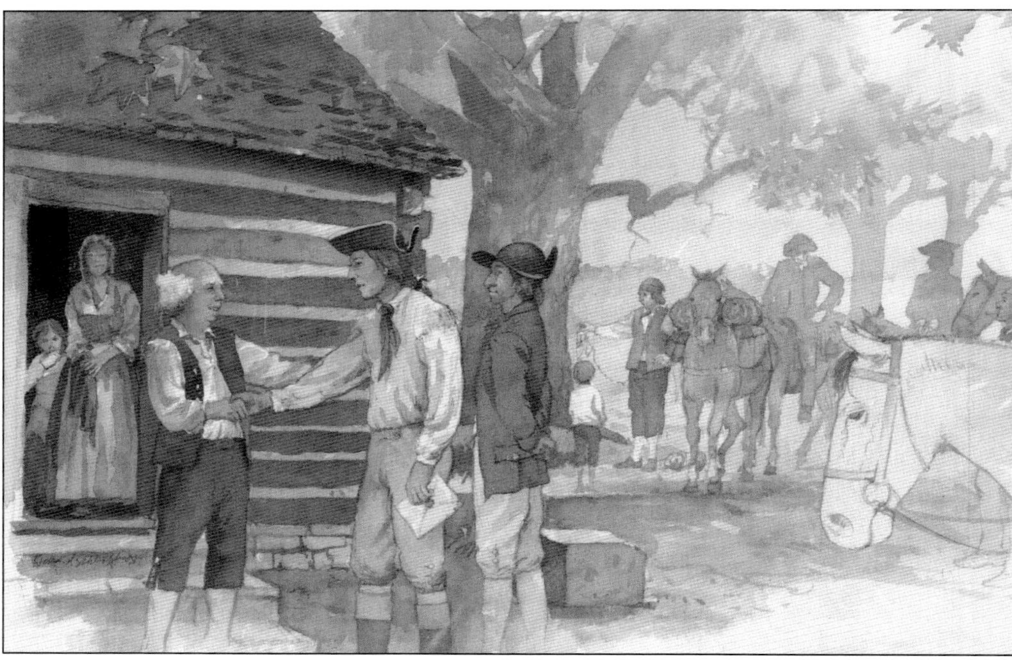

This modern watercolor depicts young George Washington's first entry into the Shenandoah Valley as a surveyor for Lord Fairfax. Washington's diary of March 12, 1748, reads: "We travel'd over ye Blue Ridge to Capt. Ashbys on Shannondoa [*sic*] River." Washington considered Fairfax a mentor and patron and while working for him accumulated important skills and knowledge about the frontier that he later used in his military service. (CCHA.)

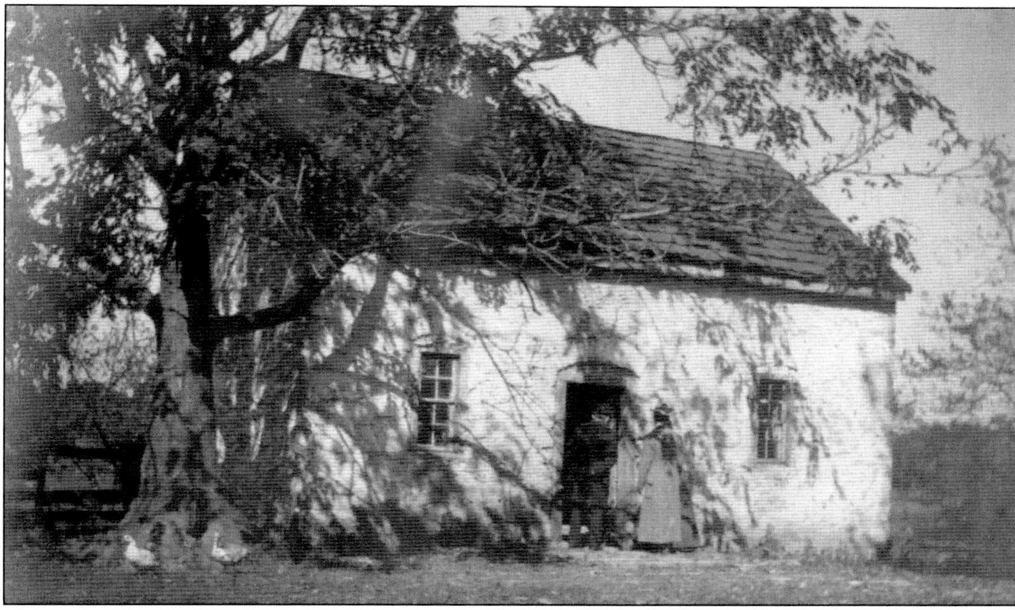

This stone building, constructed in 1761 at Greenway Court outside of White Post, was used by Lord Fairfax as a land office from which he managed his Northern Neck Proprietary holdings. The unassuming structure where quit rents were received, land records kept, and land disputes heard was a major center of colonial business in the region and is arguably one of the most significant buildings in the commonwealth. (CCHA.)

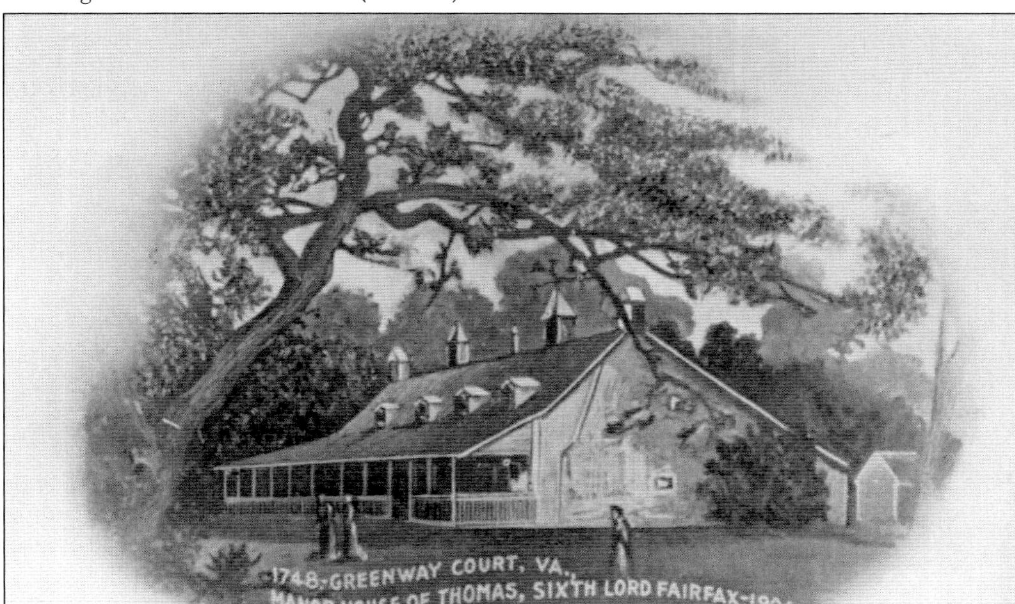

Lord Fairfax's Greenway Court was visited by many significant historical figures, even after his death in 1781. Writing in 1845, historian Henry Howe included a sketch of Fairfax's house, which had been demolished by that time, a long stone dwelling with dormers and multiple cupolas. Similar sketches of Fairfax's house appeared in other publications, including numerous postcards like this one from 1904, attesting to the continued interest in him. (CCHA.)

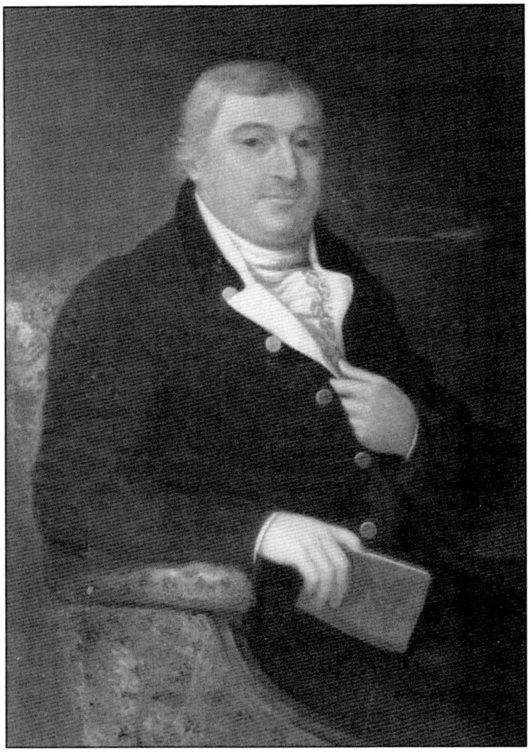

Col. Nathaniel Burwell (1750–1814) moved to Clarke in the late 18th century, built a vast estate at Carter Hall in Millwood, and played a central role in the construction of the Burwell-Morgan Mill and Old Chapel. Like many of his wealthy relatives, he relocated from the Tidewater to land in Clarke inherited from Robert "King" Carter and imported his slave-based plantation system. (CCHA.)

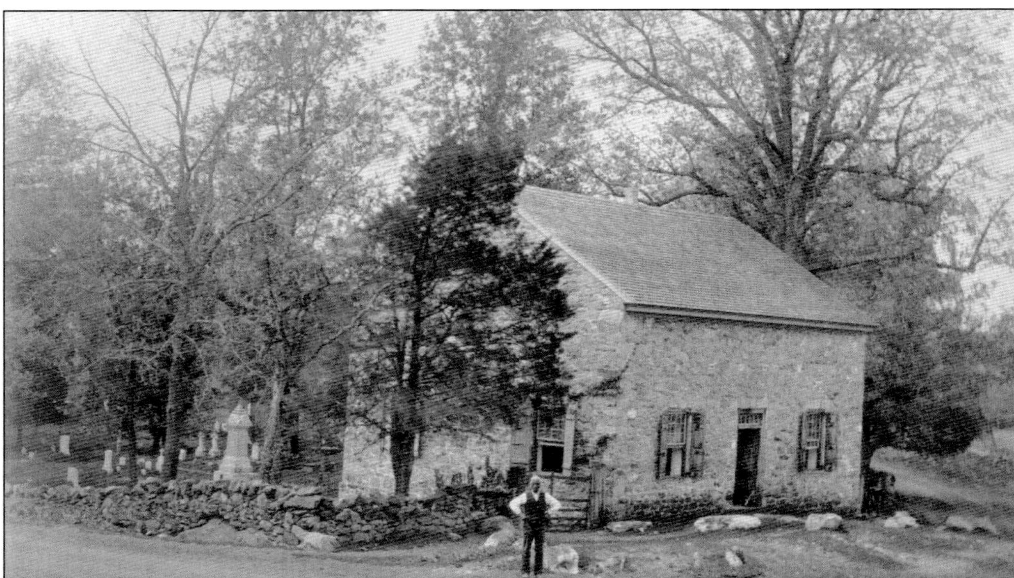

Old Chapel is considered the earliest Episcopal church west of the Blue Ridge Mountains. Built in 1793 by Nathaniel Burwell of Carter Hall, it served the local Episcopal congregation, many of whom were descendants of prominent Tidewater families. The interior of the chapel retains most of its original woodwork, including the pulpit and box pews. This postcard from about 1900 shows Nat Carter, the longtime sexton. (Author.)

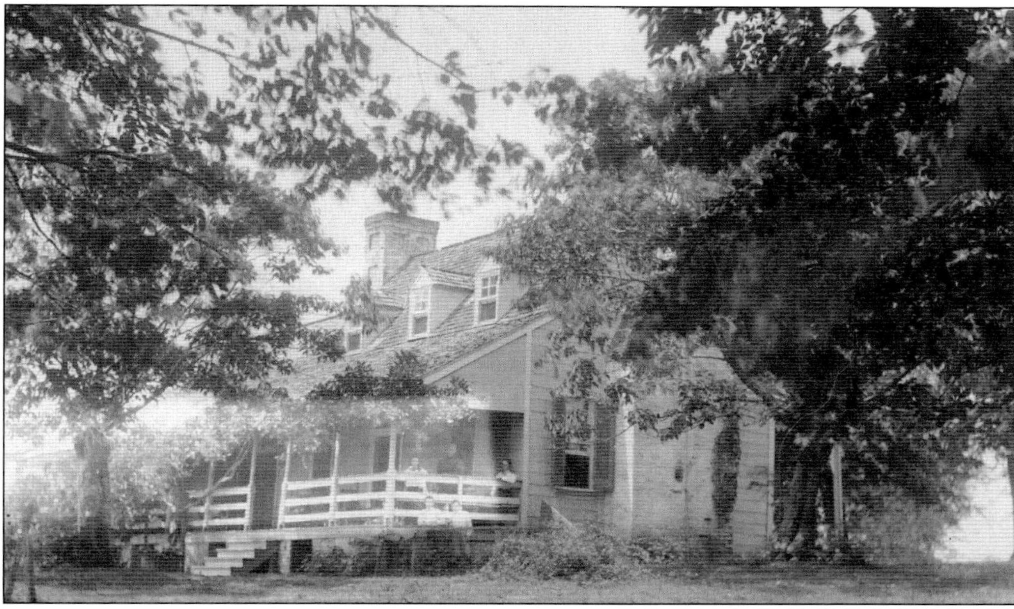

Clermont was constructed in 1756 by Thomas Wadlington, a planter from Fairfax County. Dated by experts from Oxford University in 2010, Clermont is believed to be one of the earliest surviving dwellings in Clarke. The McCormick family owned the property from 1819 until 2004, when Elizabeth Rust Williams left it to the Virginia Department of Historic Resources and a local foundation to manage it as a working farm. (Clermont Foundation.)

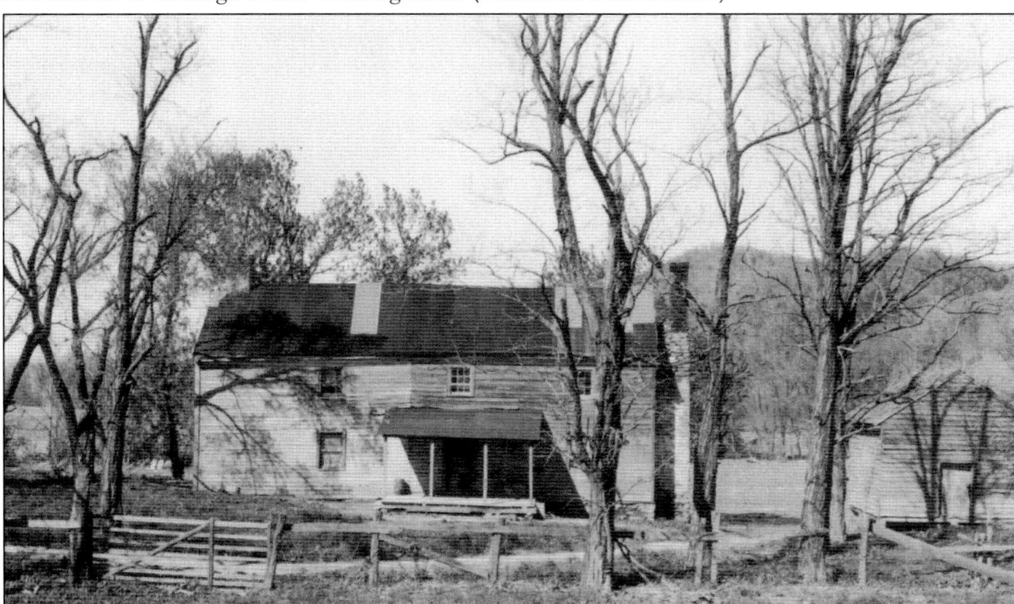

Known as the Long House because additions were made lengthways, this building is typical of early log dwellings with large exterior-end stone chimneys. Located east of the Shenandoah River near the Route 50 crossing and associated with Joseph Berry, the house was flooded on numerous occasions, finally succumbing to the massive storm of October 1942, when between 10 and 17 inches fell in a three-day period. (SBA/HRL.)

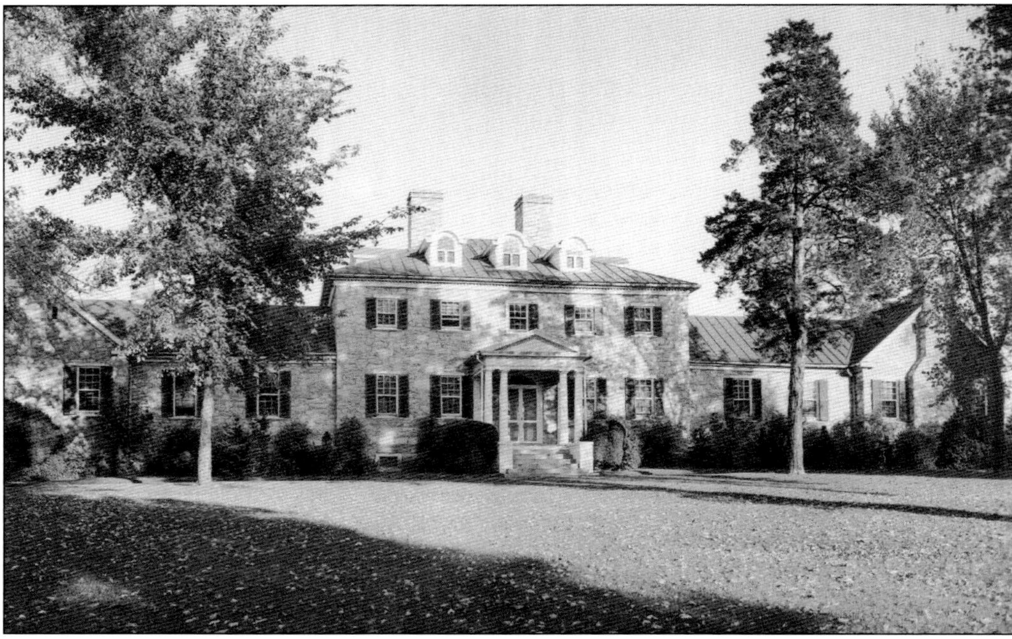

The central portion of Fairfield was constructed around 1770 by Warner Washington, cousin to George. The Washingtons held extensive acreage in northern Clarke as well as in neighboring Jefferson County, West Virginia. In contrast to the southern portion of the county, most of which was included in the Carter land grant, northern Clarke was settled by people of varying backgrounds. (SBA/HRL.)

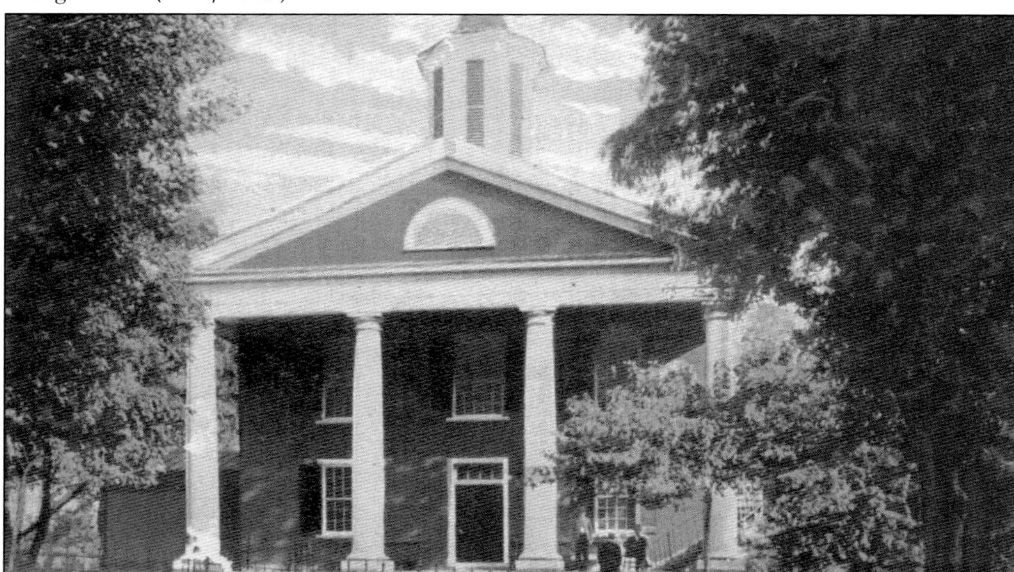

In the early 1830s, residents in eastern Frederick County petitioned the state to form their own county. Grievances included the long distance to the courthouse in Winchester and what they saw as an oppressive tax burden because of the many slaves they owned. Clarke was finally formed in 1836 and the courthouse in Berryville built around 1839 after a design by county justice David Meade. (Author.)

Two

Persons of Note

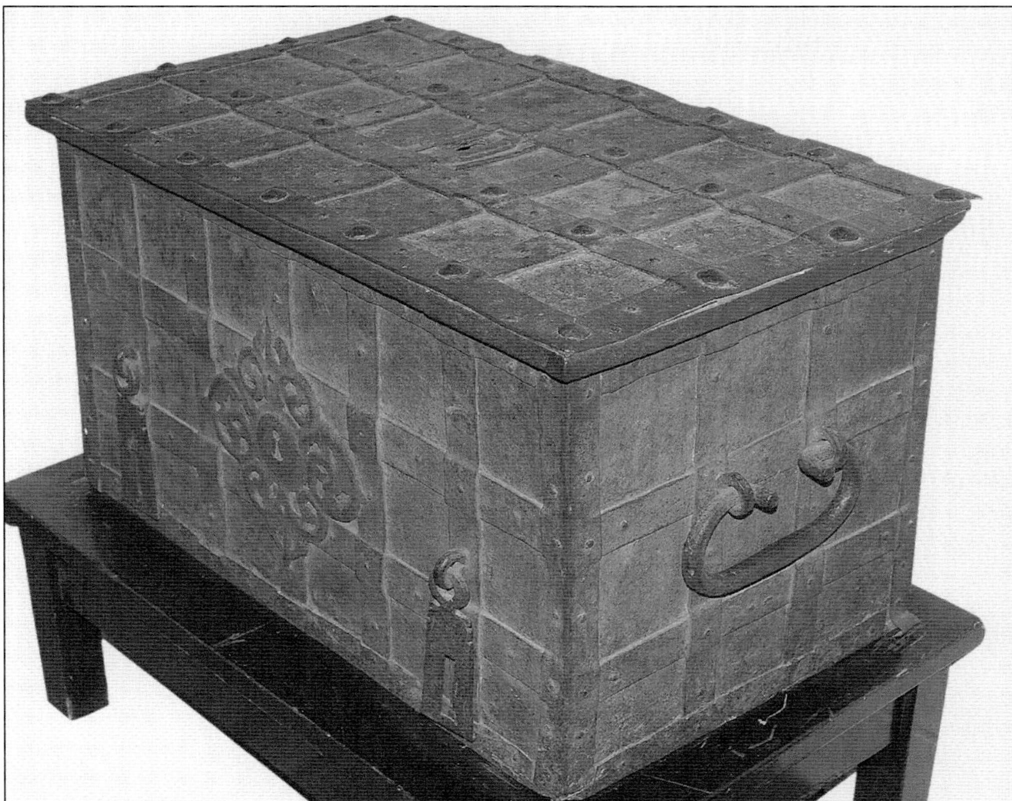

This iron strongbox belonged to Lord Fairfax, the only resident peer of the realm of Great Britain to make his home in the colonies. Known for his liberal hospitality and interest in fox hunting, Fairfax built Greenway Court, a significant center of colonial business and social activity. This money chest was donated to CCHA in 1984 by a Winchester bank that discovered the chest in one of its vaults. (CCHA.)

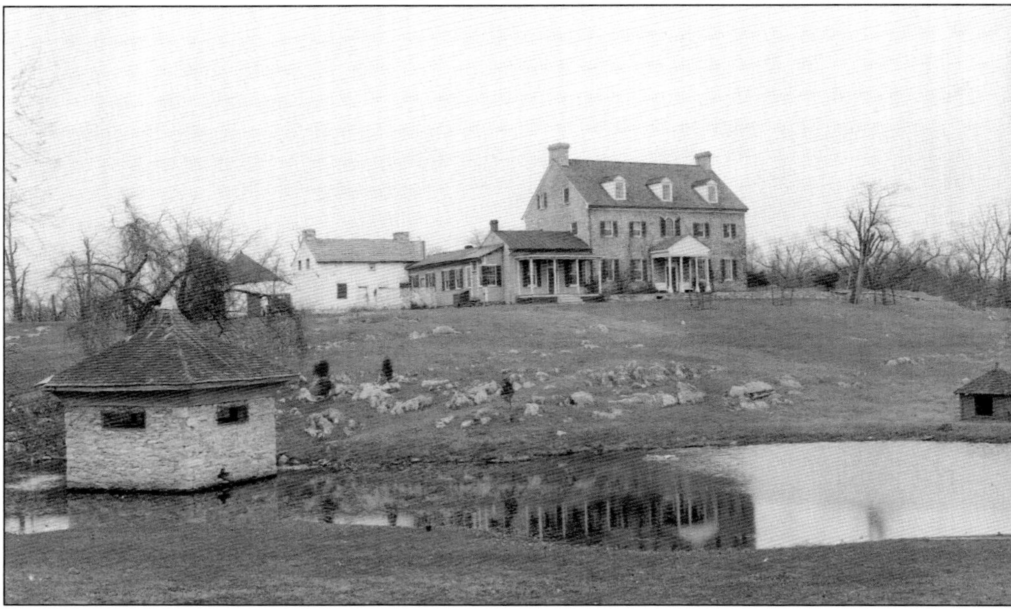

Gen. Daniel Morgan constructed Saratoga, a two-and-a-half-story stone dwelling, around 1780, using the labor of Hessian prisoners of war (German mercenaries working for the British) with which he was charged. Morgan named the house after his Revolutionary War victory near Saratoga Springs in New York. The house is one of two recognized National Historic Landmarks in the county, the other being Greenway Court. (SBA/HRL.)

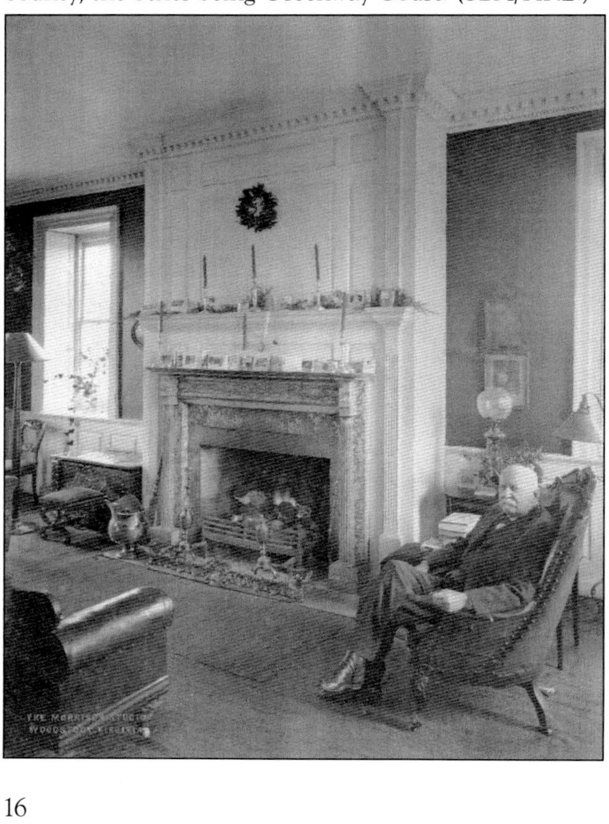

Saratoga continued to be the home of noteworthy figures even after Morgan's death. Brothers John Esten and Phillip Pendleton Cooke, prominent 19th-century writers, briefly lived here, and Stonewall Jackson made his headquarters at Saratoga in November 1862. Robert Powell Page, pictured in the living room around Christmas 1928, inherited the property through marriage to a Burwell, and the property is still in the possession of Burwell descendants. (Gin Mitchell.)

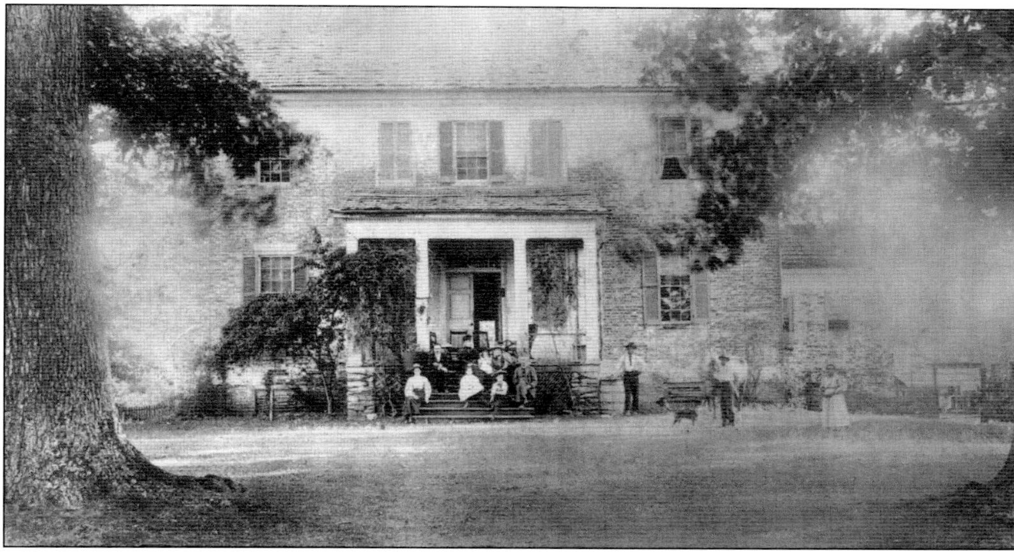

Lucky Hit, shown about 1900, was the childhood home of William Meade, third Episcopal bishop of Virginia. His father, Richard Kidder Meade, an aide-de-camp to George Washington, built the house in 1791. Bishop Meade was president of the Virginia Theological Seminary in Alexandria for 20 years and was involved in the American Colonization Society, which promoted the resettlement of freed slaves to Liberia. (CCHA.)

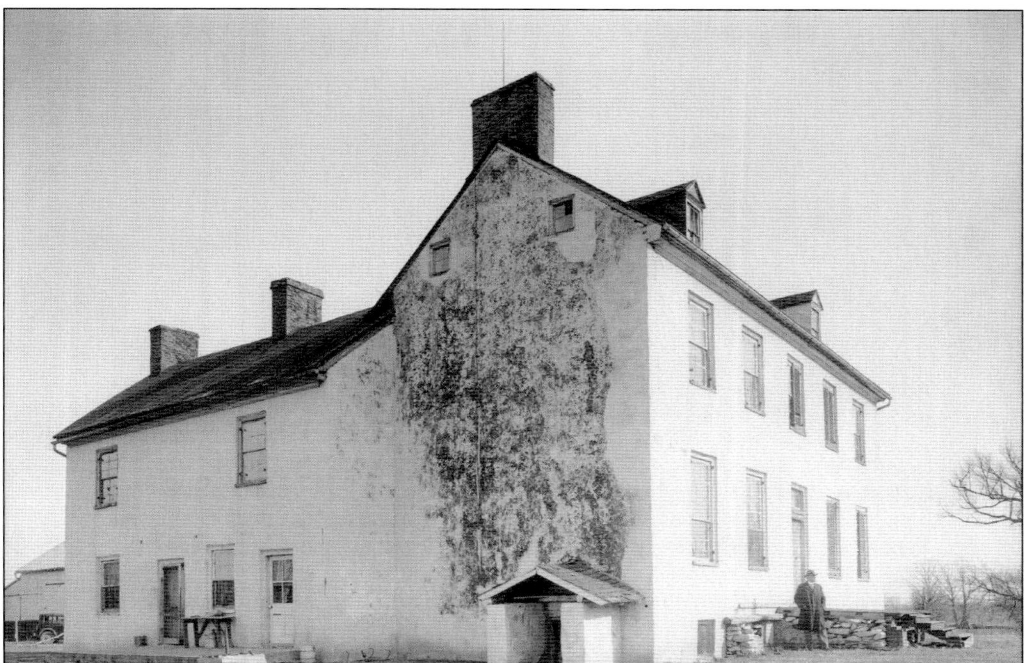

Famed 19th-century novelist and Confederate soldier John Esten Cooke lived at the Briars after the Civil War and his marriage to Mary Frances Page. It was here that he wrote many of his historical novels and other publications. This 1928 photograph shows the large, L-shaped, stuccoed stone house before it was restored. (SBA/HRL.)

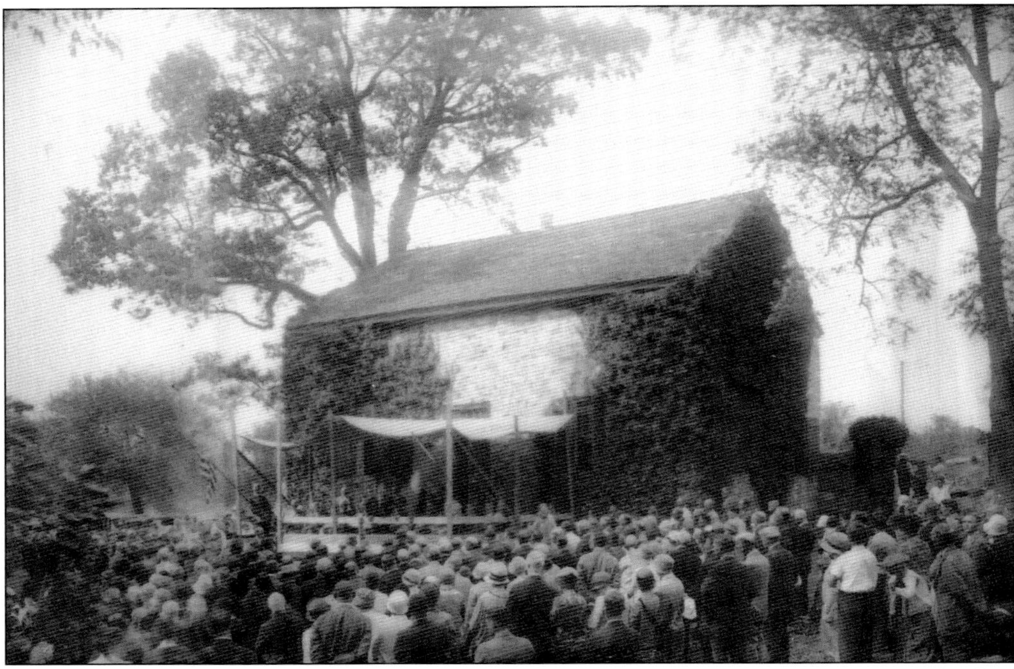

The Burwell Cemetery at Old Chapel contains the graves of distinguished county individuals as well as many Confederate soldiers and members of early Clarke County families. This scene in September 1929 marks the dedication of the Edmund Randolph monument at Old Chapel. Although Randolph, governor of Virginia and the first US attorney general, had died in 1813 while visiting Carter Hall, only a small marker was erected at that time. (CCHA.)

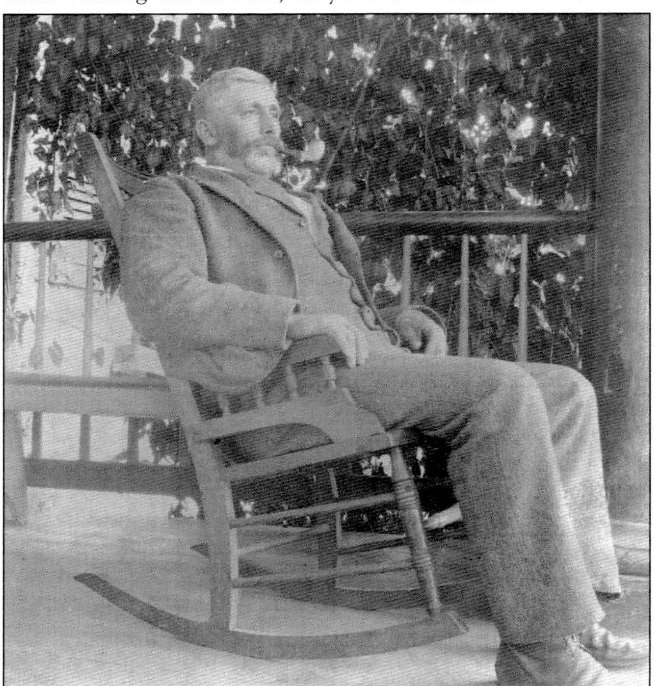

Local farmer Thomas Gold, who lived along Senseny Road at Ellwood (Avenel), is best known for his *History of Clarke County*, published a year before his death in 1914. Gold served in the 2nd Virginia Infantry during the Civil War and was captured twice. Although his book focused primarily on county Civil War engagements, Gold also included histories of local communities prepared by others. (CCHA.)

One of the county's most prominent and charismatic black leaders, Edward T. Johnson, came to Clarke in 1919 as pastor of St. Luke Baptist Church on Liberty Street. He was instrumental in rallying the community to build a high school for African Americans. Johnson-Williams Middle School honors him as well as W.T.B. Williams, a Clarke County native and first dean of Tuskegee Institute. (Josephine School Community Museum.)

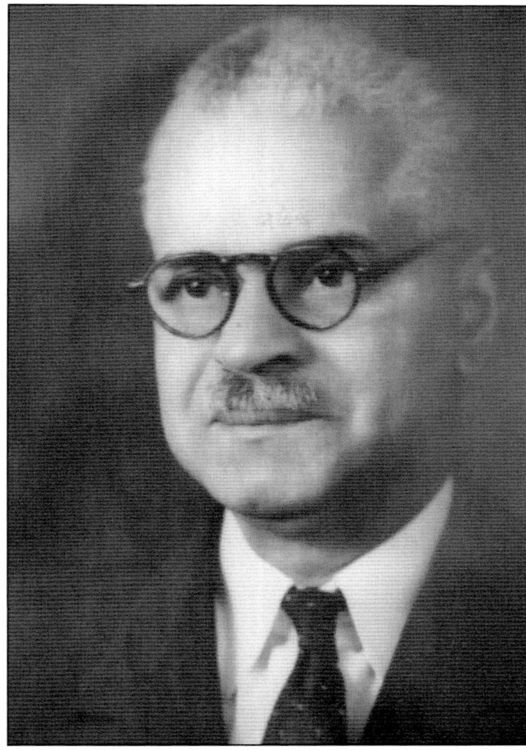

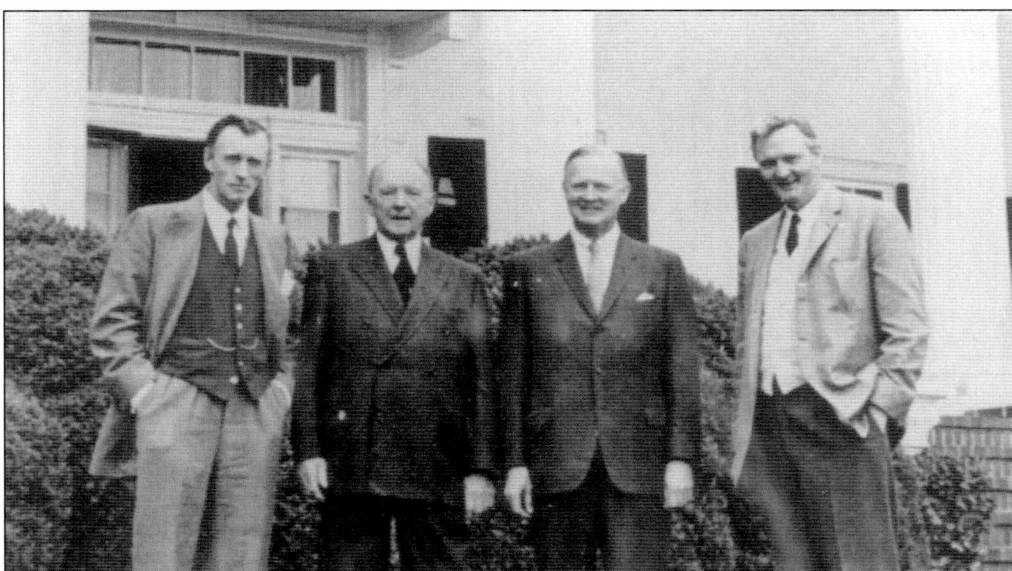

Shown with their father at Rosemont, the Berryville family home, are, from left to right, Beverly, Senator Harry F. Byrd, Harry Jr., and Richard. Among Virginia's most prominent families, they cultivated vast apple orchards, published newspapers, explored the North and South Poles, and served as senators and governors. The elder Harry Byrd initiated the pay-as-you-go system of government and the extensive highway building program in the commonwealth during the 1920s and 1930s. (CCHA.)

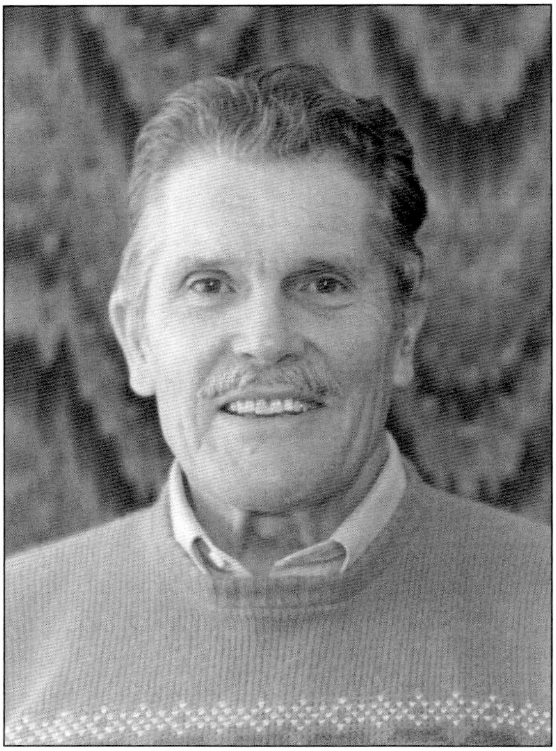

Charles Burwell is the great-great-grandson of Col. Nathaniel Burwell and one of Clarke's leading community figures. He and his family created the Burwell–Van Lennup Foundation Wildlife Preserve along the Shenandoah River and have lovingly maintained the Vineyard, the family home where 19th-century poet Phillip Pendleton Cooke lived. In the 1980s, Charles, along with Marjorie Digges, helped establish a Clarke branch of the Handley Library. (Belinda Burwell.)

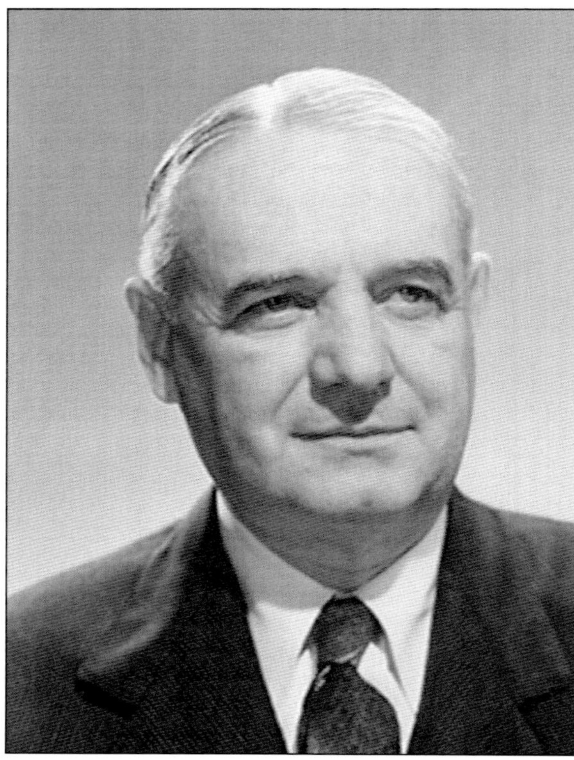

Gen. William J. "Wild Bill" Donovan served as director of the Office of Strategic Services (OSS). Established by Pres. Franklin D. Roosevelt in 1942 to gather and interpret intelligence during World War II, it later evolved into the CIA. During the 1940s and 1950s, Donovan owned Chapel Hill Farm, located near Old Chapel. Although he traveled a great deal, his family maintained it as their primary residence. (CIA.)

Joe P. Jones and his wife, Betty Smith, known for her successful book *A Tree Grows in Brooklyn*, are shown in 1947 in Davos, Switzerland. Jones, who died in 1986, was a Berryville native and editor of a newspaper in Chapel Hill, North Carolina. After his retirement and divorce from Smith, he returned to Berryville and wrote articles on birds and regional history for the local newspaper. (Author.)

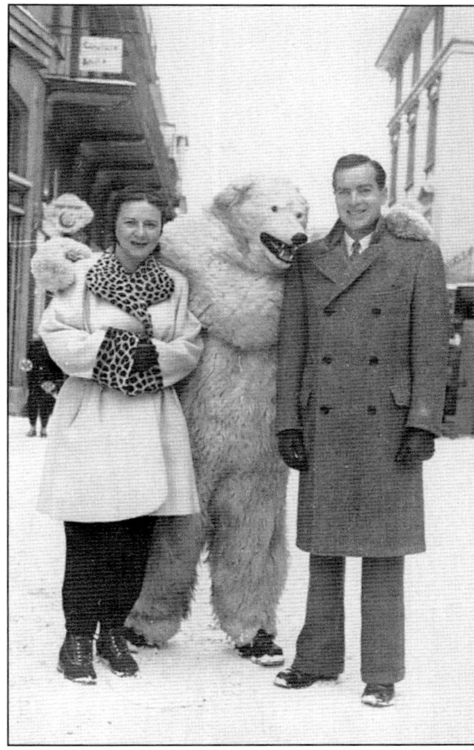

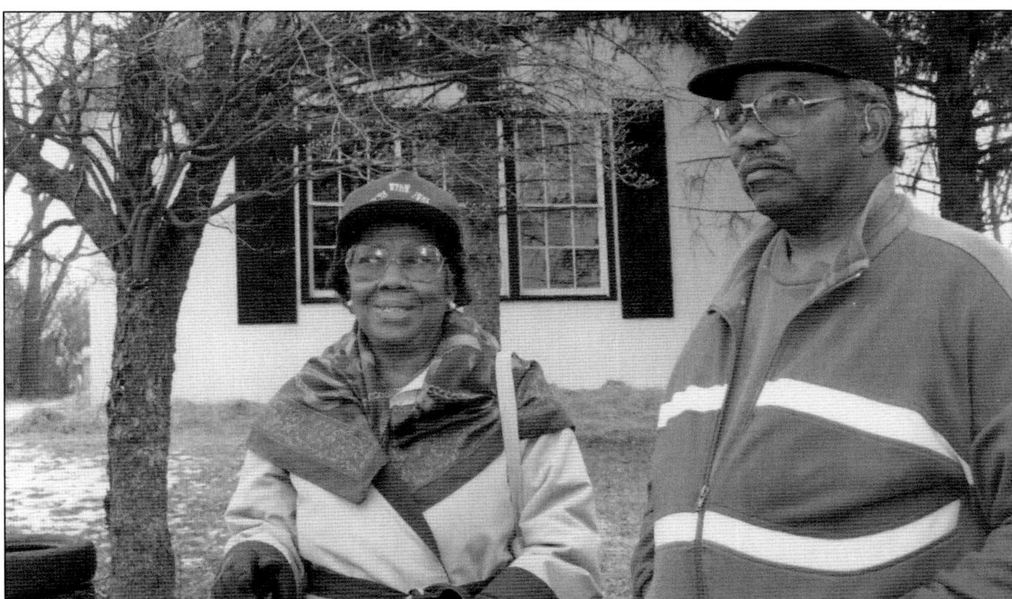

Through the tireless efforts of Rosetta Clay and Marcellus Harper as well as many others, the story of Clarke's African Americans was fully realized with the establishment of the Josephine School Community Museum. Housed in the former Josephine City School, which was built in 1882, the African American museum is also a cultural center providing information about the county's heritage and the legacy of its black residents. (Josephine School Community Museum.)

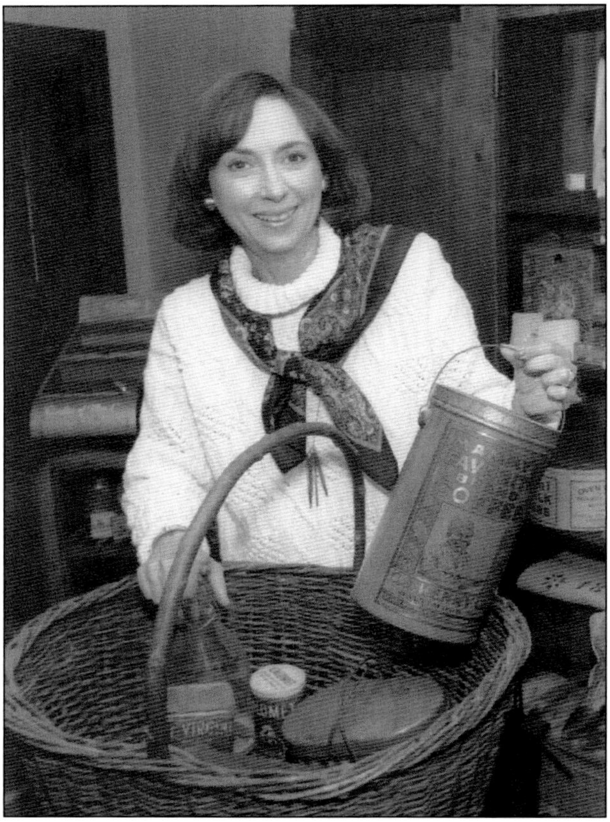

During the 1990s, the name Sally Trumbower was synonymous with historical activities in Clarke. The longtime chair of the Historic Preservation Commission and president of the Clarke County Historical Association, Trumbower invigorated both with her inspired and committed leadership. She restored and lived at Avenel, the historic home of the Gold family. Sally passed away in 2003, but many of her visions, including the semiannual Art at the Mill shows, still thrive. (CCHA.)

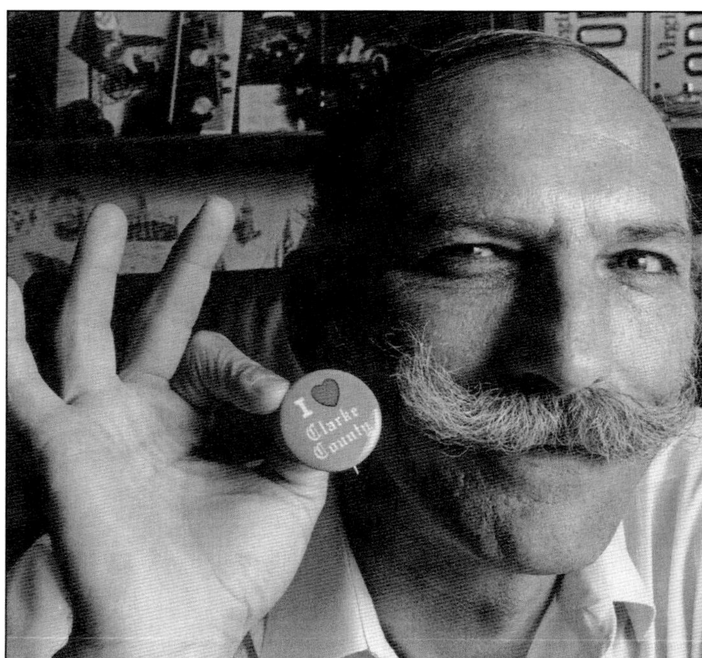

A lifetime resident of White Post, Billy Thompson was influential in establishing a historic district in the village and creating a county historic preservation commission. He chaired the Clarke sesquicentennial celebration in 1986 and organized the fabulously successful White Post Celebrates festivals in the late 1980s. Billy also operated White Post Restorations, a world-renowned automotive restoration company in White Post. (Billy Thompson.)

Renowned author, historian, and horseman Alexander Mackay-Smith moved to Clarke in the 1930s. He served as the master of the Blue Ridge Hunt for 16 years and was editor of the *Chronicle of the Horse* for 25 years. Mackay-Smith helped found the Clarke County Historical Association and authored 10 books dealing with both the history of horses and fox hunting. He died in 1998 at age 95. (CCHA.)

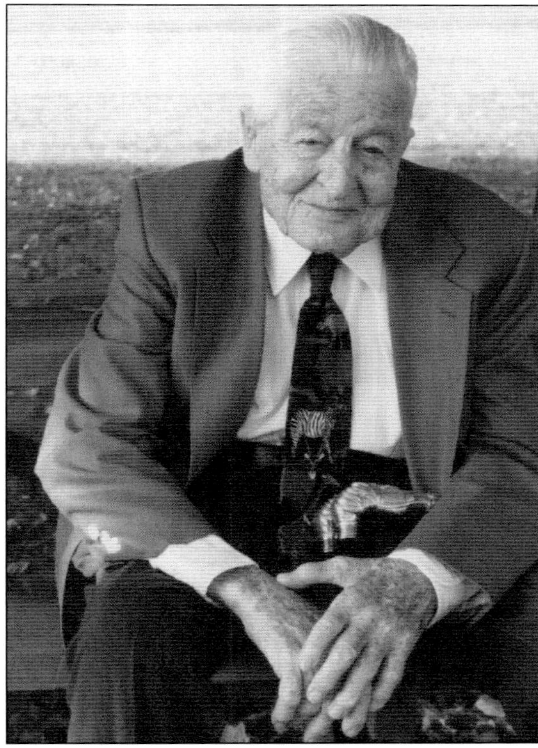

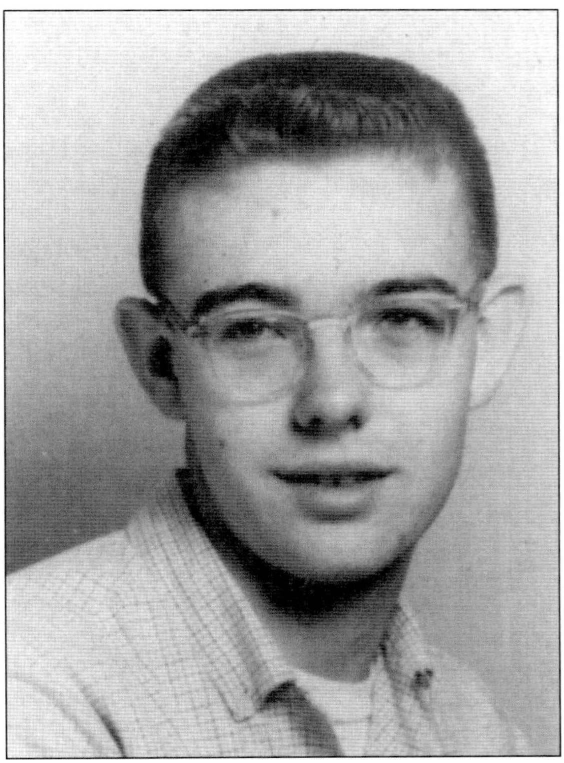

Rennard "Rennie" Cordon Davis was the 1958 valedictorian of Clarke County High School. A leader during the anti-war movement, he helped organize massive civil disobedience demonstrations, including protests at the 1968 Chicago Democratic National Convention. Indicted afterwards as one of the "Chicago 7," Davis was a principal figure in what the *New York Times* has called "the most significant political trial in US history." (Clarke County High School.)

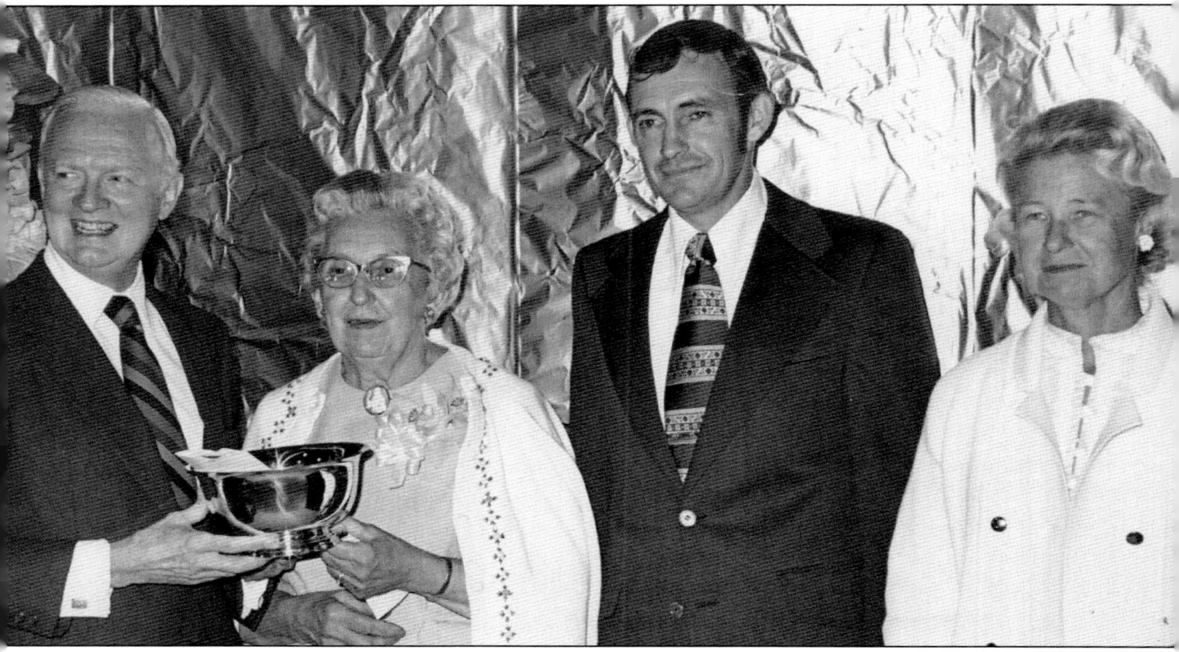

This photograph records the 1973 retirement of Mary Hardesty as Clarke County's public health nurse, a position she held for 25 years. The Mary Hardesty House, an assisted living facility in Berryville, is named in her honor, and she was tapped as Citizen of the Year by the *Clarke Courier* in 1992. Presenting her award is Clarke County native Senator Harry F. Byrd Jr. To the right of her is son Jack Hardesty, a prominent and well-respected local dairyman, who served on the Clarke County Board of Supervisors for 30 years, 17 as chairman. Next to him is Virginia "Vaida" Boy-Ed Lloyd, one of the founders of the Clarke County Visiting Nurses Association, established in the 1940s to provide health care to the needy. Lloyd, also a local philanthropist, was instrumental in the creation of the county animal shelter. (*Clarke Courier.*)

Three

The African American Story

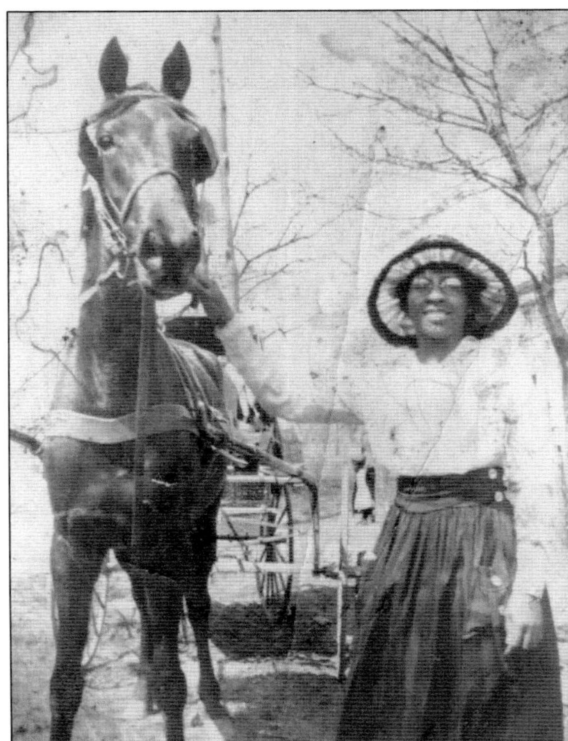

Fanny Jenkins was a longtime teacher at the Josephine School and the Josephine Training School in Josephine City. Always fashionably dressed and sporting a gregarious attitude, Jenkins, shown with a horse and carriage, was extremely popular among the students. The 1930 census lists her as a 40-year-old teacher living in Berryville with her parents and other family members. (CCHA.)

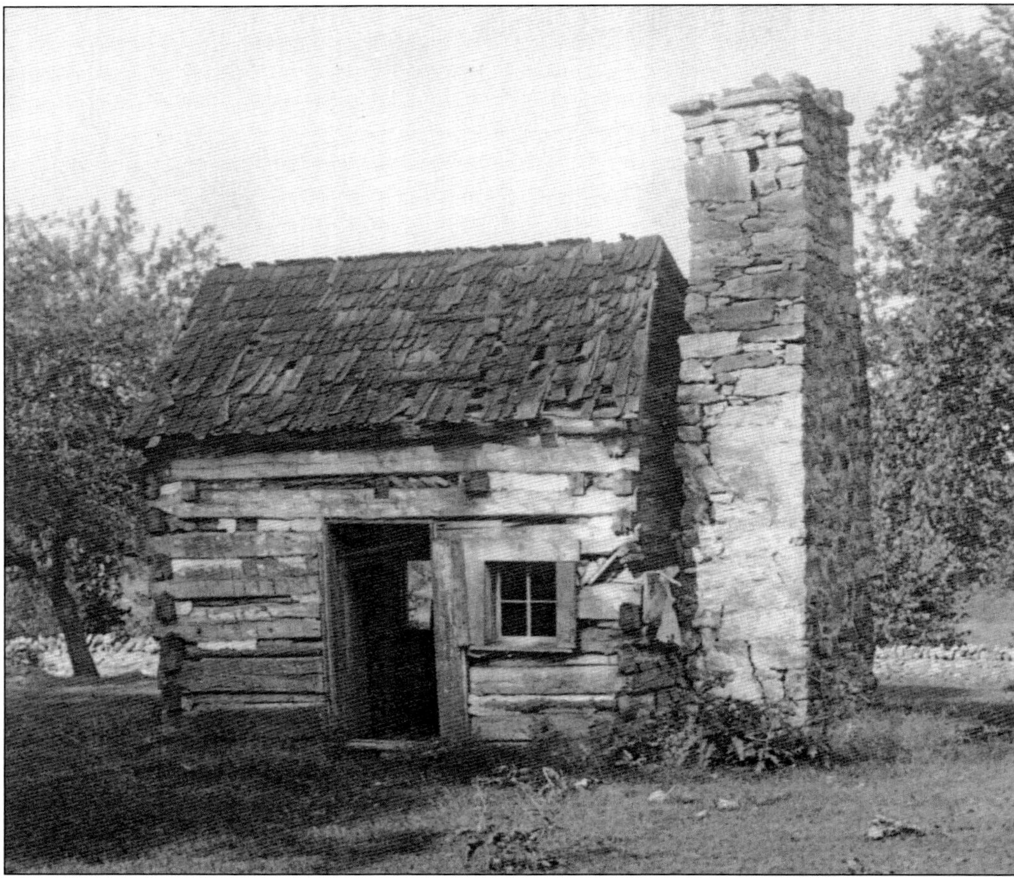

This 1958 photograph of a slave cabin at Pagebrook, an estate outside of Boyce, shows a one-and-a-half-story log building with a large exterior-end stone chimney. According to the 1860 census and personal property records, John E. Page of Pagebrook owned 28 slaves and three slave houses—an average of nine inhabitants per cabin. (CCHA.)

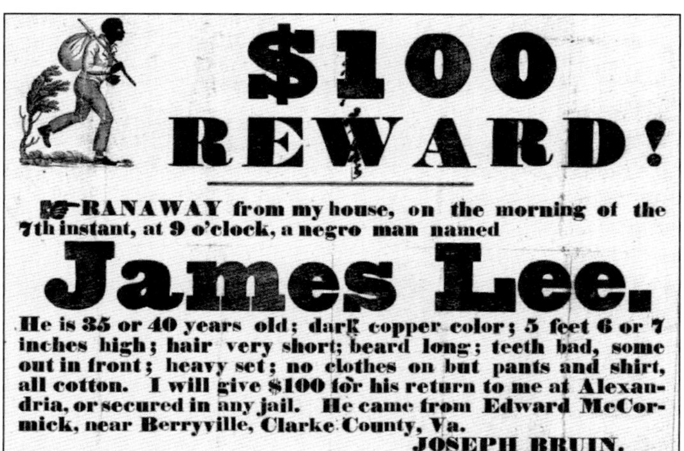

$100 REWARD!

RANAWAY from my house, on the morning of the 7th instant, at 9 o'clock, a negro man named

James Lee.

He is 35 or 40 years old; dark copper color; 5 feet 6 or 7 inches high; hair very short; beard long; teeth bad, some out in front; heavy set; no clothes on but pants and shirt, all cotton. I will give $100 for his return to me at Alexandria, or secured in any jail. He came from Edward McCormick, near Berryville, Clarke County, Va.

JOSEPH BRUIN.

[*Alexandria Gazette, print.*] *West End, Fairfax County, Va., Sept. 7, 1855.*

Broadsides advertising runaway slaves, such as this one from 1855, often appeared in newspapers. James Lee was a slave from Clermont, outside of Berryville, and belonged to Edward McCormick. A reward of $100, later increased to $300 (the equivalent of almost $7,000 today), was offered for his return—a measure of his value to the operation of McCormick's plantation. (Clermont Foundation.)

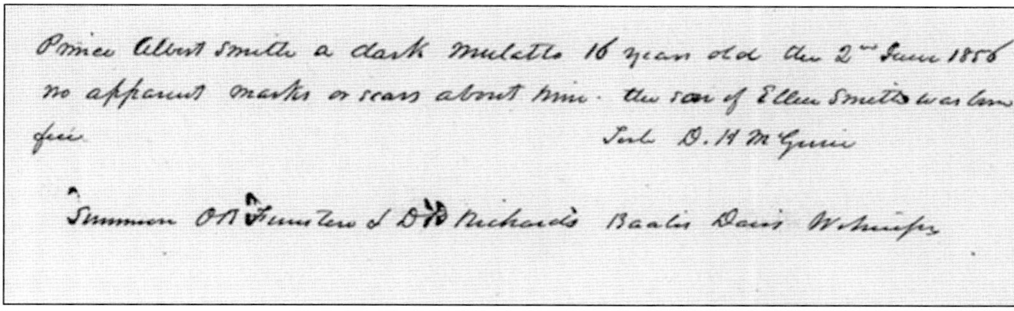

Prince Albert Smith a dark mulatto 16 years old the 2nd June 1856 no apparent marks or scars about him. the son of Ellen Smith was born free

Teste D. H. McGuire

Summoner O.R. Funsten & D.H. Richards Baalis Davis Witnesses

Emancipation certificates, like this one for Prince Albert Smith dated June 2, 1856, would have been carried by free African Americans in the antebellum South. The precious document included a description of the bearer and validated his or her right to freedom. Smith was described as "a dark mulatto" with "no apparent marks or scars about him." The 16-year-old was the son of Ellen Smith, and he was born free. (Clarke County Circuit Court.)

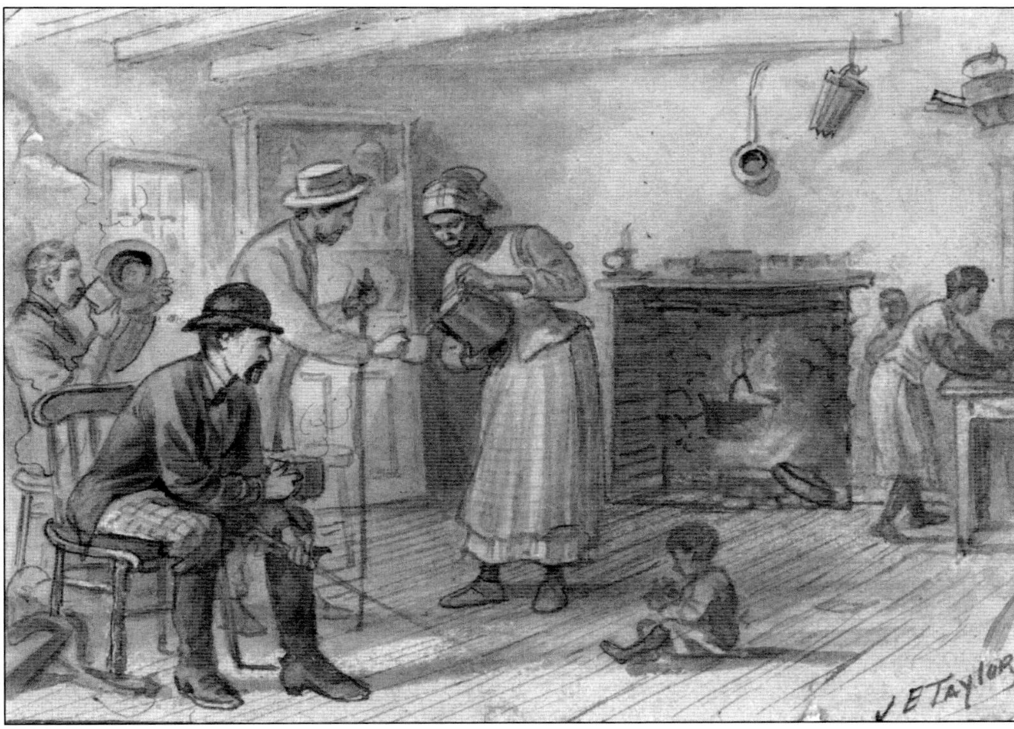

This 1864 sketch by Civil War illustrator James E. Taylor provides a rare glimpse into the interior of an African American house. The log cabin, located near White Post, had wooden floors, a corner cupboard, exposed ceiling rafters, and an open fireplace containing a crane and topped by a simple wooden mantel. Taylor wrote of the hospitality of his hostess, who served him and his party coffee. (Western Reserve Historical Society.)

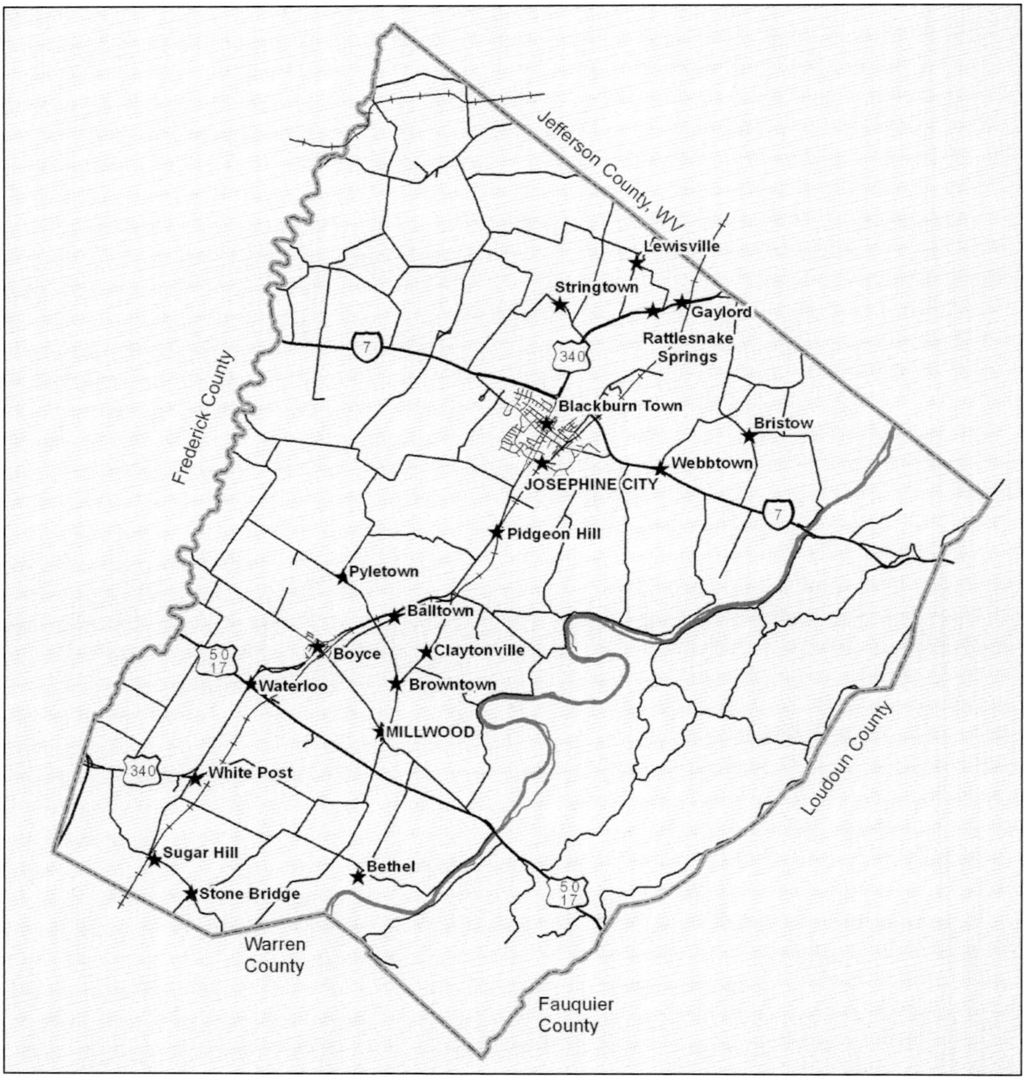

By 1840, Clarke's population was 55 percent African American, compared to 22 percent in neighboring Frederick County. This map shows 20 Clarke communities developed by African Americans after the Civil War. Many of these were established in the 1870s by former slaves who had purchased land at auction from financially strapped whites—often at the edge of existing communities—and then subdivided the land, regularly selling to others of their race. By the 1890s, many of these communities, some of which were named for their earliest African American owners, were anchored by a church and school. The two largest were Josephine City, outside of Berryville, and the village of Millwood. Over the second half of the 20th century, out-migration has dramatically altered the county's racial mix. A majority in pre–Civil War Clarke County, African Americans today account for less than seven percent of the county's population. (Clarke County Planning.)

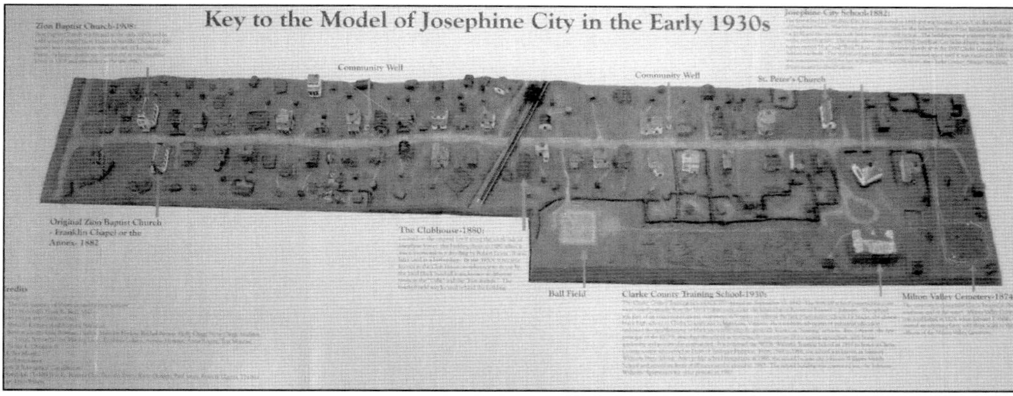

This model, created in 2008 and housed in the Josephine School Community Museum, depicts Josephine City in the early 1930s. It both captures the buildings that existed at the time and illustrates the vibrancy of the neighborhood. Created in 1870 when 32 acres belonging to Ellen McCormick of Clermont were sold as lots to African Americans, Josephine City developed into a self-sufficient community. (Josephine School Community Museum.)

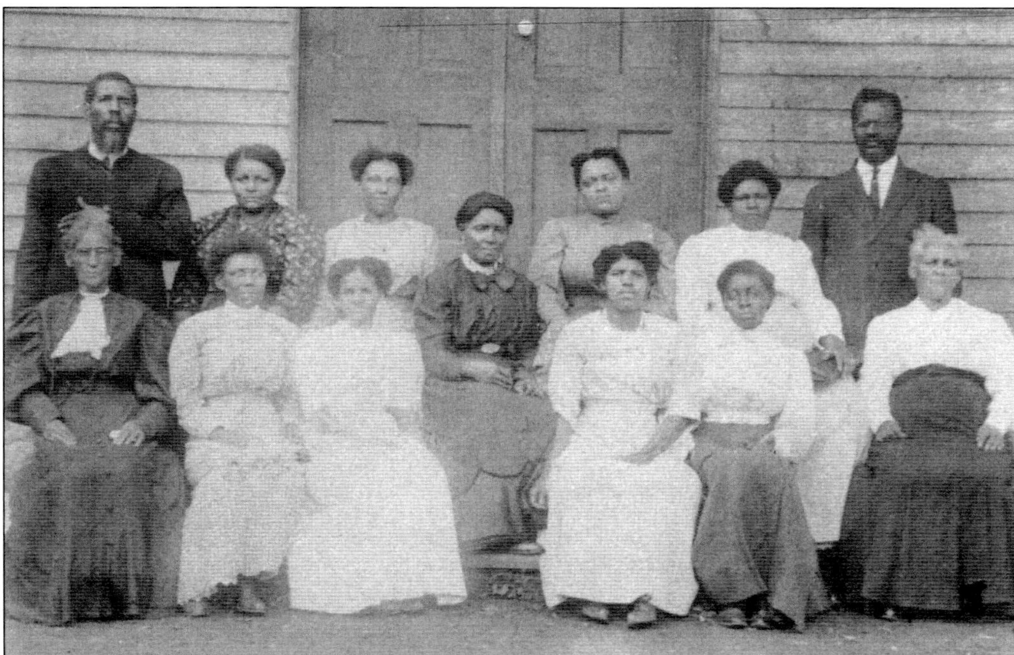

The Woman's Union Light Company of Josephine City was formed in the late 1800s to raise the necessary funds to install and maintain gas lights along Josephine Street. Shown are, from left to right, (first row) Mrs. Burns, Violet Morris, Julia Nickens, Lucy Franklin, Jamie Laws, Edna Paige, and Mandy Reed; (second row) Rev. Spotswood Brown, Bert Willis, Betty Boss, Kelly Crutchfield, Emma Brown Hall, and Rev. John Wanzer. (CCHA.)

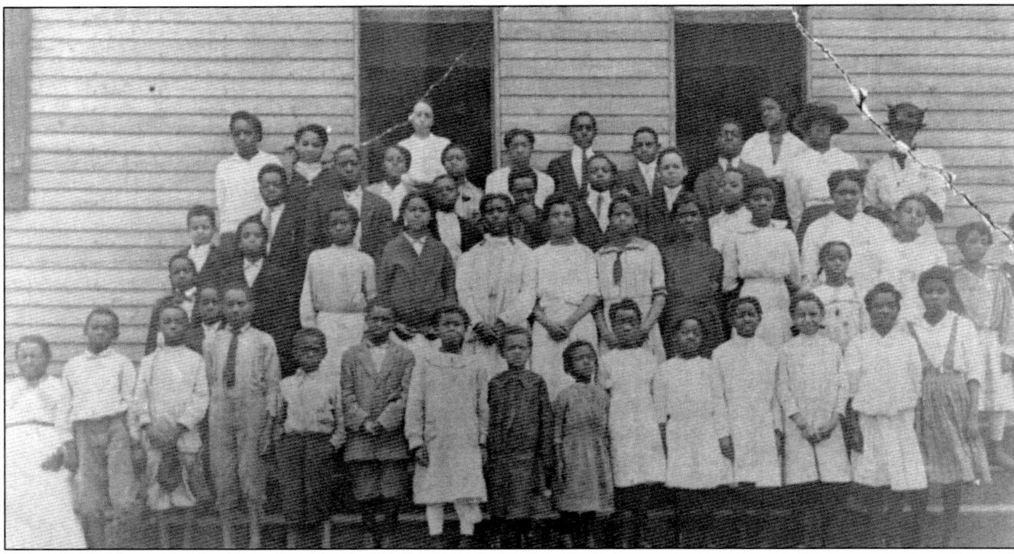

Teachers and students are pictured in 1911 in front of the Josephine School, which reopened as a museum in 2003. None of the county's black public schools taught at a level beyond the seventh grade until the construction of the Clarke County Training School in 1930, which followed years of hard work by the African American community and fulfilled its dream for improved educational opportunities for the county's black youth. (CCHA.)

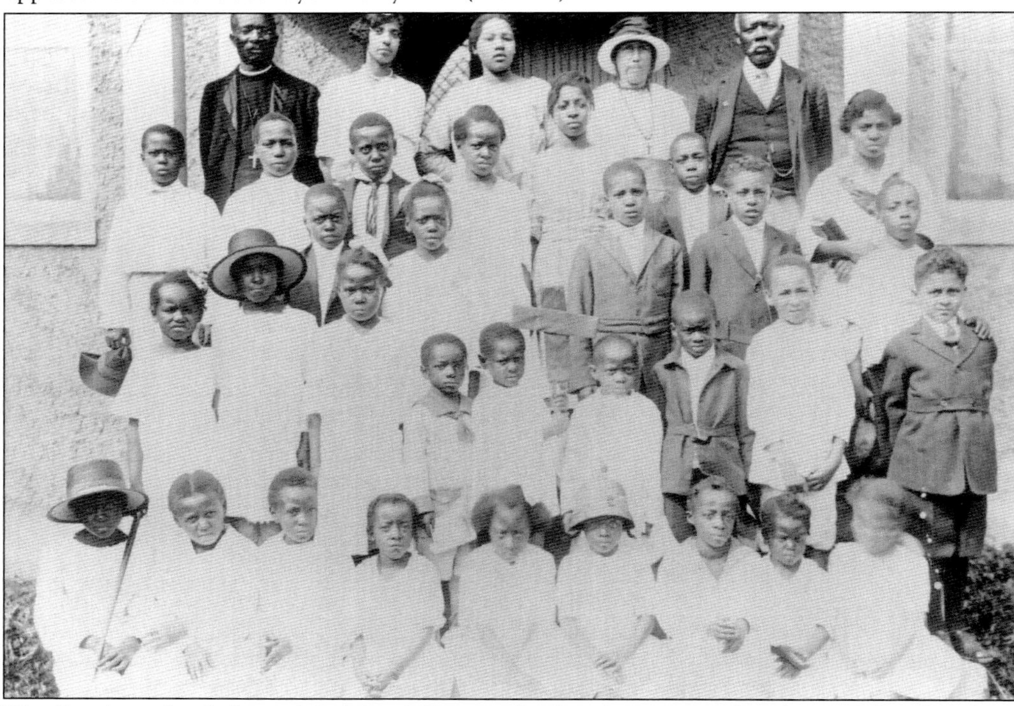

The Sunday school class of St. Mary's Episcopal Church is pictured in front of the church on dedication day in September 1916. The 30 children are accompanied by (top from left to right) Rev. Joseph Mitchell and teachers Helen Mott, Lessie Coxen, Julia Nickens, and William Lightfoot. Still a vibrant and active part of the community, St. Mary's is located in Berryville. (CCHA.)

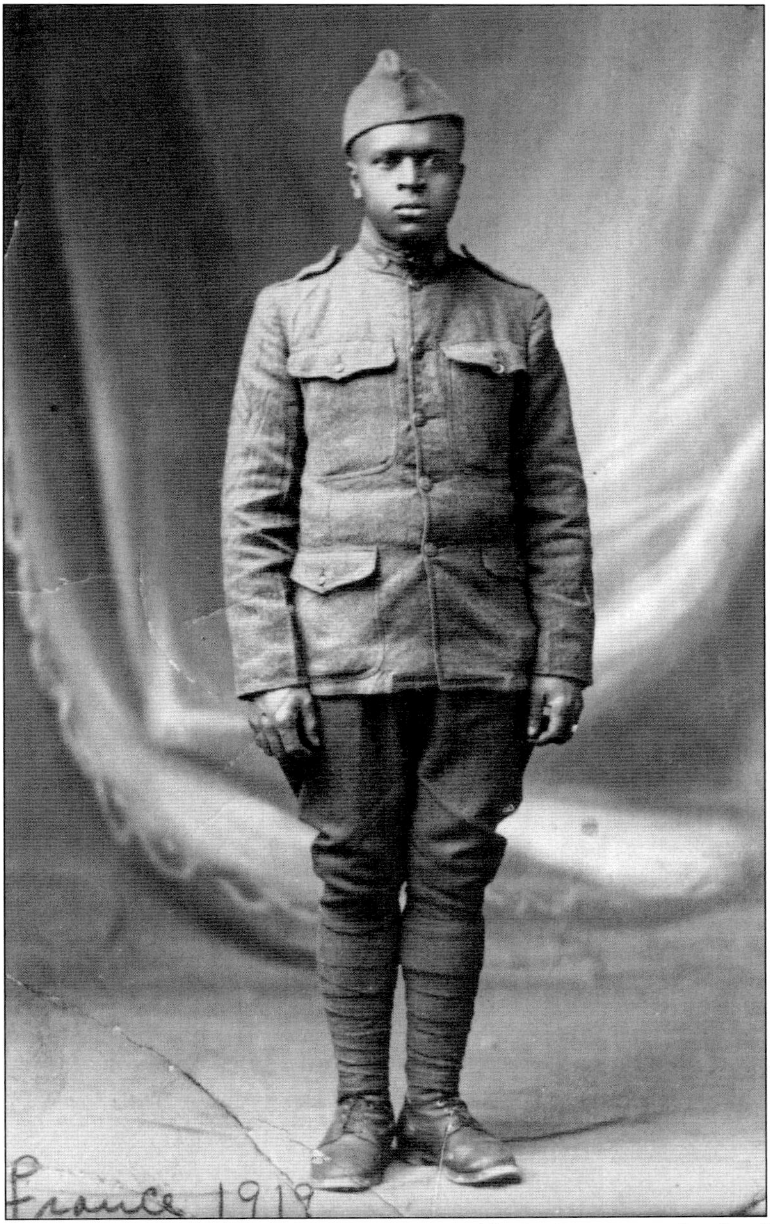

Robert Jenkins, pictured in uniform in 1919, was a World War I veteran who fought in France and is buried at Milton Valley Cemetery on Josephine Street in Berryville. African Americans from Clarke have been well represented in many of the nation's conflicts. In 1866, Congress officially formed the 9th and 10th Cavalry Regiments and the 24th and 25th Infantry Regiments as all-black regiments. Later dubbed Buffalo Soldiers, these regiments continued in existence until the Korean War, when the US military was finally desegregated on orders of President Truman. Buffalo Soldiers from Clarke include Charles Davis, who served in the Indian wars in the West; Thomas Wheeler, who served in the Spanish-American War; Edward Cross, who served between World Wars I and II; Sgt. Jessie B. Williams, who served in World War I; and Albert Young, who was part of the 25th Regiment during the Spanish-American War. (CCHA.)

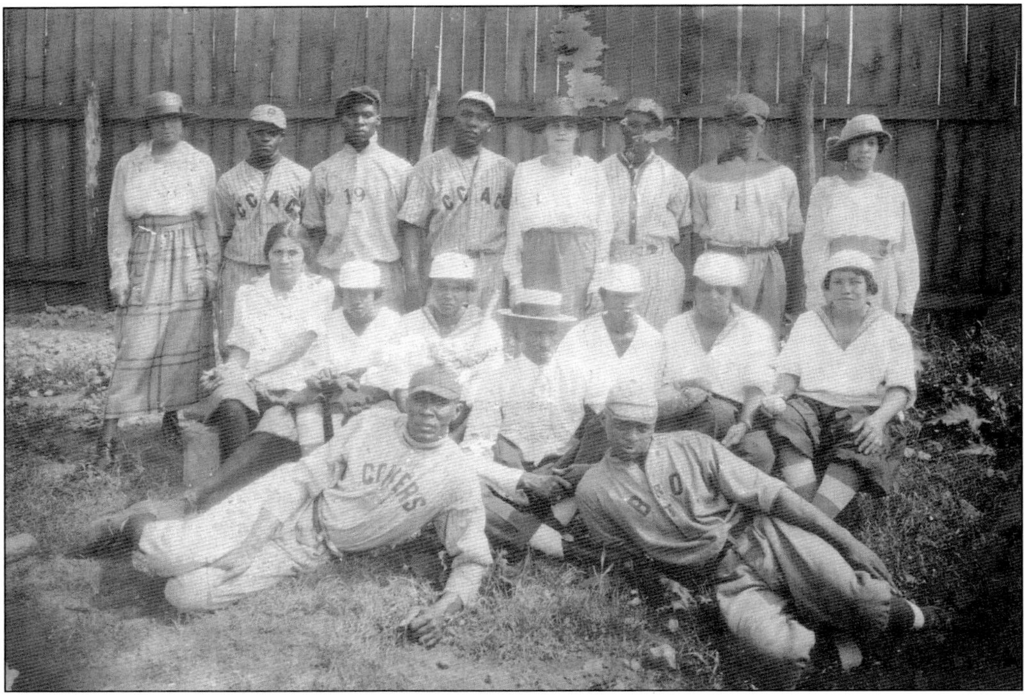

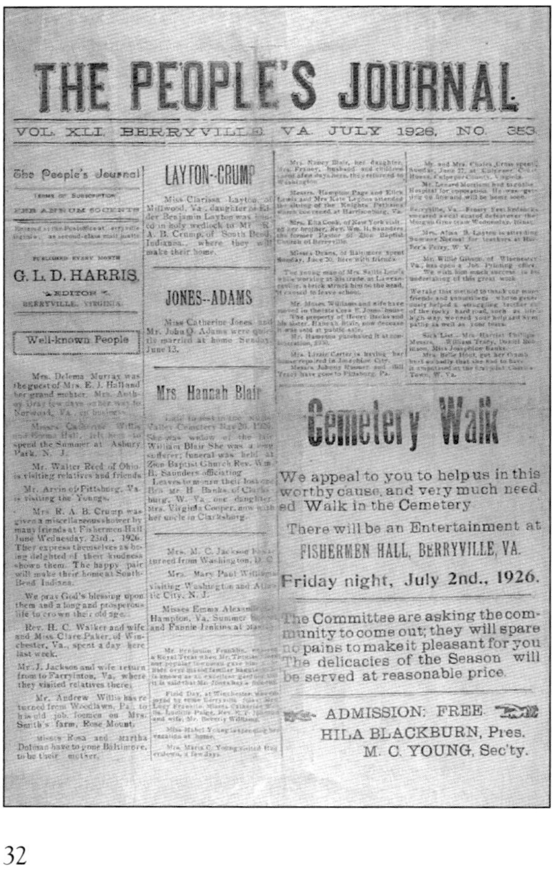

THE PEOPLE'S JOURNAL

VOL. XLI. BERRYVILLE VA. JULY 1926. NO. 353.

The People's Journal

PUBLISHED EVERY MONTH

G. L. D. HARRIS,

EDITOR

BERRYVILLE, VIRGINIA.

Well-known People

Mrs. Delema Murray was the guest of Mrs. E. J. Hall and her grand mother.

Mr. Walter Reed of Ohio is visiting relatives and friends.

Mr. Arvin of Pittsburg, Va. is visiting the Youngs.

Mrs. R. A. B. Crump was given a miscellaneous shower by many friends at Fishermen Hall June Wednesday. 23rd., 1926. They express themselves as being delighted of their kindness shown them. The happy pair will make their home at South-Bend Indiana.

We pray God's blessing upon them and a long and prosperous life to crown their old age.

Rev. H. C. Walker and wife and Miss Clare Paker, of Winchester, Va., spent a day here last week.

Mr. J. Jackson and wife return from to Farryinton, Va. where they visited relatives there.

LAYTON--CRUMP

Miss Clarissa Layton of Millwood, Va., daughter of Elder Benjamin Layton was united in holy wedlock to Mr. R. A. B. Crump, of South Bend, Indiana., where they will make their home.

JONES--ADAMS

Miss Catherine Jones and Mr. John Q. Adams were quietly married at home Sunday June 13.

Mrs Hannah Blair

She was widow of the late William Blair She was a long sufferer; funeral was held at Zion Baptist Church Rev. Wm. B. Saunders officiating.

Cemetery Walk

We appeal to you to help us in this worthy cause, and very much needed Walk in the Cemetery

There will be an Entertainment at

FISHERMEN HALL, BERRYVILLE, VA.

Friday night, July 2nd., 1926.

The Committee are asking the community to come out; they will spare no pains to make it pleasant for you The delicacies of the Season will be served at reasonable price.

ADMISSION: FREE

HILA BLACKBURN, Pres.
M. C. YOUNG, Sec'ty.

This early-1900s photograph of African American baseball players in Berryville shows both men and women in uniform. Some wear jerseys with the names of local businesses such as Coiners, while others bear CCAC for the Clarke County Athletic Club. Baseball really was the national pastime in those days. Games were played on Pulliam's Field off East Main Street and on a field off the south side of Josephine Street. (CCHA.)

Two newspapers were published by African Americans in Clarke. The *Berryville News* was a small newspaper whose first edition was in 1883. The monthly *People's Journal*, established in 1895, also reported on the activities of the black community. It ceased operations with the 1927 death of its editor, George Harris. (Josephine School Community Museum.)

Four

The Civil War Years

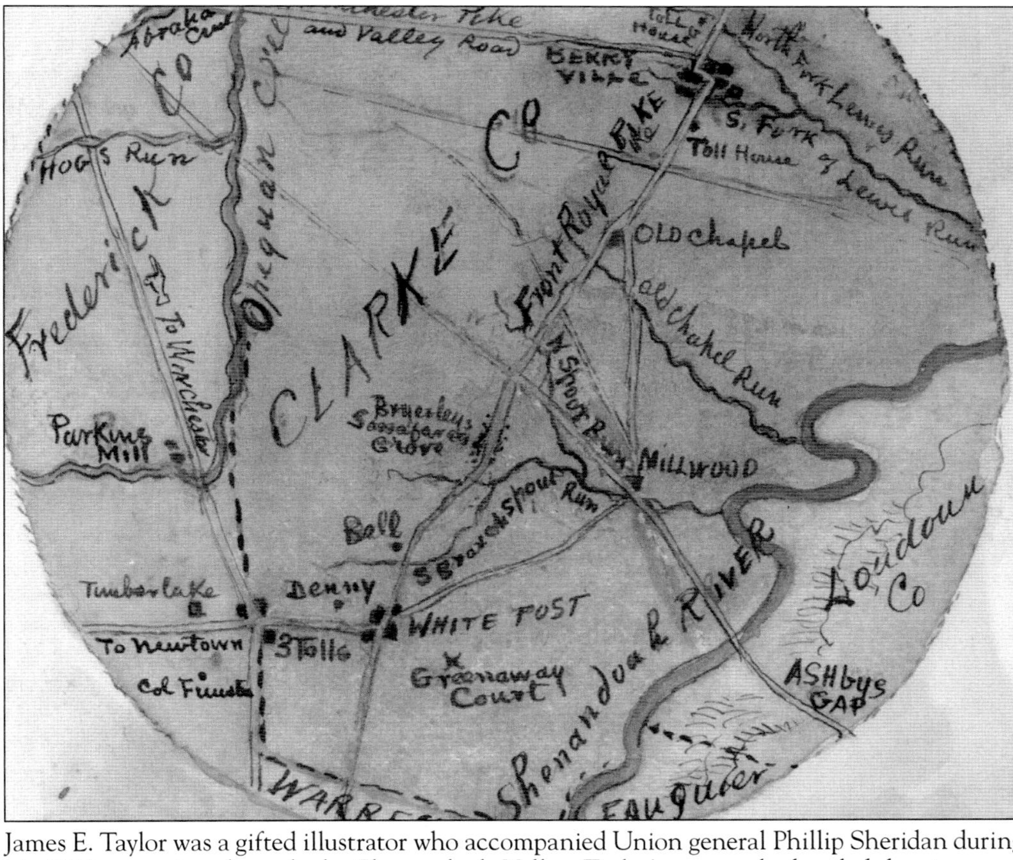

James E. Taylor was a gifted illustrator who accompanied Union general Phillip Sheridan during his 1864 campaign through the Shenandoah Valley. Taylor's extremely detailed drawings and complementary text, eventually published in the 1880s, provide valuable documentation of the area. This map of a section of Clarke shows the major roads, watercourses, towns, homesteads, and landmarks of that time. (Western Reserve Historical Society.)

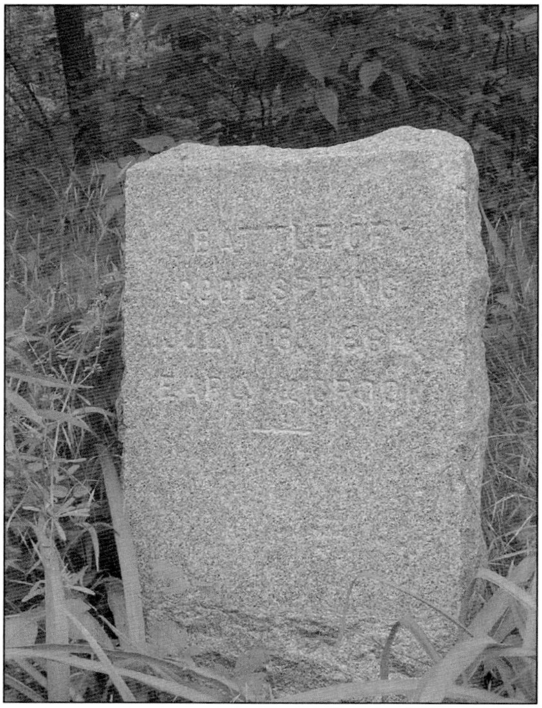

This simple granite marker commemorates the Battle of Cool Spring on July 18, 1864, the largest Civil War engagement in Clarke. It was installed in 1914 by the J.E.B. Stuart Camp of Confederate Veterans; nine similar monuments mark the sites of Confederate victories. At Cool Spring, Gen. Jubal Early's men forced the withdrawal of Union forces across the Shenandoah River, resulting in the drowning of many Federal soldiers. (Simon McKay.)

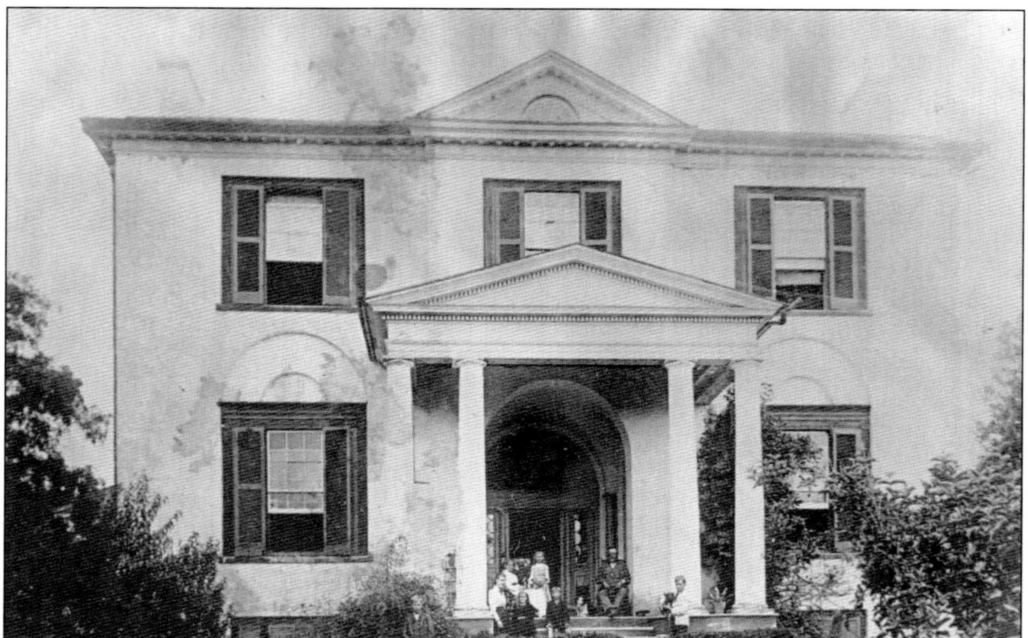

Constructed in 1827 by successful farmer Josiah Ware, Springfield was one of five dwellings targeted to be burned in August 1864 by Union troops in retaliation for an earlier loss in Berryville in which General Sheridan's wagon train was destroyed. The fire at Springfield was extinguished by quick-thinking family and slaves. Destroyed by a later fire in 1904, the house was rebuilt the following year. (CCHA.)

Warren Cophenhaver was one of countless Clarke men who fought in the Civil War. He joined the 2nd Virginia Infantry, known as the Nelson Rifles, commanded by Capt. William Nelson of Millwood. After the Battle of Manassas in July 1861, Copenhaver contracted typhoid and was found by his family trying to walk back to Clarke. He was only 18 years old when he died at home several days later. (David Copenhaver.)

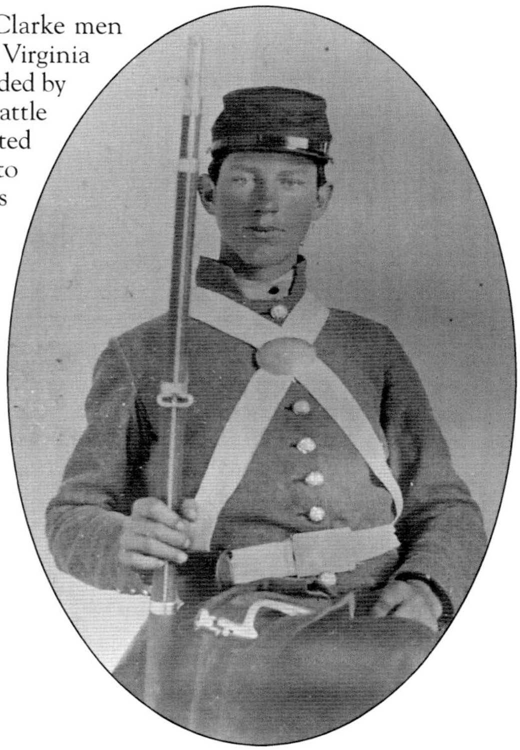

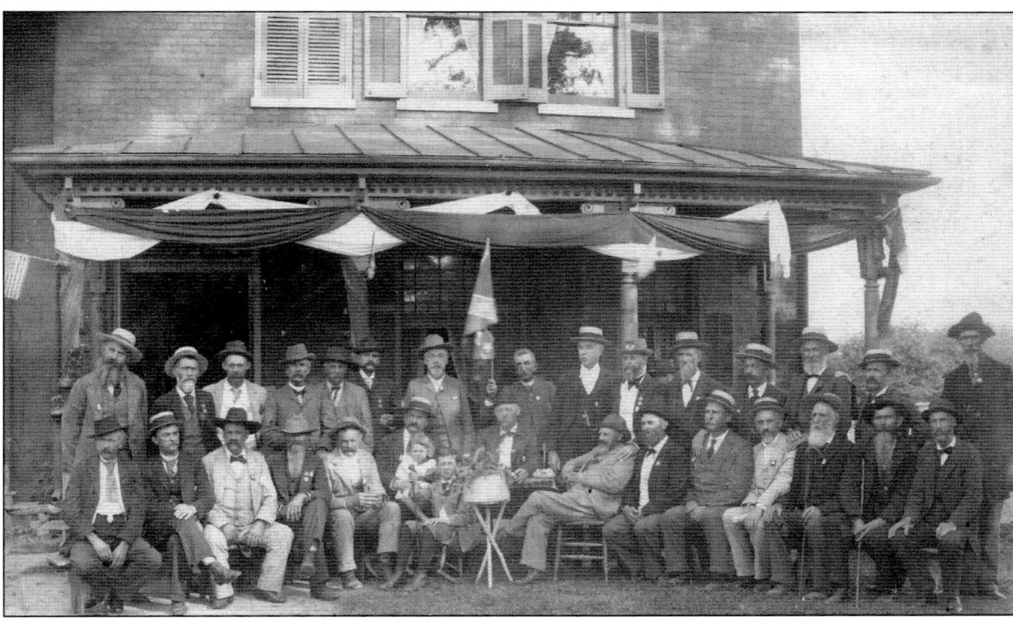

Reunions, such as this one of Clarke Cavalry Survivors, were common in the late 1880s. This shows a group of 29 veterans along with a young girl and boy (front row center) and is thought to have been taken at the home of Ammishaddai Moore on Main Street, now the location of the Family Dollar Store. A cake rests on a wooden tripod, and flags and banners adorn the porch. (CCHA.)

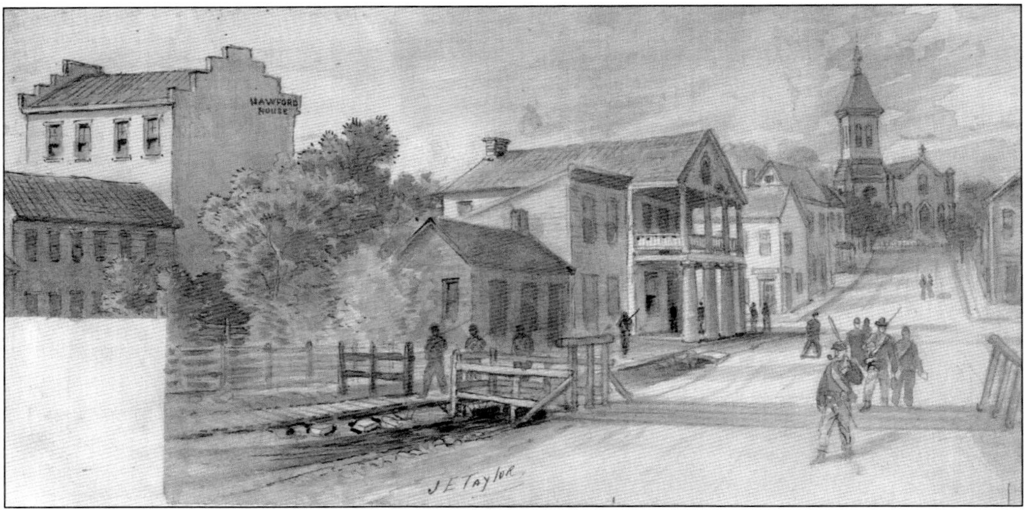

Drawn by James E. Taylor in 1864, this scene of Berryville captures the view north along Church Street. Taylor describes the picturesque scene with "the imposing Episcopal Church planted seemingly . . . at the top of the slope . . . the store in the middle ground with its plaster-bespattered gable and pillared gallery supports. . . . The foreground accessory was the bridged crossing of Lewis Run." (Western Reserve Historical Society.)

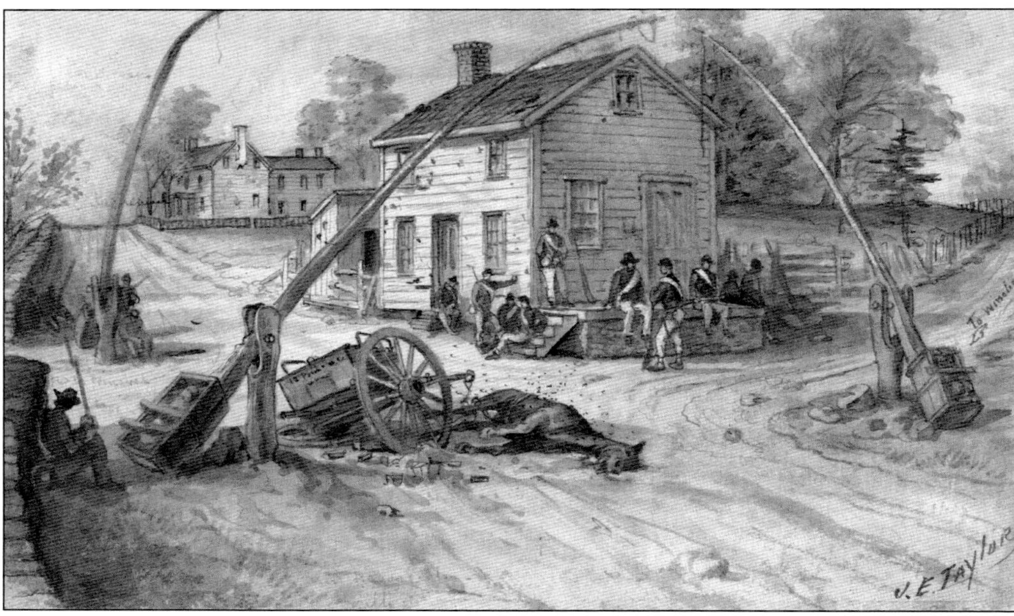

James E. Taylor's *Highland Cross Road* was drawn the day following an August 11, 1864, skirmish when Confederate troops under the command of Gen. John Imboden sparred with Union cavalry. The resulting scene shows a wrecked caisson and a horse carcass. The multiple tollgates in the drawing give the crossroads its current name, Double Tollgate. (Western Reserve Historical Society.)

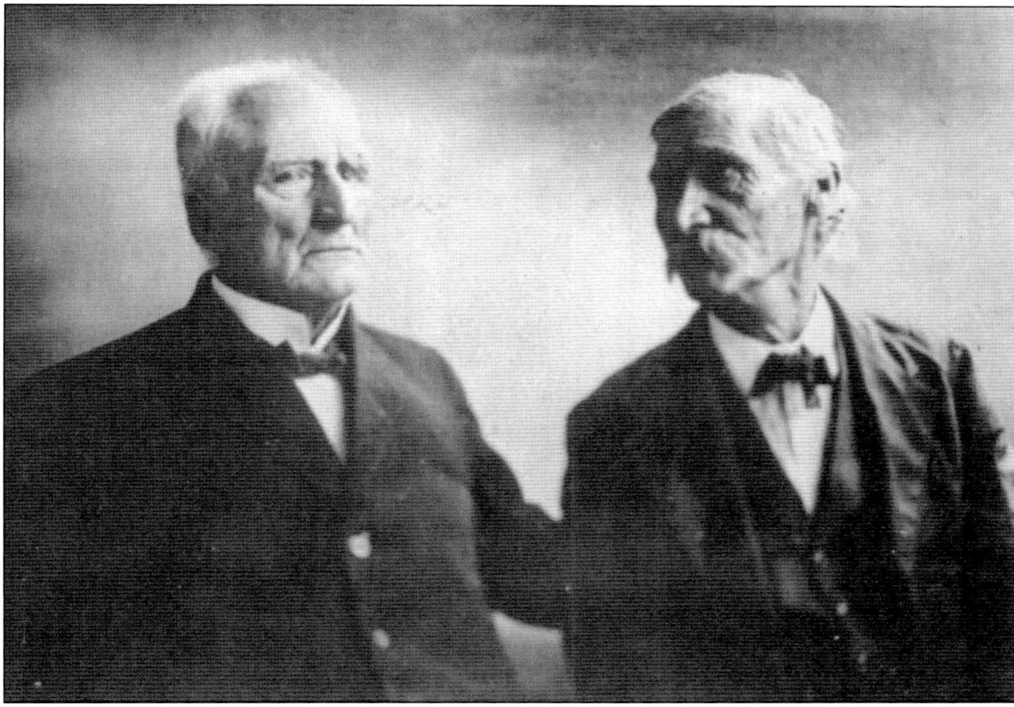

Col. John Singleton Mosby was the leader of Mosby's Rangers, a Confederate unit that raided many Union troop positions and often succeeded because of the speed of its attacks. Mosby (left) is pictured about 1915 with his former lieutenant, John Russell of Berryville. Mosby was also known as the "Gray Ghost" in honor of his ability to elude pursuing Union troops by blending in with the locals. (CCHA.)

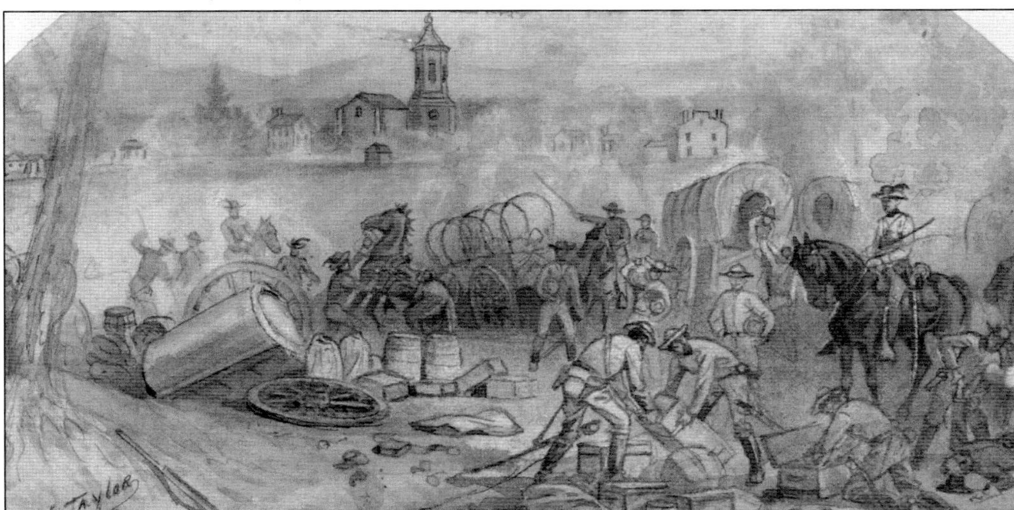

Although he was not a witness to the battle, James E. Taylor drew this scene of Colonel Mosby and his men destroying Sheridan's supply train at Berryville on August 13, 1864. Arriving the day after the fight, Taylor noted the wreckage, which included burned wagons, ruined supplies, and slaughtered mules. (Western Reserve Historical Society.)

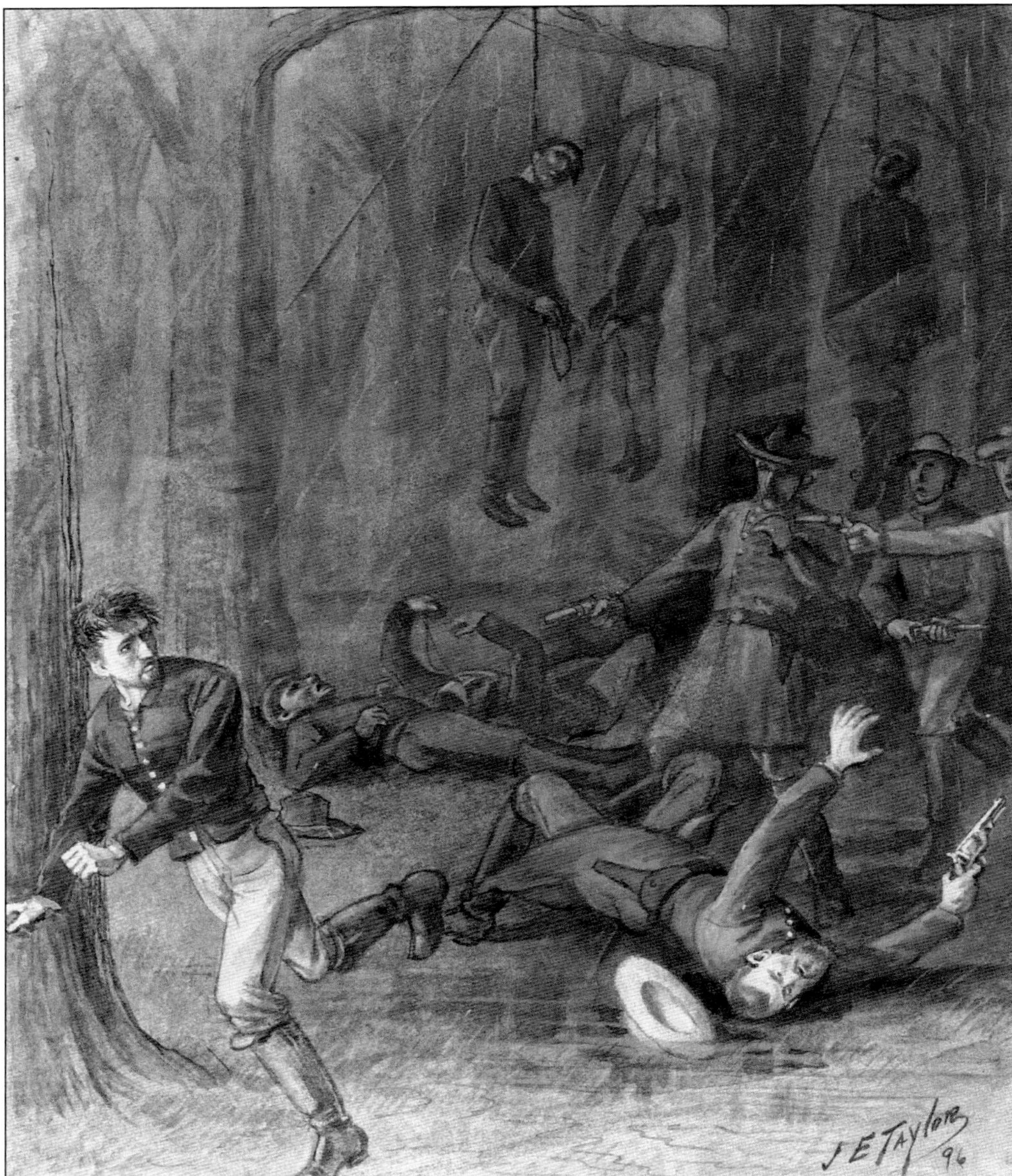

This gruesome scene took place in November 1864 at Beemer's Woods along Route 7 west of Berryville. Under Custer's command, seven of Col. John S. Mosby's rangers had been executed in Front Royal two months earlier. In retaliation, Mosby ordered the hanging of an equal number of men to be drawn by lot from the 27 prisoners he held in Rectortown (Fauquier County). The seven doomed Federals were being marched toward Winchester when two escaped, so it was decided to proceed with the deed immediately. Ultimately, three men were hanged and another two ran away. James E. Taylor's sketch depicts the fleeing of one prisoner, who had requested time to pray but instead attacked the ranger and ran off while his comrades were left hanging. The hanging tree, which for years stood along the north side of Route 7 across from Rosemont near the present entrance to the new Clarke County High School, was cut down in the late 1940s, although pieces were saved as souvenirs. (Western Reserve Historical Society.)

Five

Towns: Berryville and Boyce

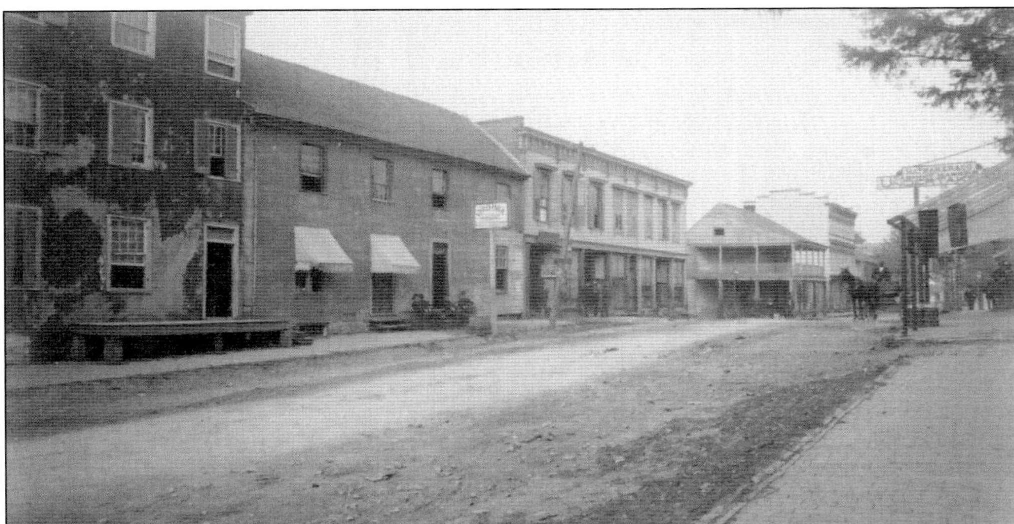

Berryville began as an 18th-century crossroads—the intersection of the highways between Winchester and Alexandria and between Old Chapel and Charles Town, West Virginia. The land on which the town stands belonged originally to Charles Smith, who sold part of it to Benjamin Berry, the founder of the town, in 1798. This 1888 photograph is looking southwest on East Main Street. (SBA/HRL.)

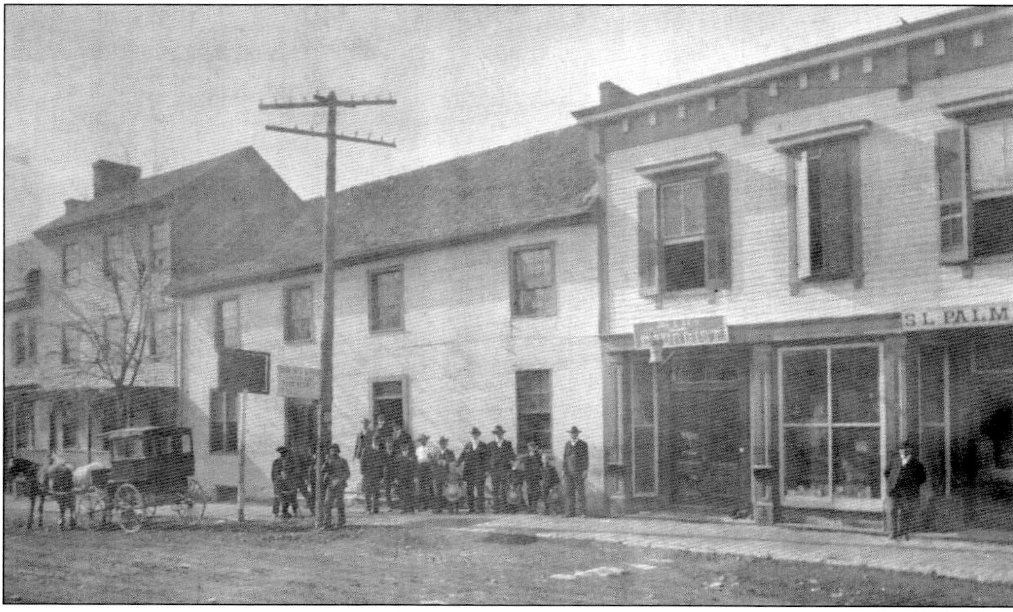

This 1890s view of East Main Street shows men gathered in front of the Virginia House, the infamous inn where Gen. Daniel Morgan was known to have engaged in rowdy behavior. Local lore maintains that Berryville was also called Battletown because of the frequent brawls on its streets. Note the raised stepping stones across the dirt road to allow pedestrians to cross without getting their shoes or skirt bottoms muddy. (CCHA.)

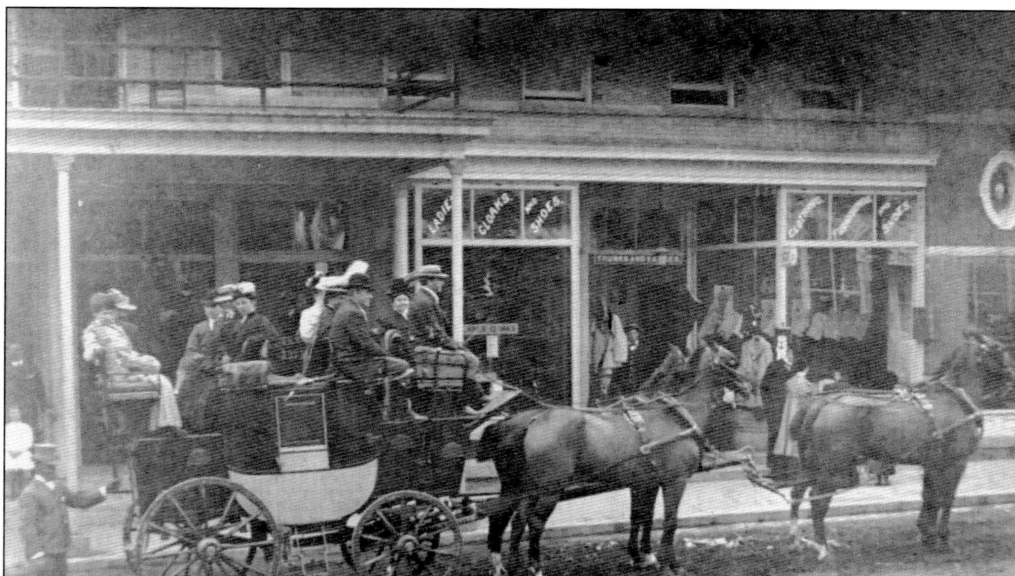

Several stagecoaches like this one, pictured around 1900, ran through Berryville, transporting passengers to other towns or train stops where they could connect to even more distant destinations. The building to the left was the Battletown Inn until it moved to its current location on West Main Street. The one to the right, 9 East Main Street, was a clothing store and is now the Berryville Grill. (Jack Stark.)

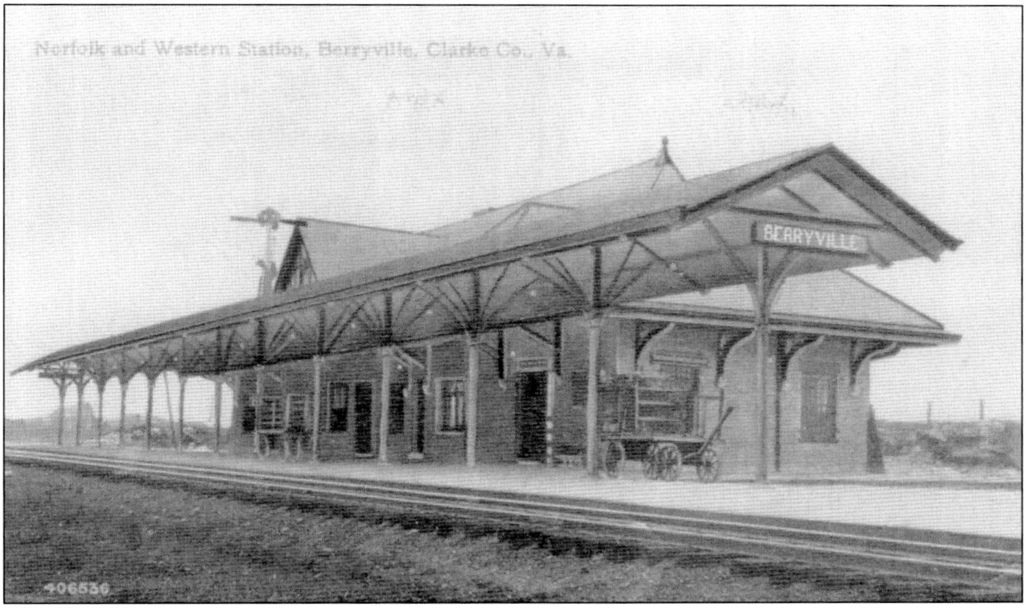

This unusually elegant brick passenger-train station in Berryville (pictured about 1910) featured deep overhanging eaves designed to protect travelers from the weather. The long steel-and-glass canopy in front contained overhead lights, a relatively recent innovation at the time. The Shenandoah Valley Railroad was completed through Berryville in 1879. The station had been vacant for many years when it was unexpectedly demolished by the railroad in the 1990s. (CCHA.)

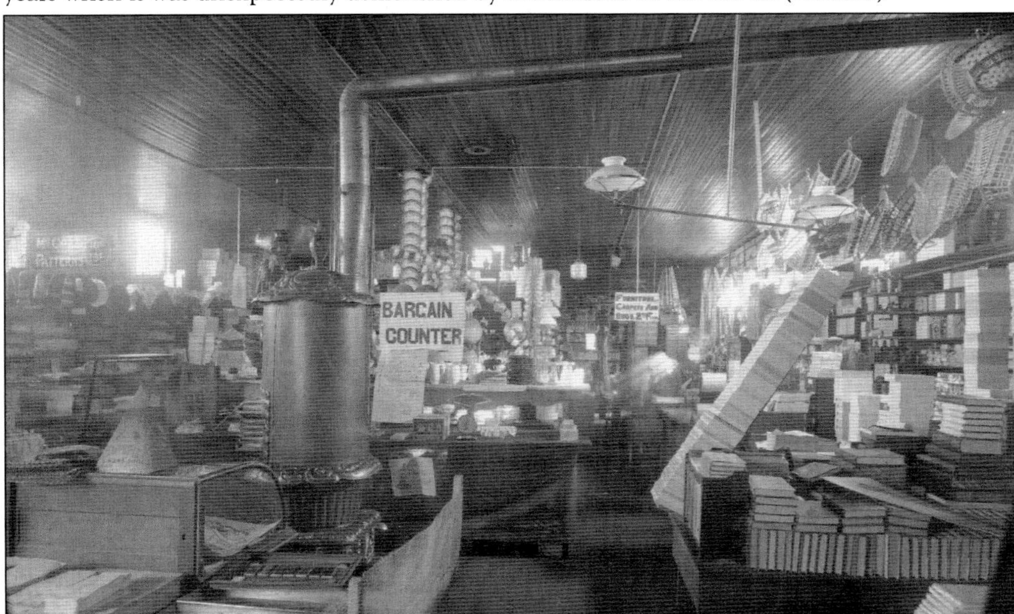

This interior view of Coiner's Department Store, 24 East Main Street, shows the plethora of goods available for purchase, including baskets, books, and clothing, as well as furniture and rugs displayed on the second floor. The store opened in 1896 and operated continuously until it closed in 1995. The potbelly stove was the only source of heat, and the lights were gas-powered. (CCHA.)

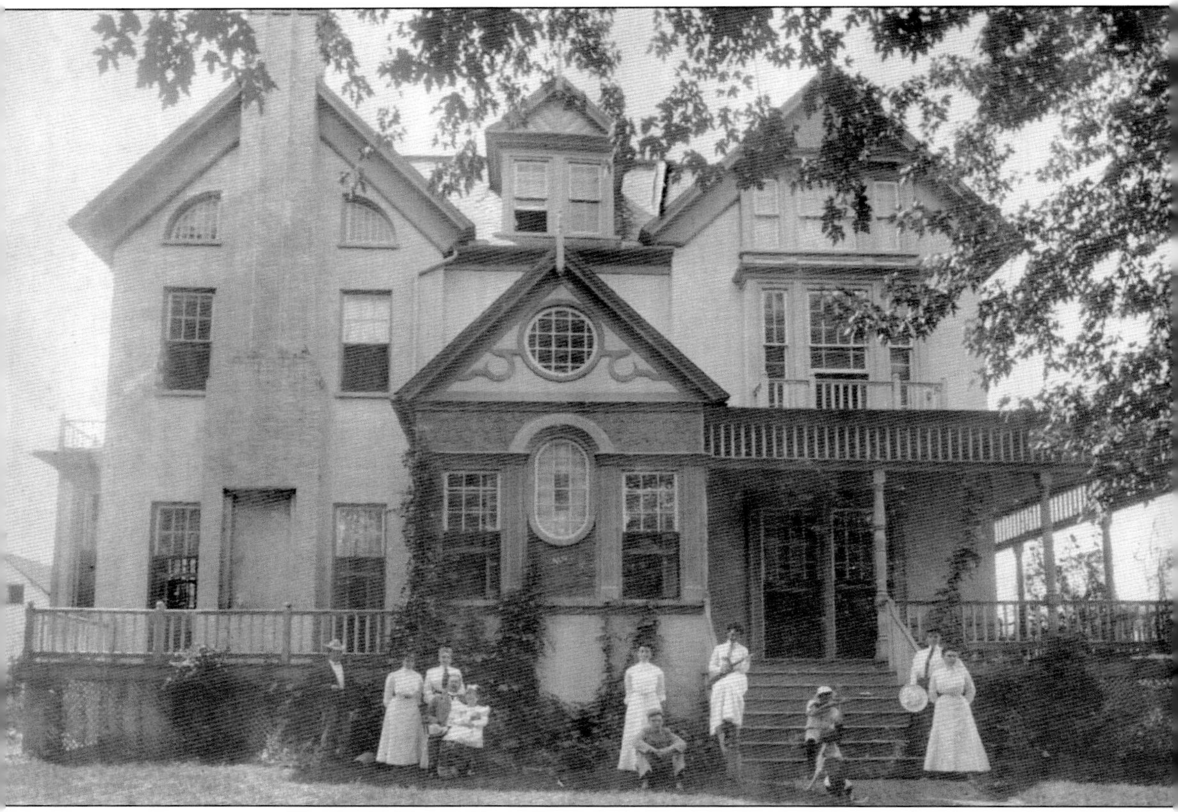

Pictured around 1900 is Rose Hill, a beautiful mid-19th-century brick mansion that was once the centerpiece of Berryville. Located on East Main Street, Rose Hill had been constructed by the Neills and enlarged and remodeled by the McCormicks, who gave the house its Victorian appearance. The Smithey family, shown in a variety of activities, donated the three-and-a-half-acre property to Berryville in 1964. Although plans to convert the Smithey Mansion into a cultural center and the accompanying dairy barns into a teen center were considered, the house was left vacant, burned by vandals, and demolished in 1978. Since then, the property has served as Rose Hill Park, containing tennis courts and a gazebo near the site of the mansion. The dairy barns, which were spared from the fire, were renovated and opened in 2011 as a community cultural and arts center. (CCHA.)

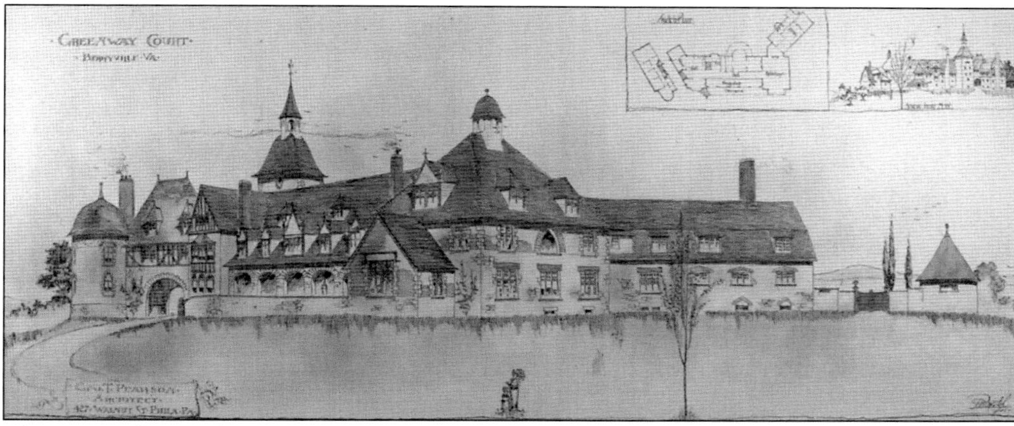

The Berryville Land and Improvement Company planned the Greenway Court Hotel, rendered in an 1892 drawing, to stand along the railroad tracks off Boom Road. Designed by Philadelphia architect George T. Pearson, the rambling Victorian-era stone structure was never built but reflects the real estate boom that seized the valley during this period, only to quickly fade after financial downturns later in the decade. (CCHA.)

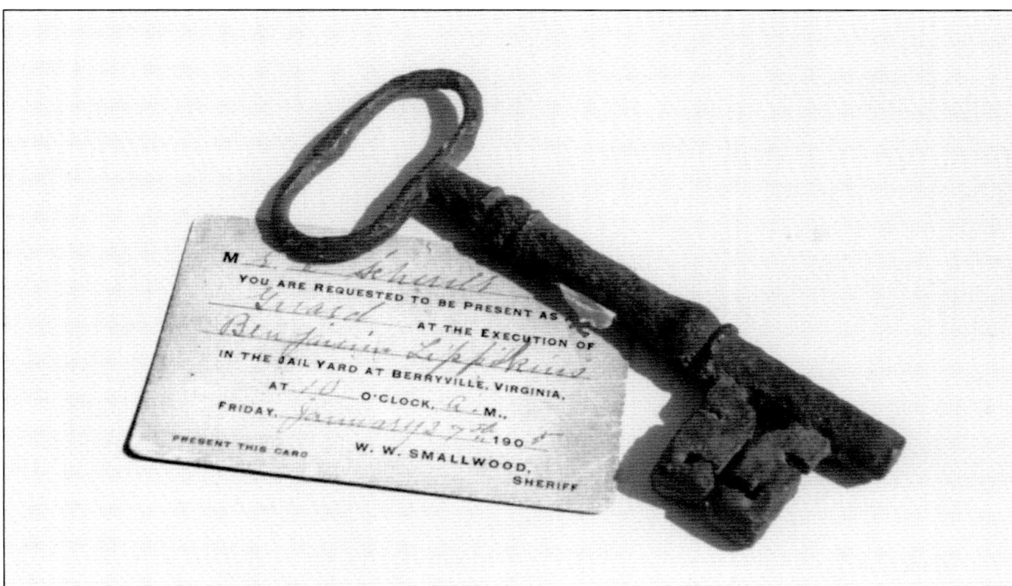

The last public execution in Clarke County took place in the jail yard near the courthouse on January 27, 1905. The invitation to the hanging is accompanied by the large iron key to the criminal's cell. The case involved a fatal shooting at a local bar where two men had argued over a woman. (CCHA.)

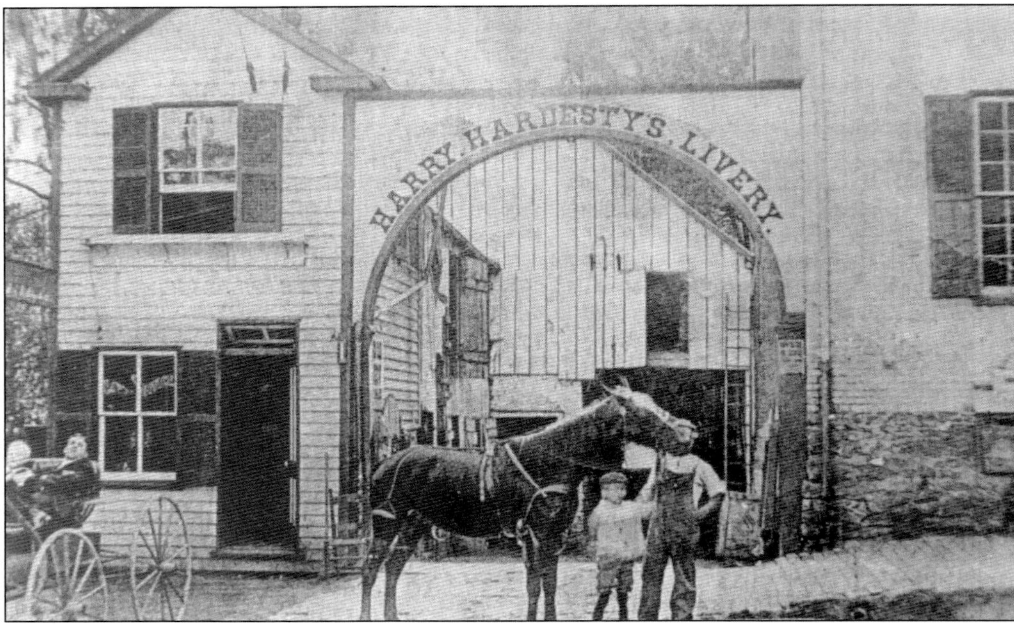

Harry Hardesty's Livery was one of two stables in Berryville where travelers could board their horses for the night. The rear of the building was incorporated into the Enders Fire Company, later used as the town office and now home to the Firehouse Gallery at 23 East Main Street. The left portion of the building was moved to Josephine Street and converted into a residence. (CCHA.)

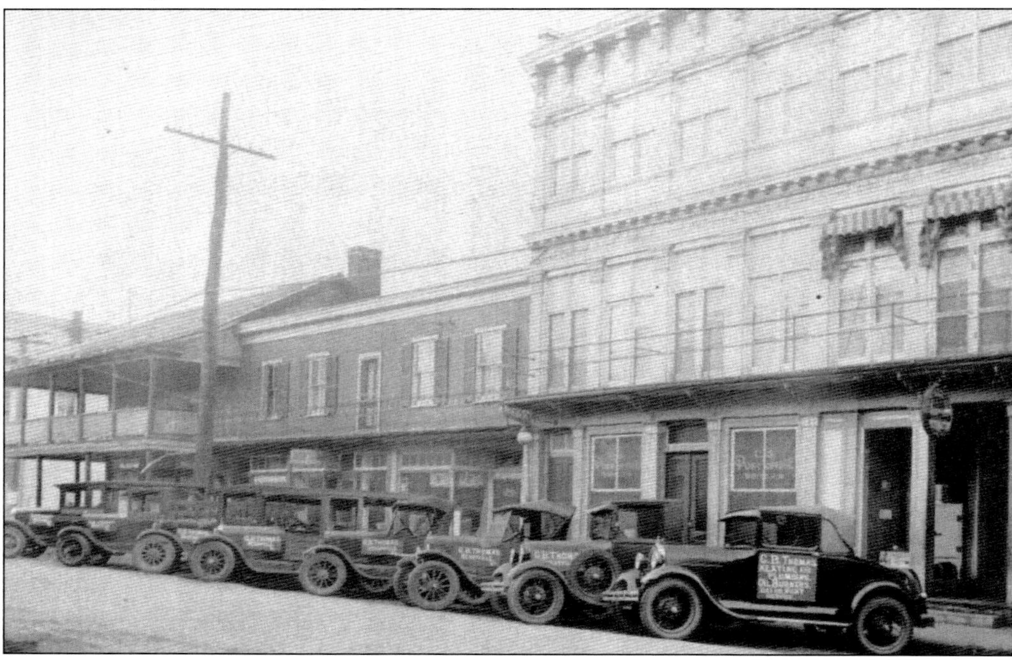

This 1931 view of Main Street shows a fleet of cars and pick-up trucks belonging to G. and B. Thomas's Heating and Plumbing Company. Angled parking clearly was preferred at that time. The post office was located in the first floor of the three-story Masonic building, originally the Harford House, a hotel and tavern. (CCHA.)

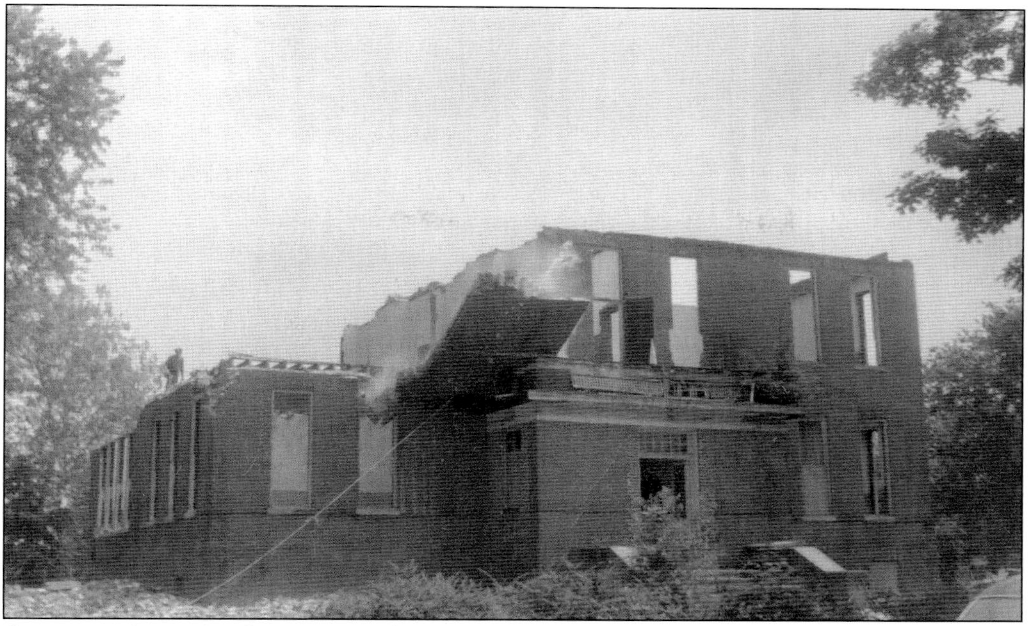

Constructed in 1901, the two-story, brick Berryville High School stood on Academy Street on the site of two earlier schools that had burned. It became an elementary school in 1924, when a new high school was constructed on West Main Street. The second-story auditorium had a seating capacity of 300. This shows the school's demolition in 1962. (CCHA.)

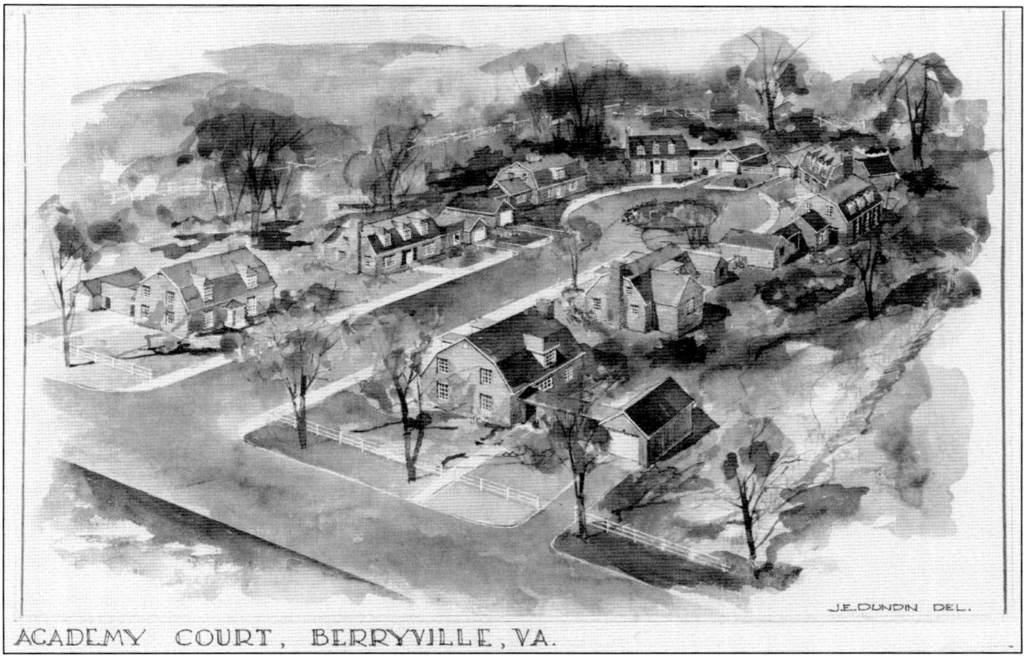

This 1963 architect's sketch depicts the Academy Court development that was built on the site of Berryville High School using bricks from the demolished school. Designed by architect George L. Howe and constructed by builder George Hummer, each three-bedroom, two-bath house had a full basement with a fallout shelter. (*Clarke Courier.*)

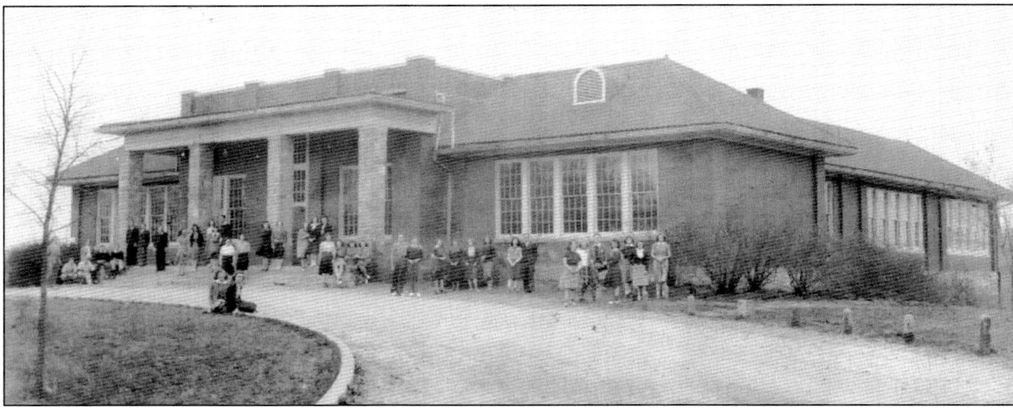

A new Berryville (later Clarke County) High School was constructed on West Main Street in 1924, replacing the one on Academy Street. In 1954, another high school was built on Swan Avenue, and this building was eventually demolished. When a subsequent high school on Westwood Road was completed in 1987, the Swan Avenue building became Johnson-Williams Middle School. The current high school will be replaced in 2012 by a more modern facility. (CCHA.)

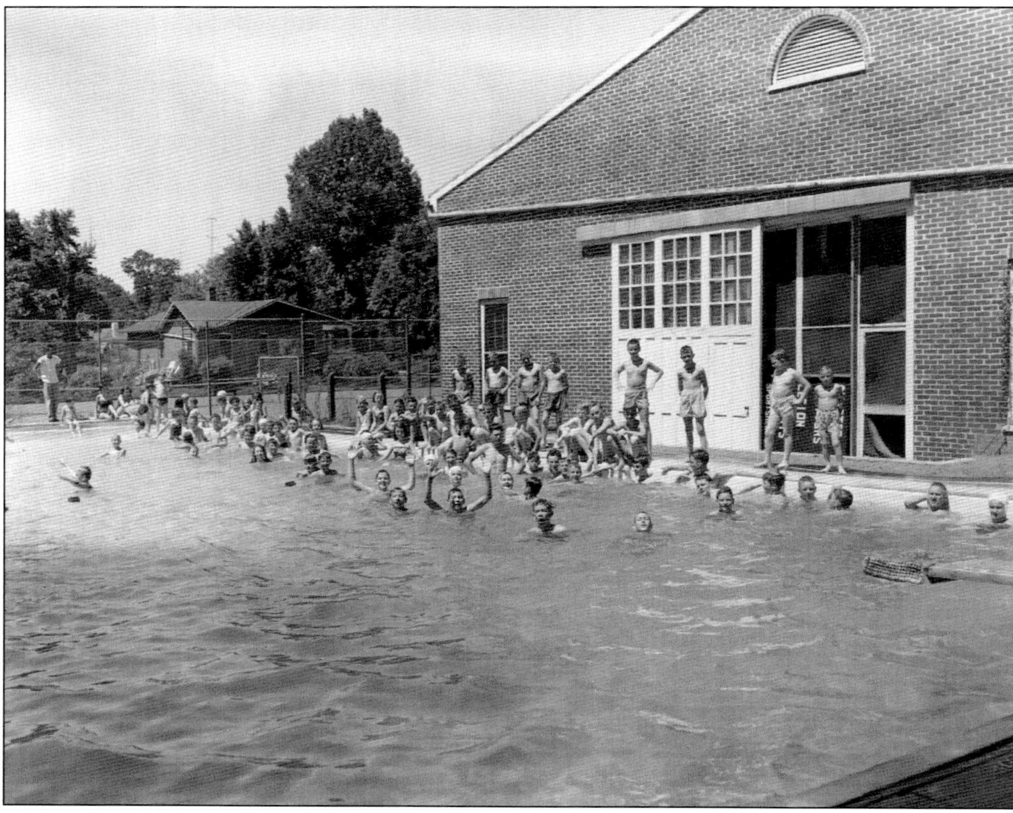

This photograph from around 1950 shows the public swimming pool that opened in 1941 behind the town's community center, a building that now houses the Dollar General Store, at 20 South Church Street. Eventually filled in and paved over, the pool site is now a parking lot. The sliding doors led into the rear of the center, where Winchester native Patsy Cline sang on multiple occasions. (Herman Lloyd.)

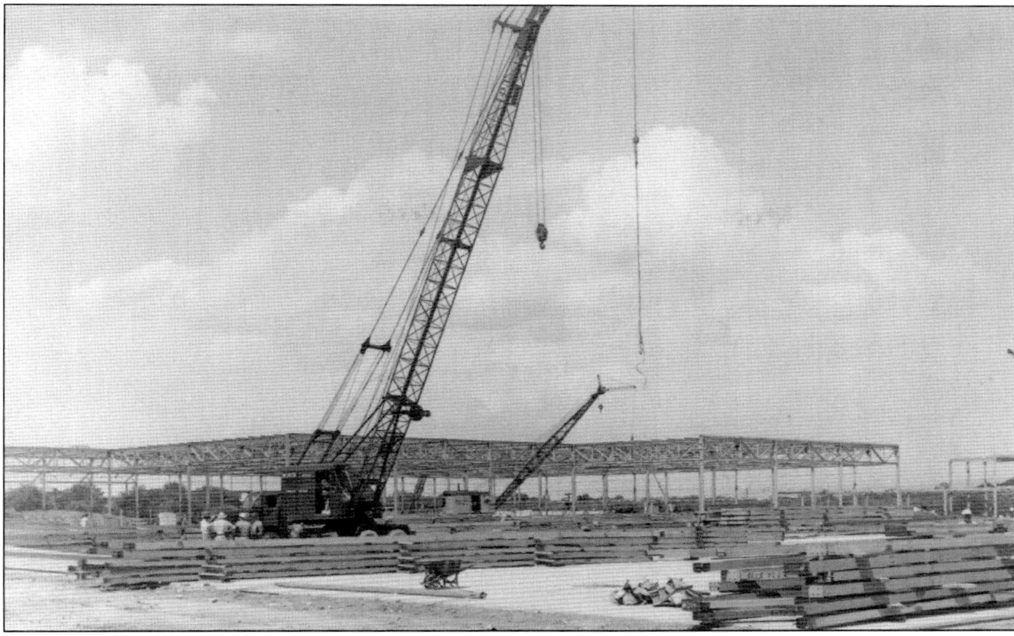

Constructed in 1956 in the middle of an apple orchard on the southeast edge of Berryville, Doubleday Publishing is now Berryville Graphics. The plant prints more than 100 million books a year, making it one of the largest of its kind in the United States and the county's largest employer. (CCHA.)

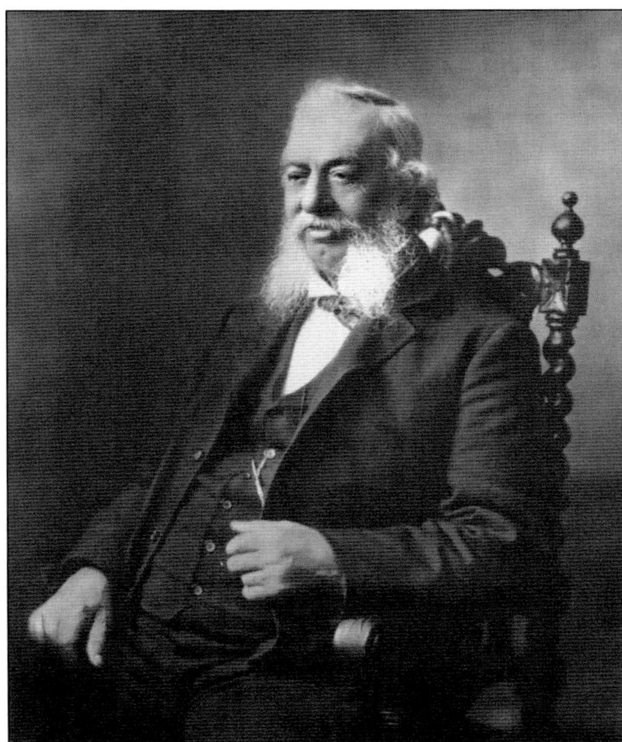

Established in 1880 at the intersection of the newly constructed Shenandoah Valley Railroad and the Winchester–Berry's Ferry Turnpike, Boyce was originally known as Boyceville. The town was named after Col. Upton Boyce (pictured), a local resident and a railroad vice president who, despite economic hard times, was able to get the rail project completed through Clarke County. (Bonnie Jacobs.)

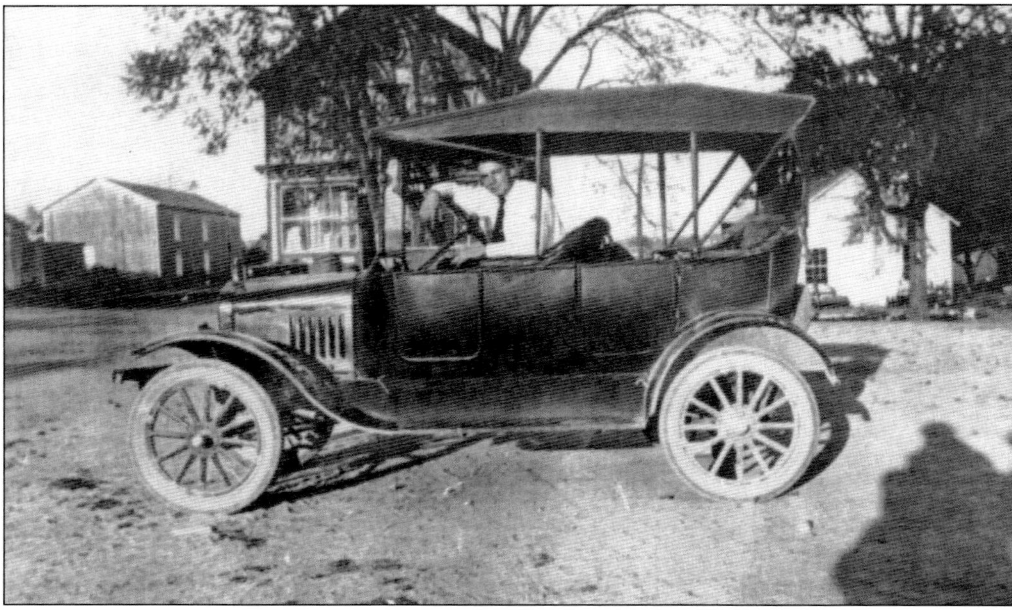

The earliest building activity in Boyce was at the crossing of the newly laid railroad and the Winchester–Berry's Ferry Turnpike. This 1920s image of Bill Thompson in his car on East Main Street shows commercial buildings in the background. When the town was incorporated in 1910, it encompassed 232 acres with a population of 312. Much of the land for the town came from five surrounding farms. (Billy Thompson.)

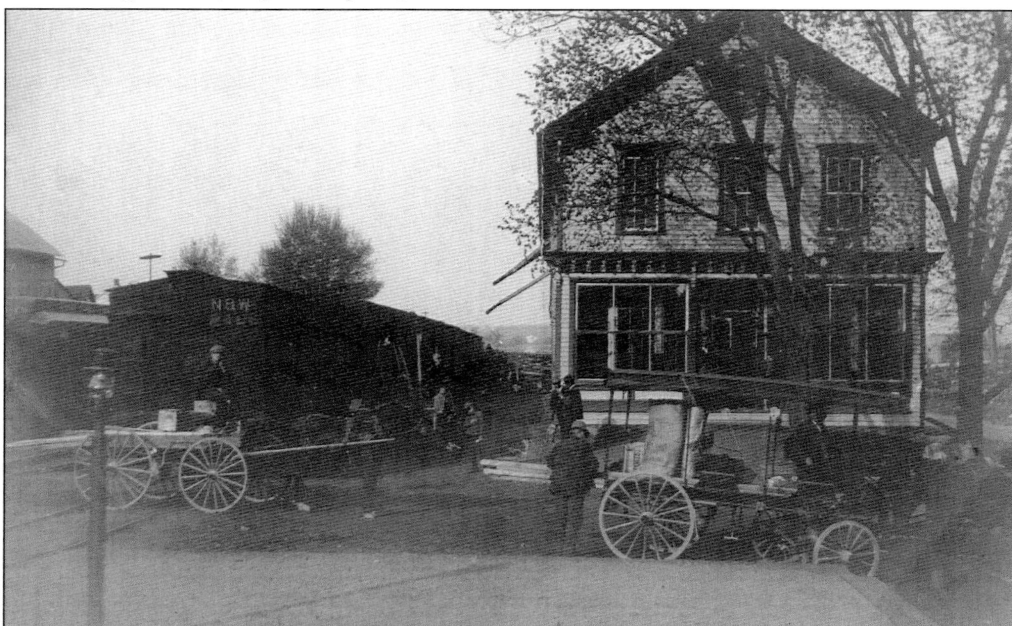

This image from around 1900 shows George Garvin's grain elevator and feed store at what is now 108 East Main Street. Thanks to the railroad, Boyce became a major commercial center and shipping point for local farmers, some of whom are pictured loading their long open wagons. Note the post in the foreground fitted with a kerosene lantern to illuminate the crossing. (CCHA.)

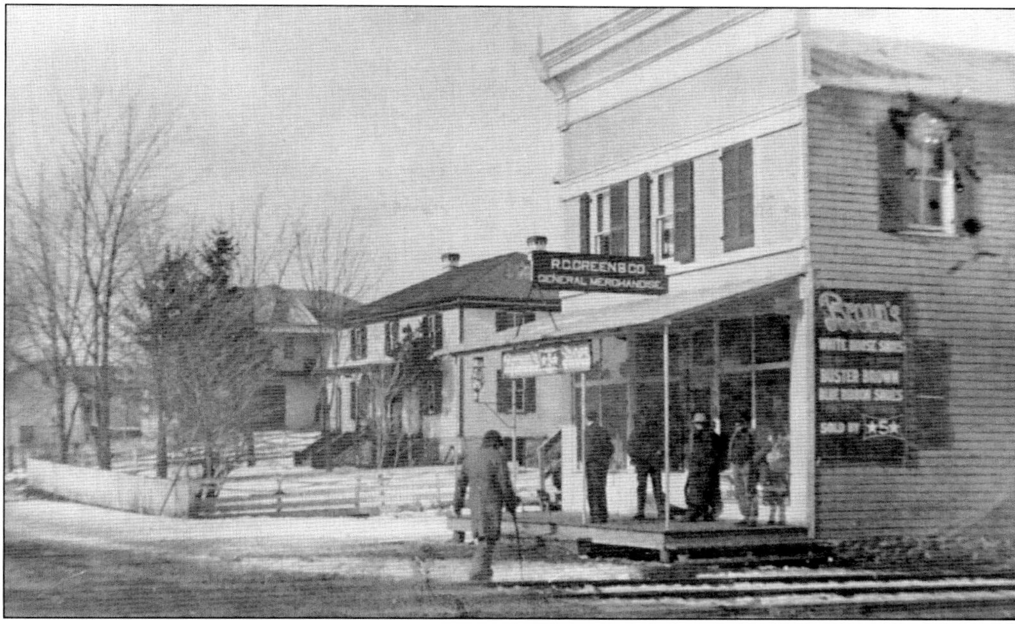

The 1881 Virginia Business Directory listed three general stores, two iron works, a hotel, a meat dealer, a saddler, and a wool dealer in Boyce. By the mid-1880s, the town added two attorneys, a sawmill, another saddler, and a physician to its list of businesses and professionals. This image from around 1910 shows Green's Store and was taken from the tracks, looking northwest along Main Street. (CCHA.)

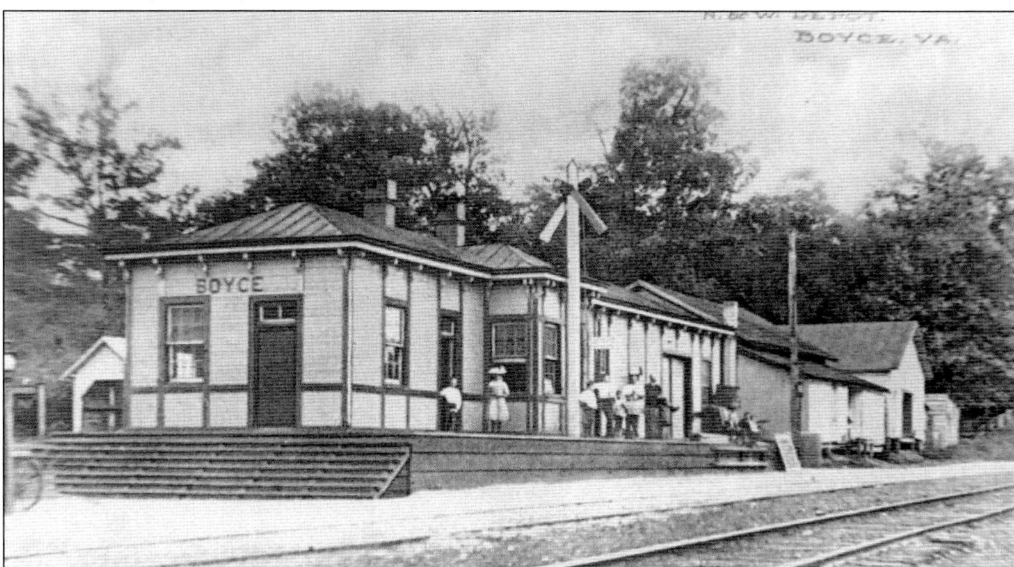

This postcard of Boyce's first train station (no longer standing) shows the hip-roofed frame building with a raised platform and full-width steps. When the railroad wanted to improve the station, locals were dissatisfied with the proposed design, preferring a more "pretentious" facility. With the help of funding from wealthy local residents, a new station that suited their tastes was completed in 1913. (CCHA.)

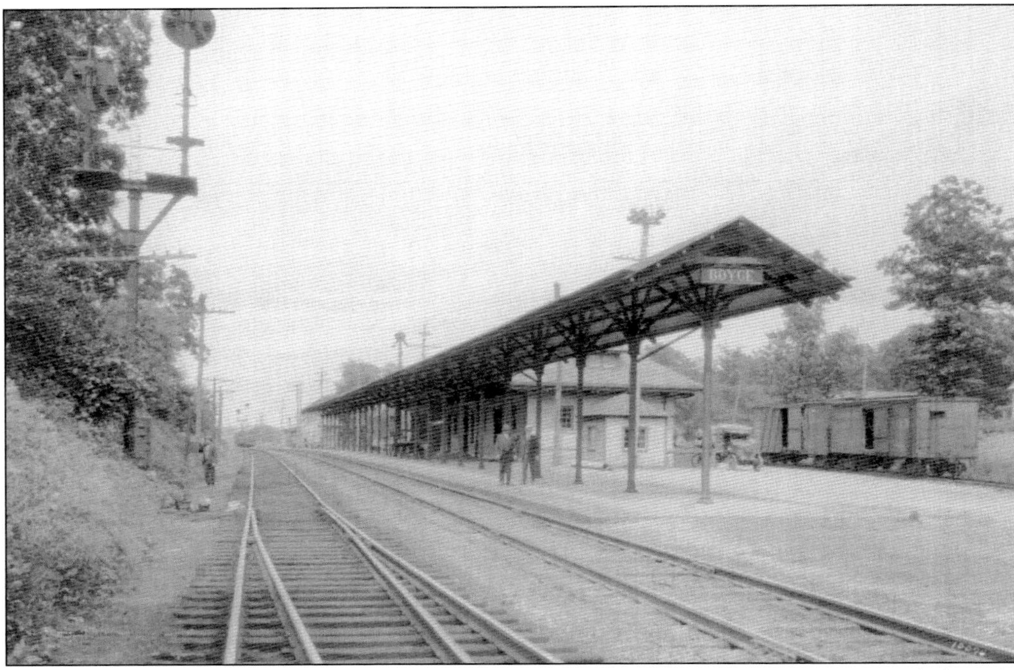

When completed in 1913, the Boyce train station was the largest and most ornate in Clarke. The elegant structure contained 11 rooms, including separate waiting and restrooms for black patrons, a large "whites only" waiting room, and a telegraph office. The station also featured iced water fountains, central heat, and electric lights. No longer used as a station, it is privately owned and houses the Railway Mail Service Library. (Virginia Tech ImageBase: Norfolk-Southern.)

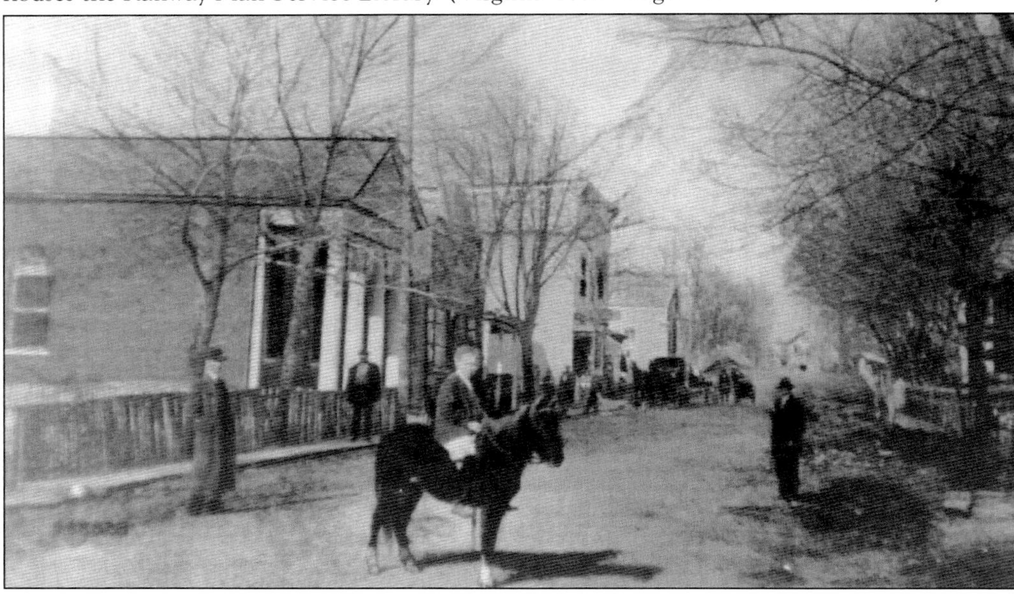

Boyce State Bank, the brick building with the portico in the foreground, opened in 1908 and touted itself as having the most modern equipment around, including a circular-shaped burglar-proof safe. Ironically, it had been robbed seven times when the bank finally moved from the building in 1983. The structure is now home to Boyce's town hall. (CCHA).

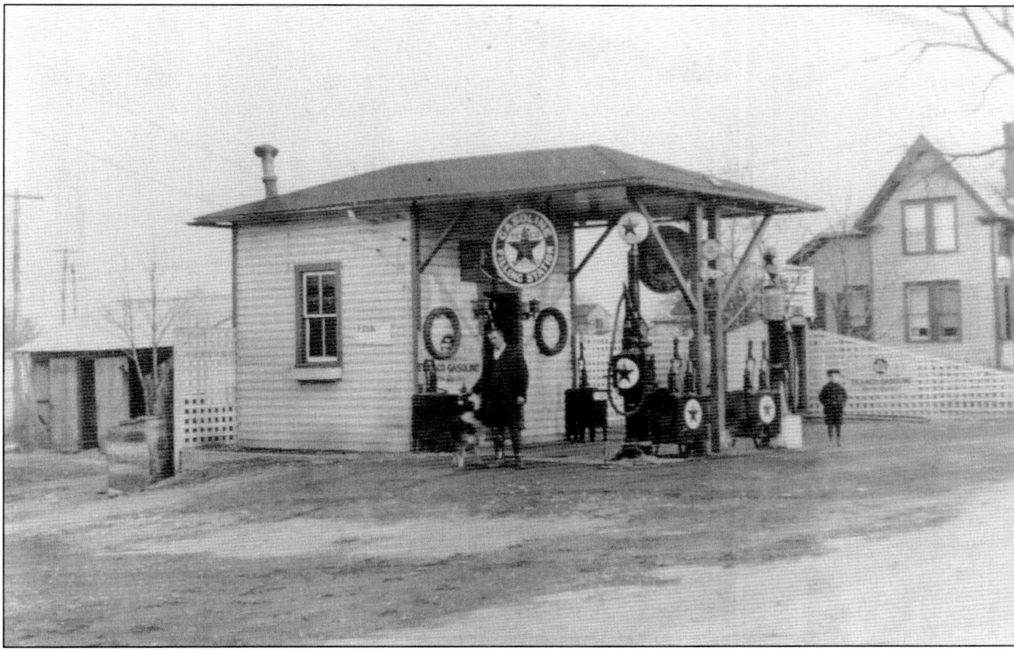

Shown about 1925 is the Texaco station, then located at the northeast corner of the junction of Main Street and Old Chapel Road. Its operator, Thomas Powell Jolliffe, also managed the Shell station on the opposite corner. He is pictured with his son Powell Jr. and his dog Major. (Shirley McKay.)

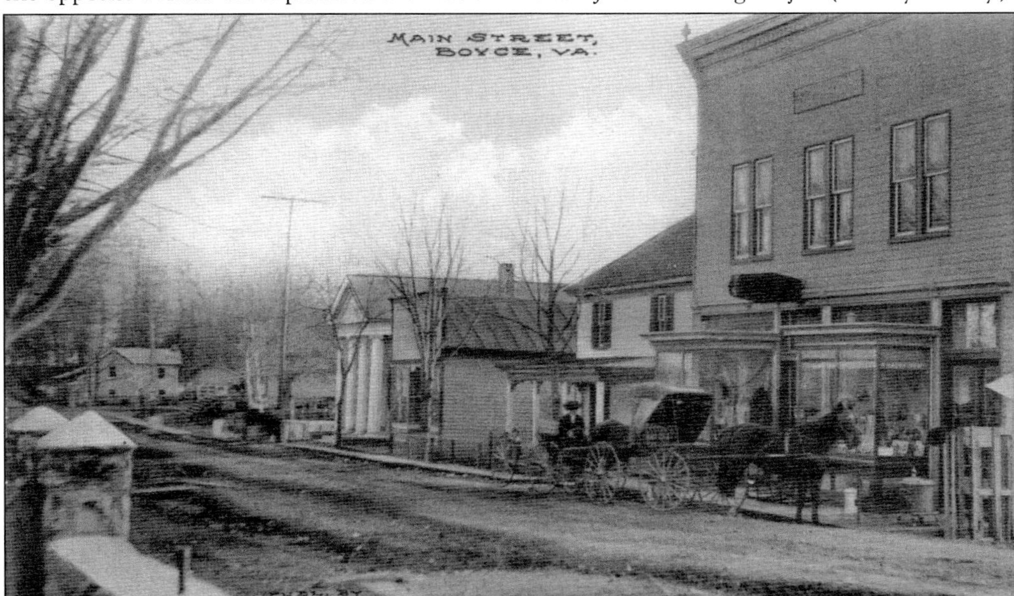

This early-1900s postcard of Boyce shows Simpson's Department Store in the foreground at 17 East Main Street. The second floor of the building once housed the town's movie theater. The building's facade was remodeled in 1999 to resemble a Venetian palace and is now the headquarters of Elizabeth Locke Jewels. A comparison of this historic view with a current one shows how little Boyce's streetscape has changed in the past century. (Author.)

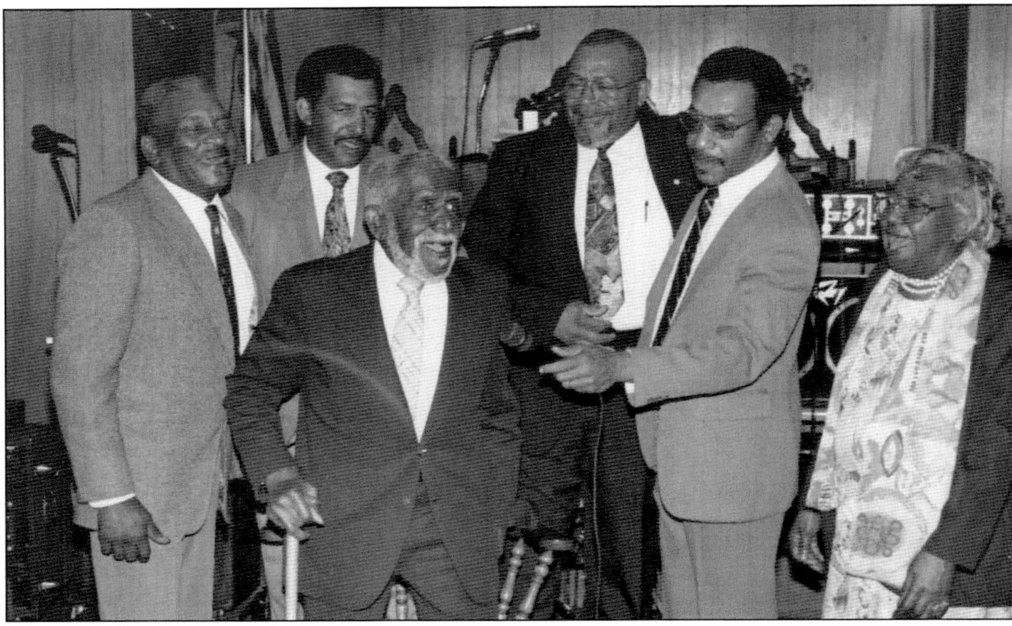

Beloved Boyce resident Abner Jackson Carey Sr. is shown in 1995 at his 100th birthday celebration. From left to right are his children Charles, Rudy, Abner Jr., Bushrod, and Roseanna. The first Boyce resident was Dennis Seals, an African American who owned land in the area by 1876, before the town was formed. An African American school opened in Boyce in 1885, and Mount Zion Baptist Church opened next to it in 1890. (*Clarke Courier.*)

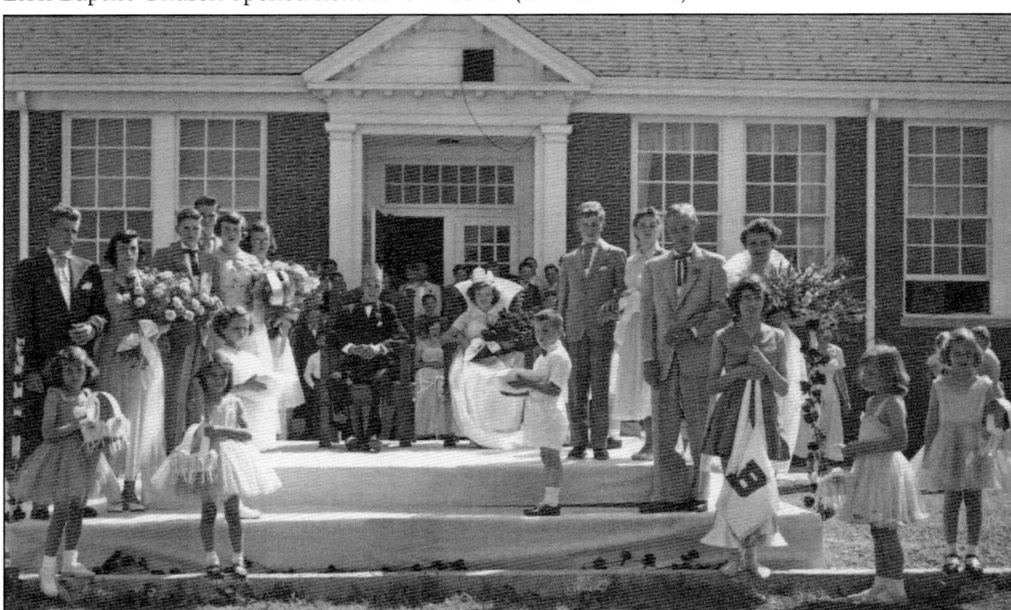

Boyce Elementary School was constructed in 1942 at a cost of $72,500, replacing the 1908 Boyce High School, later known as Boyce Agricultural School, which was eventually demolished. This 1953 scene of May Day celebrations in the front yard of the brick school shows the king, queen, and various attendants. (Herman Lloyd.)

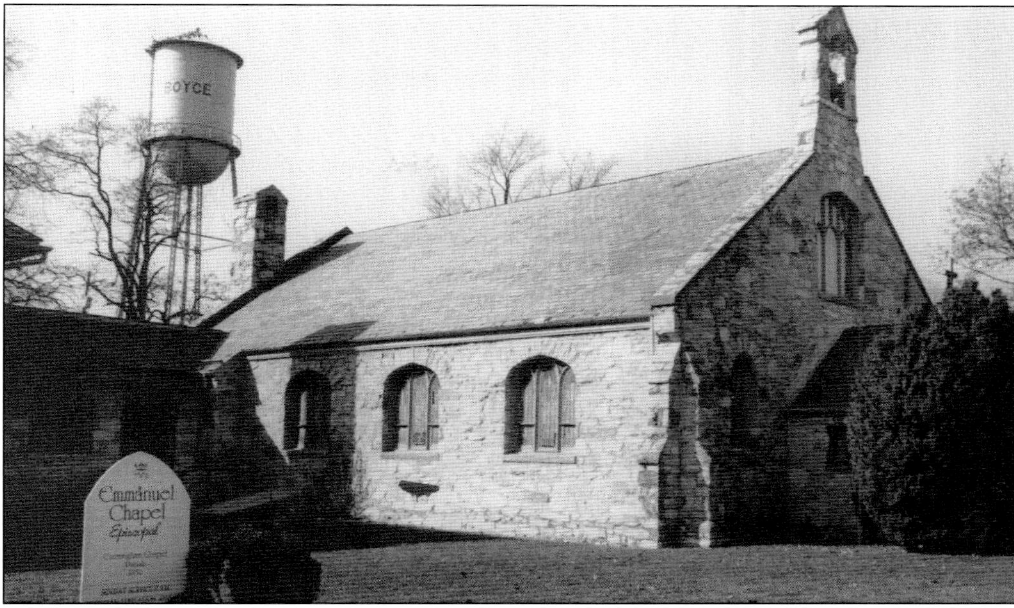

Emmanuel Chapel Episcopal Church was constructed in 1916, followed by the large stone parish hall in 1919. The hall featured an auditorium and a bowling alley and was for many years considered the community center. In 2011, both buildings were sold and deconsecrated. When a municipal water system was installed in the mid-1970s, the water tower seen in the background was erected. A new one replaced it in 2006. (CCHA.)

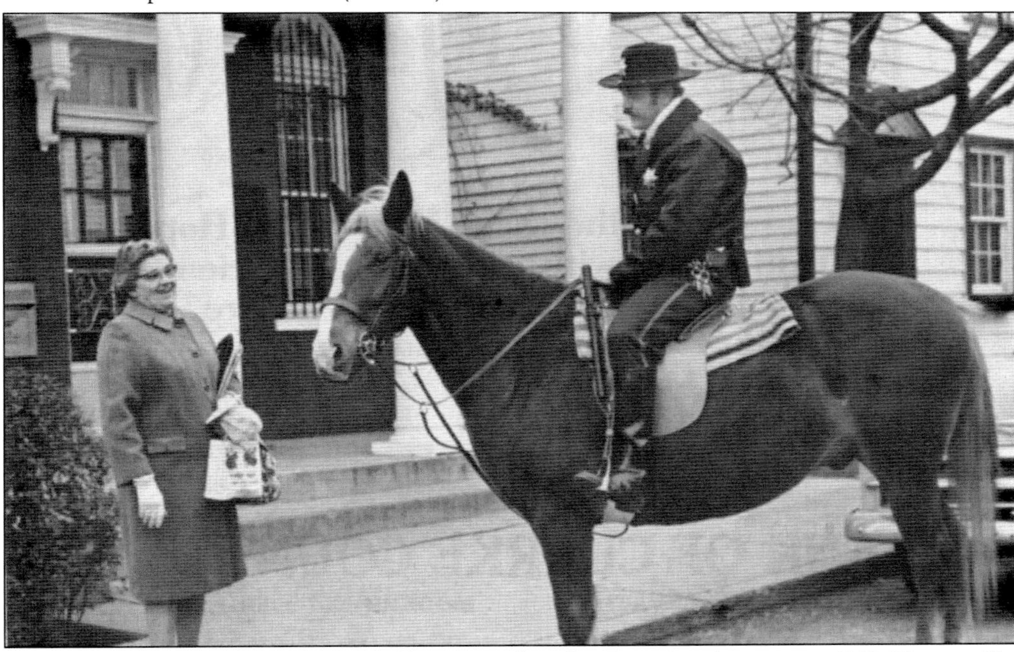

After several area robberies, Greer Fullerton was hired as Boyce's policeman in 1973. He patrolled the streets astride Roscoe, as the town lacked funds for a police car. In this photograph, Fullerton is chatting with Bank of Clarke County employee Edith Rodgers in front of her workplace. (Billy Thompson.)

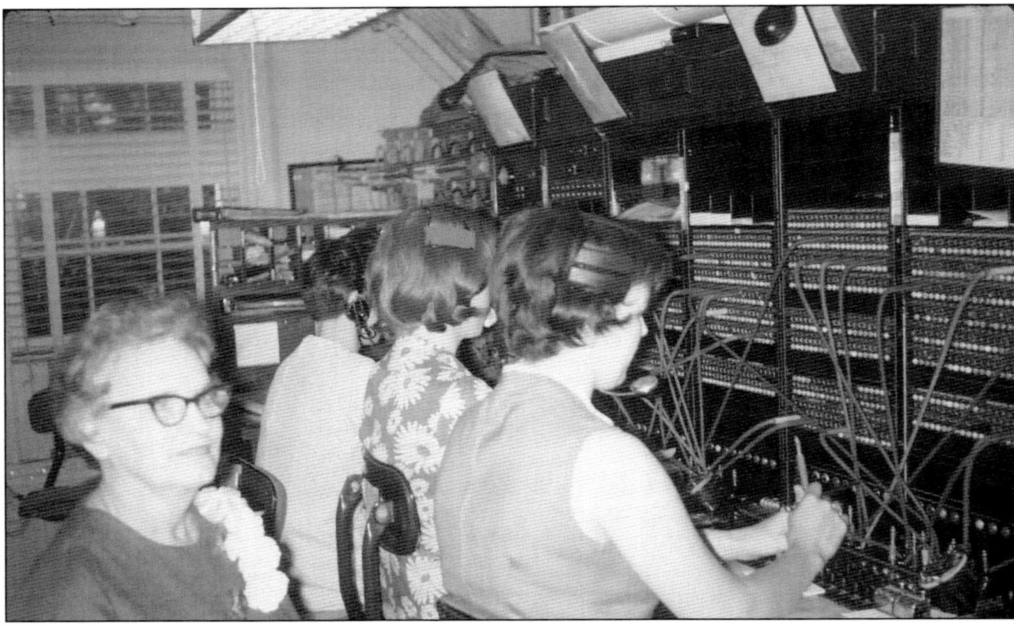

This late-1960s photograph depicts Lucy Kephart (with corsage), operator of the Boyce exchange, along with three others manning the busy phone operation. Before the telephone company converted from a manual operator to an automated dial system in 1968, all calls had to go through the switchboard. Boyce was one of the last offices in the commonwealth to convert to a mechanical system. (Author.)

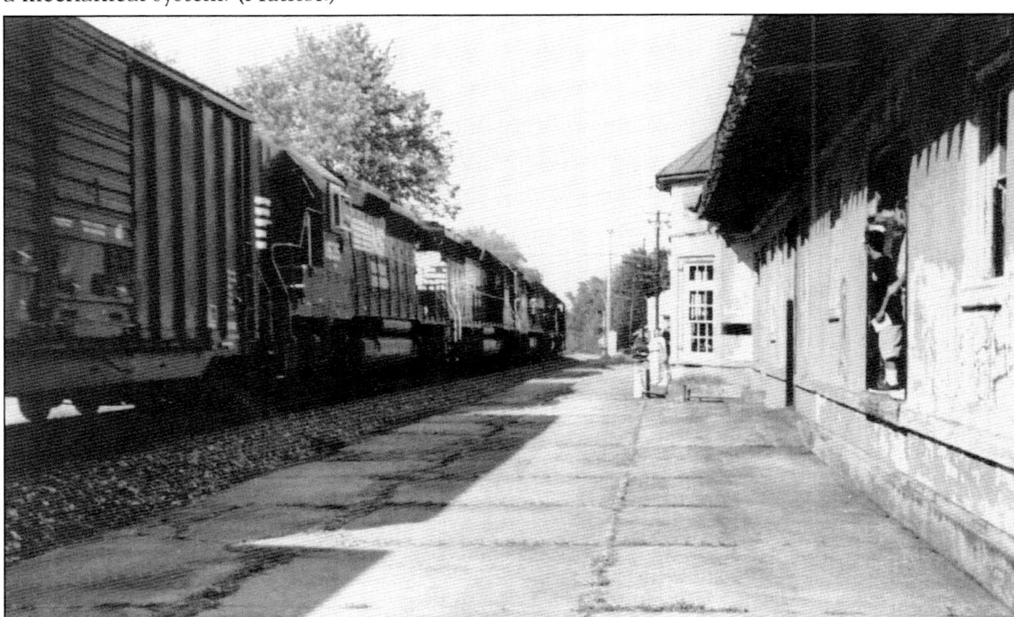

Passenger and freight rail service ceased in Boyce in the mid-20th century, and the town was bypassed when US Route 50 was constructed two miles to the south. Since then, Boyce has evolved into a residential center with only a few commercial establishments, but trains that still roll through town recall the roots of the community's development. (CCHA.)

Six

Villages: Millwood and White Post

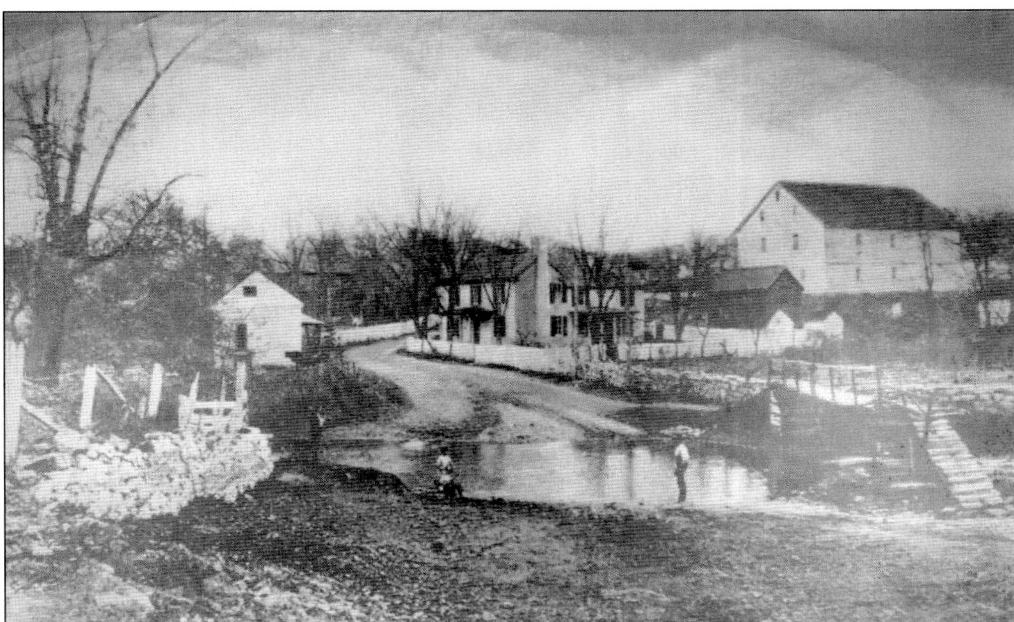

Dominating the Millwood skyline is the Burwell-Morgan Mill, constructed between 1782 and 1786. This late-19th-century view shows the pedestrian bridge and original road that forded Spout Run, passing the miller's house as it ran up to the mill. The small building to the left was constructed as a warehouse for Joseph Tuley's tanyard, which operated on the site as early as 1786. It was later used as a tollhouse on the Millwood-Berryville Turnpike. (CCHA.)

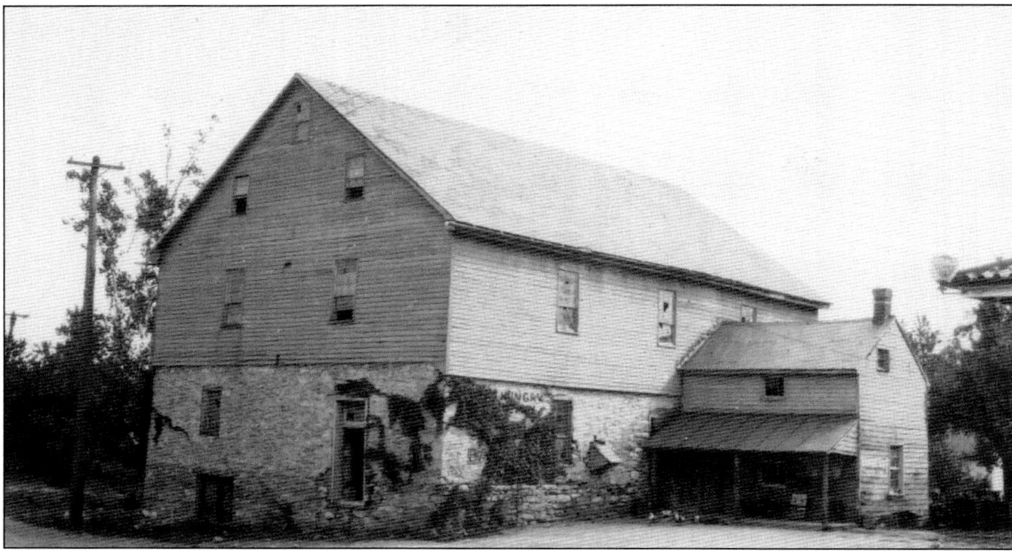

Millwood developed in the late 1780s around the newly constructed Burwell-Morgan Mill, the largest merchant mill in the area. Established by the partnership of Col. Nathaniel Burwell and Daniel Morgan, the mill was constructed by Hessian prisoners of war and contains an interior overshot wheel. The frame upper stories and side wing shown in this late-1920s view were added in 1876. The first millwright was supposedly named "Sledgehammer" Mongrul. (SBA/HRL.)

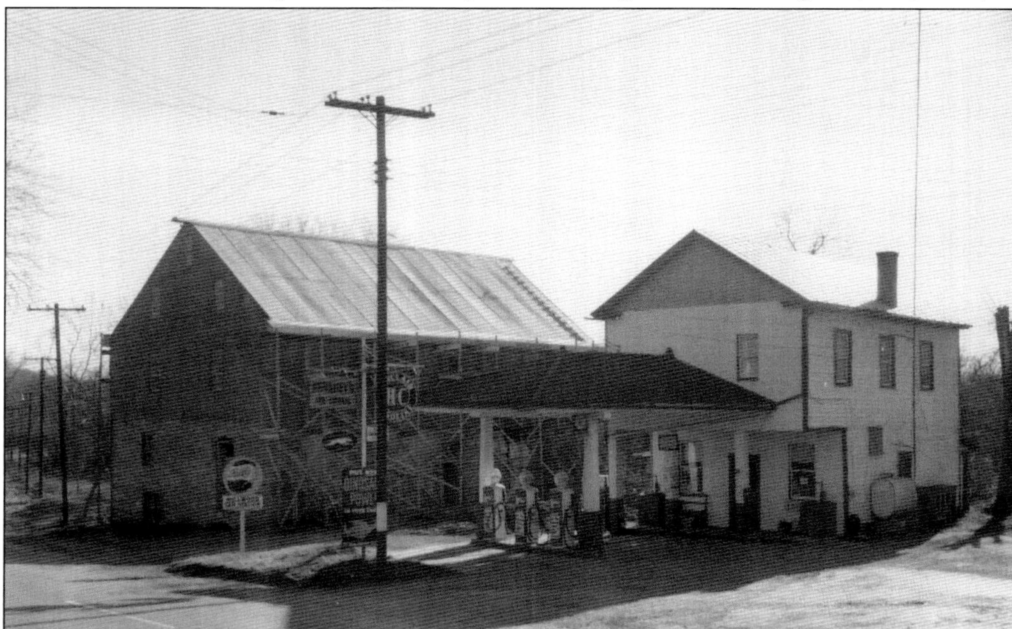

Operated into the 1950s, the Burwell-Morgan Mill fell into disrepair and was donated to the CCHA in 1964 by Leo Bernstein. The association restored the structure and in 1970 opened it as an exhibition mill and museum. Ernest Alger both ran the mill and operated the adjacent Millwood service station, shown to the right, which was located in a former grain house. The station was demolished in the mid-1960s. (CCHA.)

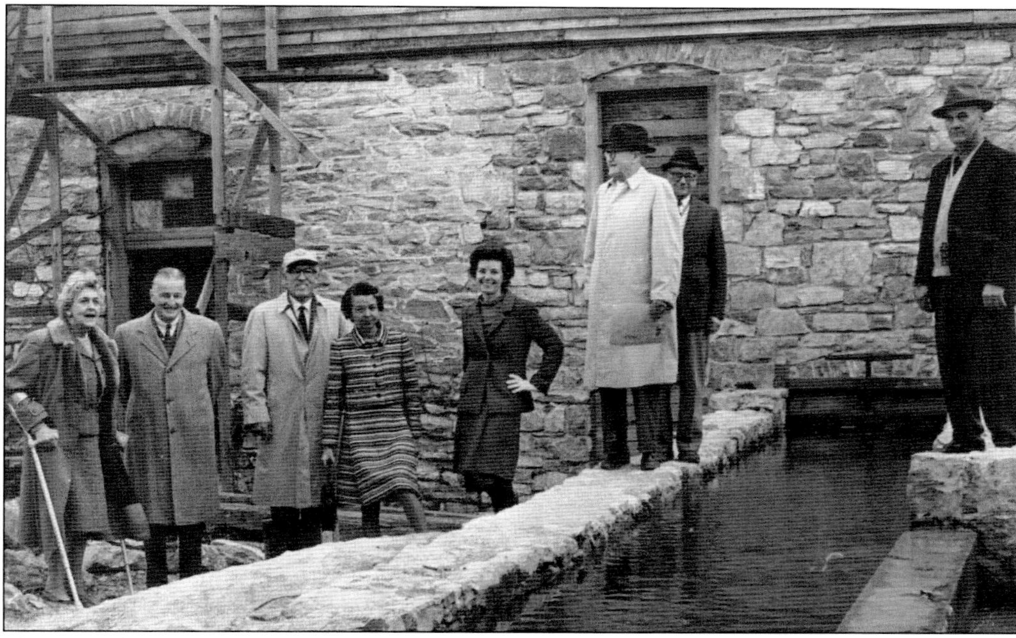

The Burwell-Morgan Mill Restoration Committee is pictured in October 1968 at the dedication of the newly restored headrace. From left to right are Mrs. Kenneth Gilpin (Isabella T.), Alexander Mackay-Smith, Richard Plater Jr. (chairman), Mrs. William West (Betty C.), Mrs. Richard Byrd (Helen), George H. Burwell, Ralph Dorsey, and William I. Groves (millwright). The mill continues to operate, grinding corn and wheat and other grain every Saturday from May through November. (CCHA.)

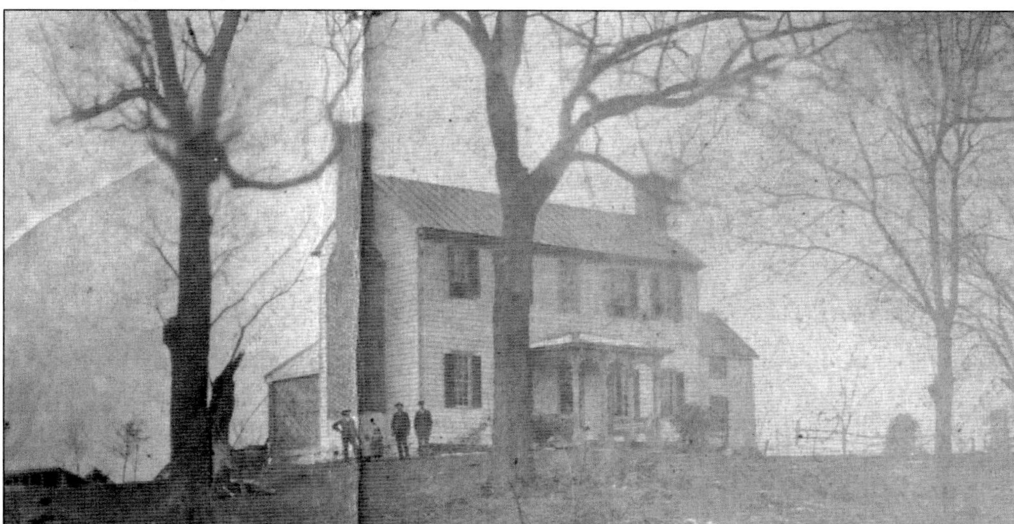

Joseph Tuley, a tanner from New Jersey, constructed this dwelling around 1795 on a bluff across Spout Run from his tannery. The name Three Pounds reflects what Tuley paid for the site. Descriptions of Millwood in 1810 tell of a population of "50 to 60 people, a large merchant mill, extensive leather manufactory, a tavern, a store, a blacksmith, a tailor, a boot and shoe maker, and wagon maker." (CCHA.)

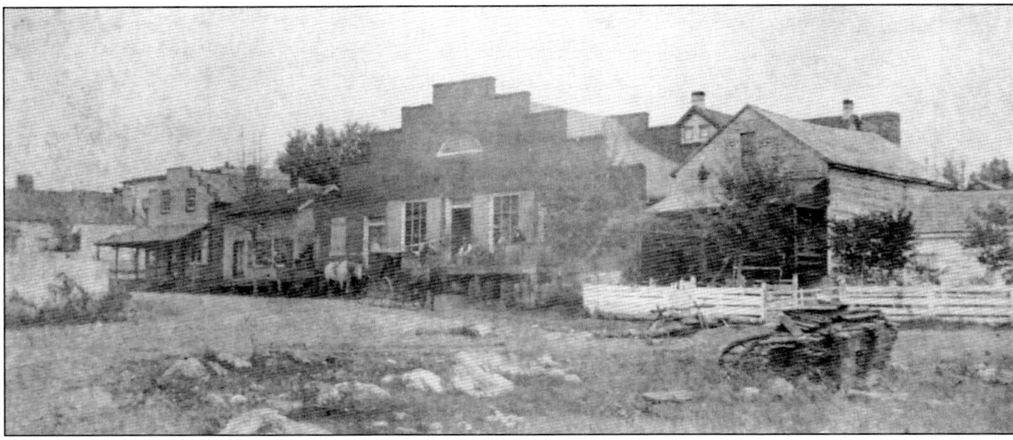

Locke Store, a brick building constructed by James H. Clark in the 1830s, stands at the center of the late-1800s photograph of "downtown" Millwood above. A 1935 fire that followed a botched robbery destroyed the tall, stepped parapet roof. The building to the right (constructed about 1805) was used to store liquor in a secure place. The stuccoed building on the left was eventually raised to two stories and housed the post office on the ground floor with a barbershop above. Farther left is a building with a stepped parapet, the Russell Brothers Store, which was later run by the Potters. The photograph below, from about 1920, shows B.B. McKay, one of the owners of the store, known at that time as McKay and Burch. Since 2002, the country store has continued to thrive under new ownership. (Both, CCHA.)

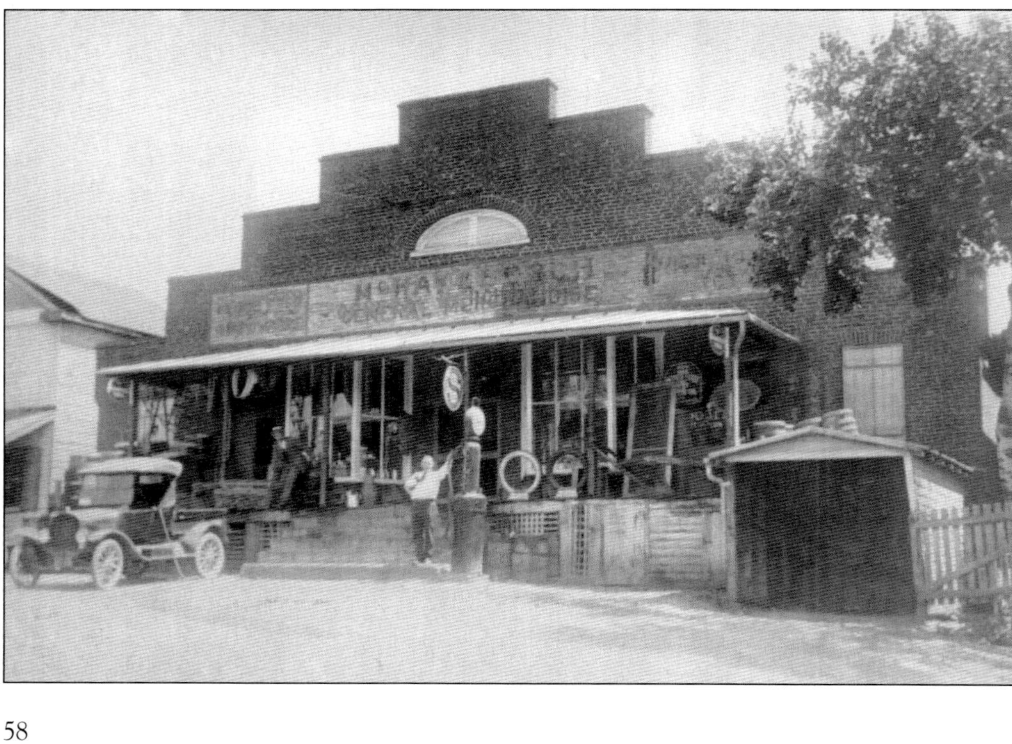

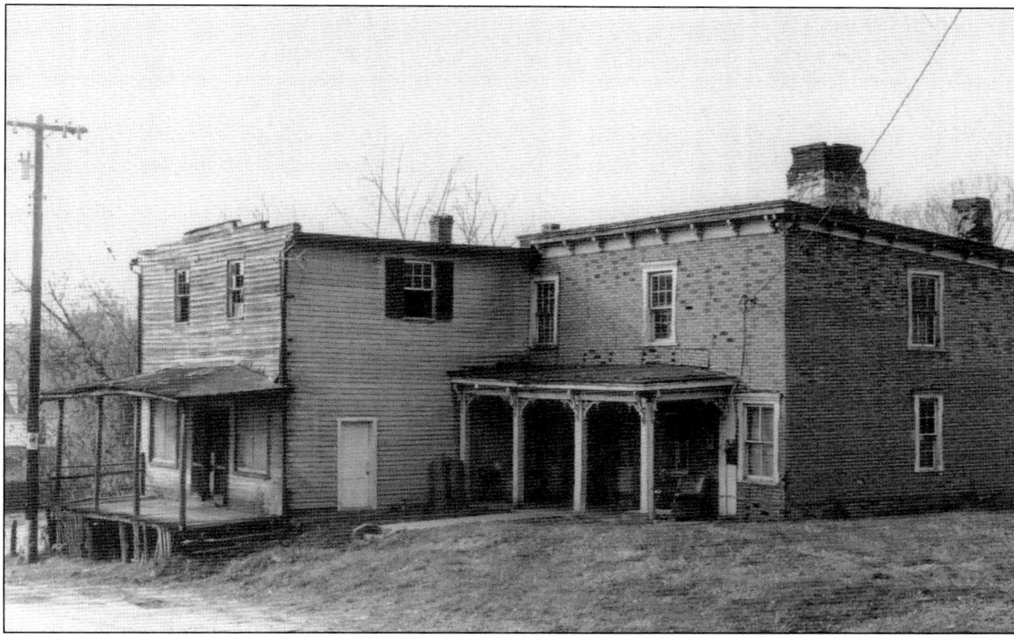

Pictured in 1976, these two buildings, which have since burned, stood on the west side of Bishop Meade Road near the bottom of the so-called Millwood Hill. The left one was the Willingham & Burch Store and later Golden Rule Grocery. The recessed building to the right was presumably a dwelling. The massive stone-and-brick chimney suggests an early construction date. (CCHA.)

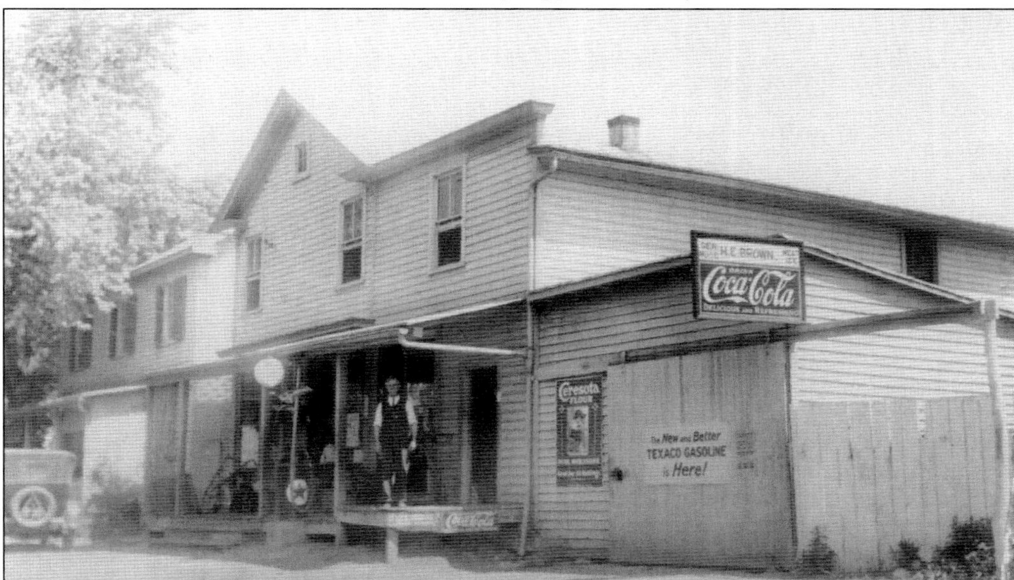

Located on Millwood Road, H.E. Brown's Store was one of multiple village businesses, confirming Millwood's importance as a commercial center. Posing on the front porch in the 1920s is proprietor Brown. With the arrival of the railroad and the establishment of Boyce just two miles to the west, Millwood faded as a market community, with commercial activity generally limited to the area around the mill. (CCHA.)

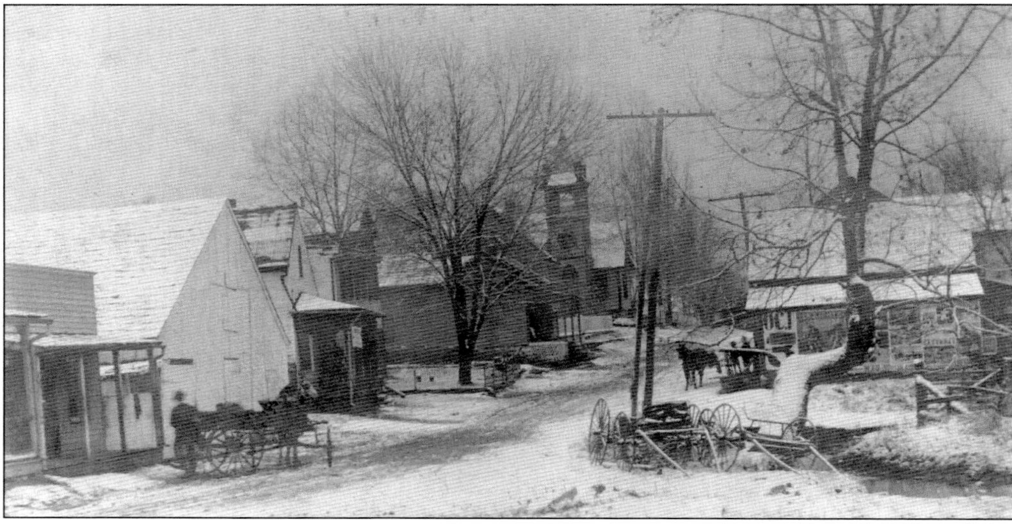

This early-20th-century snow scene of Millwood Road looking east shows Brown's Store to the left. The building to the right is pasted with broadsides advertising traveling shows. The bell tower in the background belongs to Shiloh Baptist Church, constructed in 1892 and one of two African American Baptist churches in the village. This road was also known as Water Street because of its proximity to the millrace, which is in the foreground. (CCHA.)

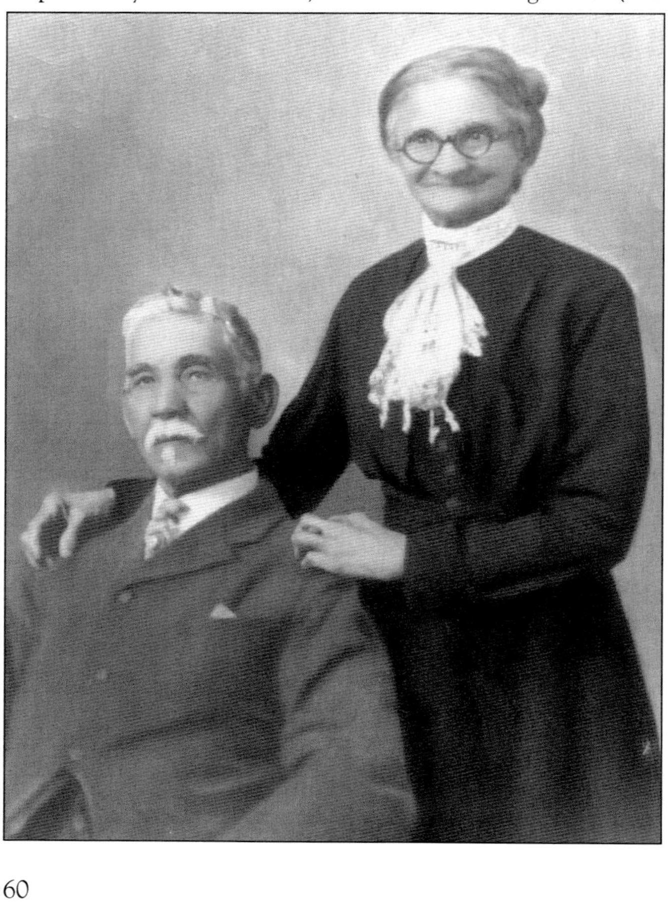

Rev. Benjamin Thomas Layton and Elizabeth Brown Layton are pictured in 1925 at the celebration of their 50th wedding anniversary. They lived at Rock Cliff across from the Burwell-Morgan Mill. Mrs. Layton taught school, and all nine of their children received full educations and pursued professions. Until his death in 2007, their grandson William W. Layton, a former government executive, writer, and philanthropist, spent summers and part of his retirement in Millwood. (SBA/HRL.)

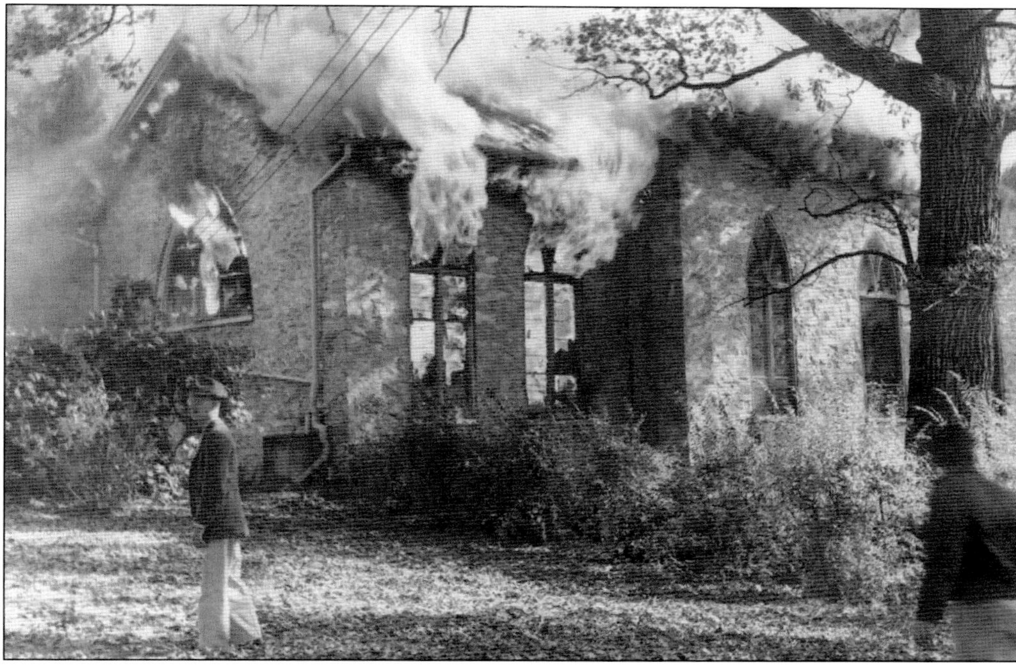

Christ Episcopal Church, constructed in 1834 on land donated by George Burwell of Carter Hall, was almost destroyed in the 1947 fire pictured. It was subsequently rebuilt. The 1914 frame rectory located behind the church was constructed with funds from a wealthy donor at about the same time that the small bishop's chapel on the property was remodeled. (CCHA.)

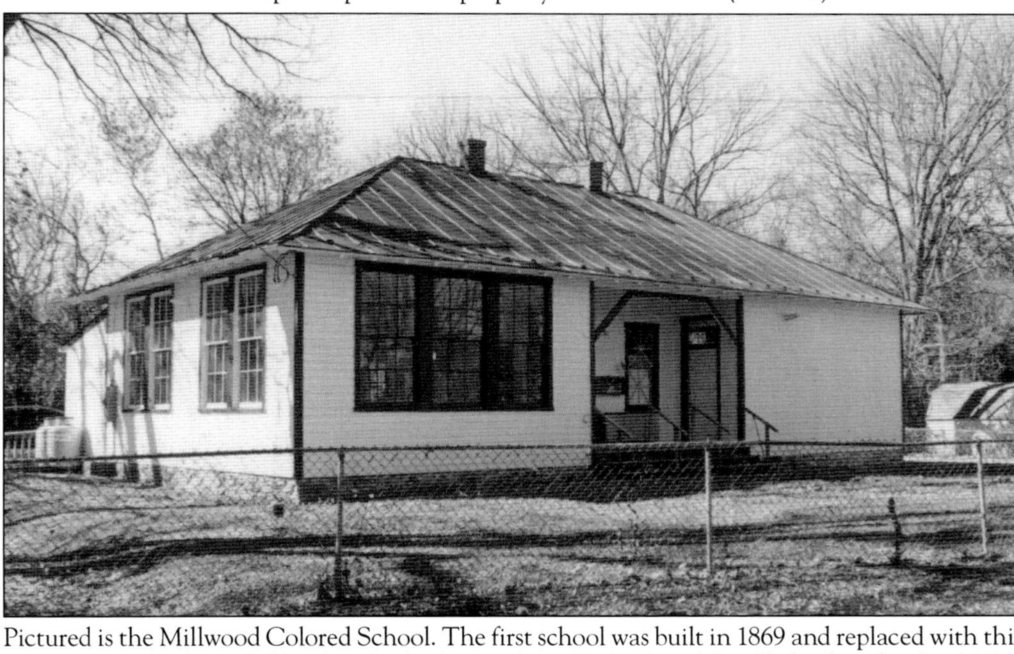

Pictured is the Millwood Colored School. The first school was built in 1869 and replaced with this one in 1910. Graham F. Blandy, who had moved to Clarke from New York after the Civil War, financed the construction of this school and one similar to it in White Post. This former school now serves as the community center run by the Millwood Goodwill Association. (CCHA.)

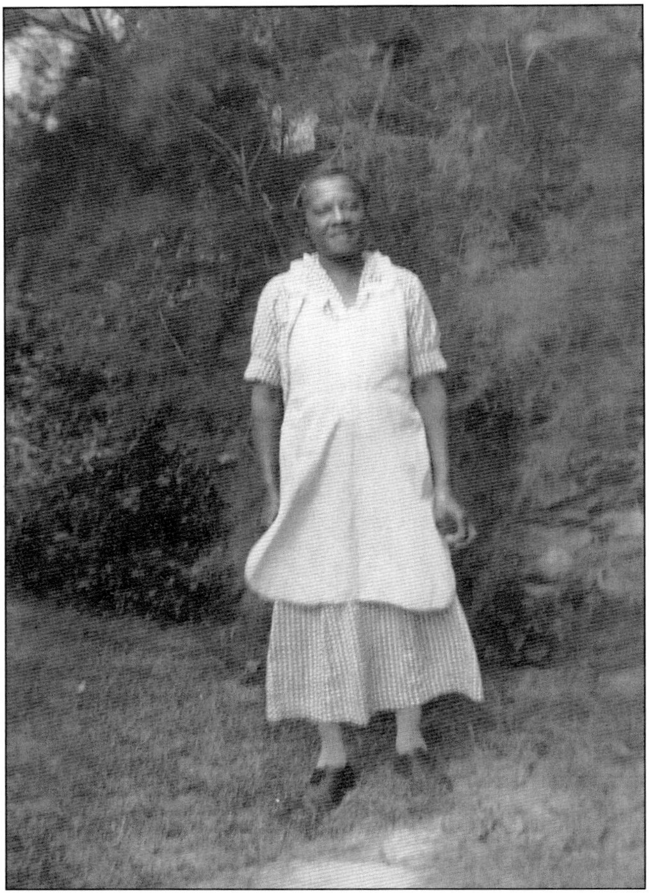

Pictured in 1938, Violet Williams Bannister was the longtime cook at Blandy Experimental Farm and much admired for her baking skills, especially a dark molasses-based sweet that she called black cake. Bannister made the four-mile round trip from Millwood to Blandy on foot almost daily. The mother of five, all of whom succumbed to childhood illnesses before their 10th birthday, Bannister lived to 95, dying in 1982. (Blandy Experimental Farm.)

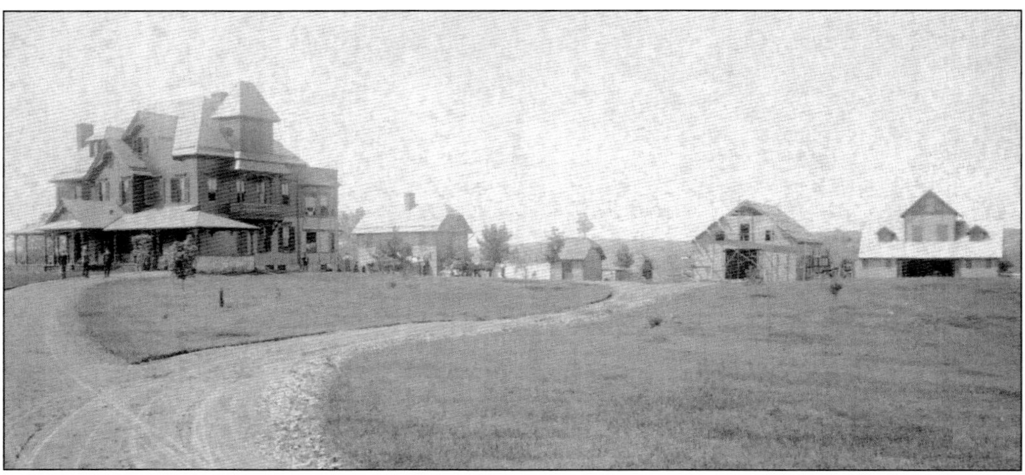

Peter H. Mayo and his wife, Isabella Burwell, of Carter Hall, built Powhatan as a summer home in 1888. The large Victorian dwelling is pictured in 1904 with multiple outbuildings and a barn under construction. When the property passed to the private Blue Ridge Country Day School in 1957, the name Powhatan was retained. The house burned in 1988, and a new educational facility was built on the site. (CCHA.)

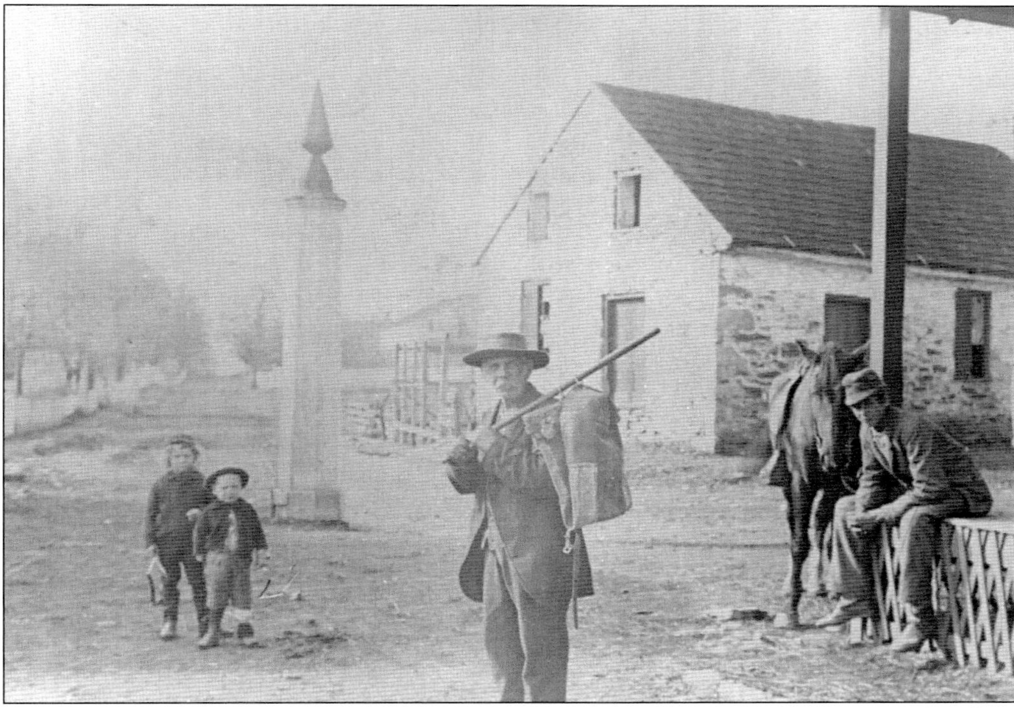

Seen in an 1880 view looking south, the crossroads village of White Post grew around a white-painted post erected in the 1760s to point the way south to Greenway Court, the nearby estate of Lord Fairfax. A post is still there today, recalling an era when it was a significant county landmark. The other roads led north to Berryville, east to the Shenandoah River, and west to Stephens City. (CCHA.)

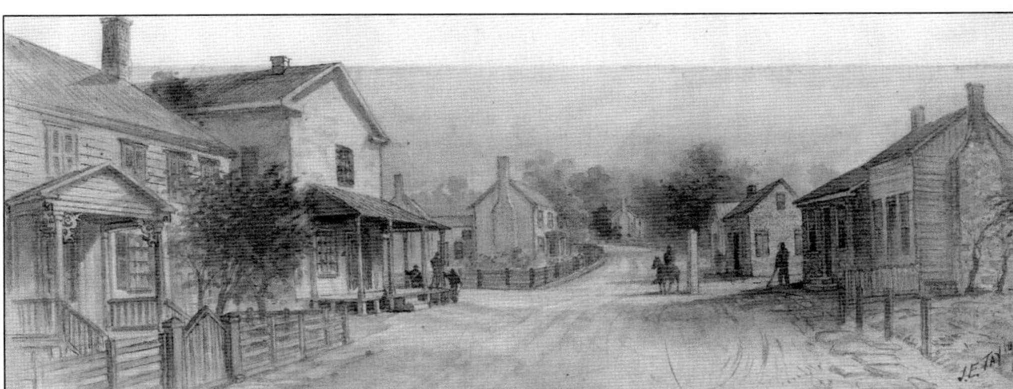

James E. Taylor's 1864 sketch of the hamlet of White Post (looking east) shows Jane Meade's residence and the adjacent Meade's Store (left foreground), a residence on the northeast corner, a stone office of the justice of the peace on the southwest corner (right side), and a brick inn at the southeast corner. None of these buildings survive. (Western Reserve Historical Society.)

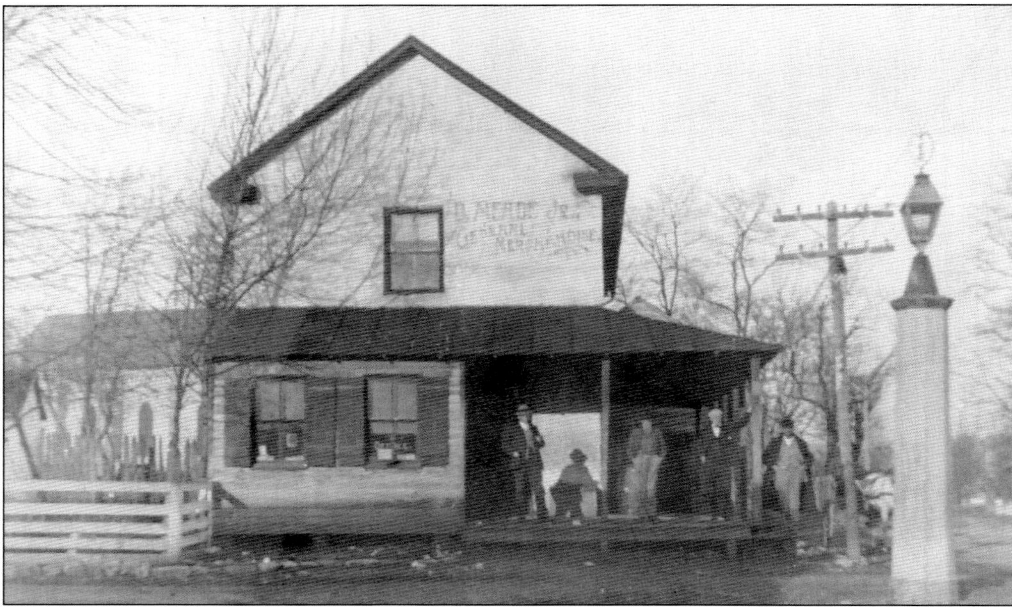

This view looking north from about 1910 shows D. Meade Jr. General Merchandise, a store that stood at the northwest corner of the crossroads. In notes accompanying his 1864 sketch of White Post, James E. Taylor describes the building as a "general store . . . of Bishop Meade's son." The white post is topped by a kerosene lantern that replaced an earlier wood finial. (CCHA.)

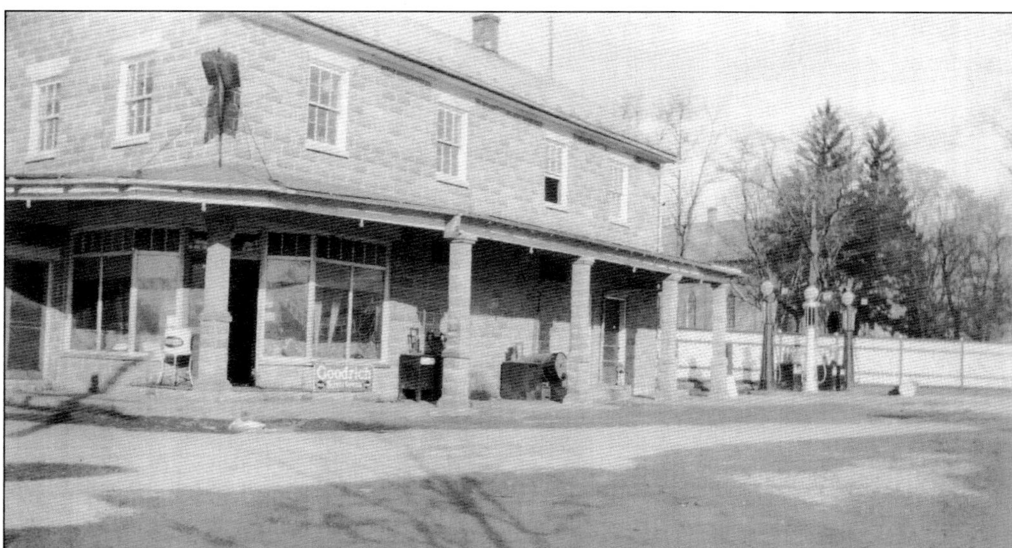

George R. Green's Store replaced Meade's at the northwest corner of the crossroads around 1920. The two-story building with a wraparound porch and corner entryway pictured was constructed of rock-faced concrete blocks, a popular material of the time. The store closed in the mid-20th century and was eventually demolished. Three gasoline pumps stood along the east side of the building. (Billy Thompson.)

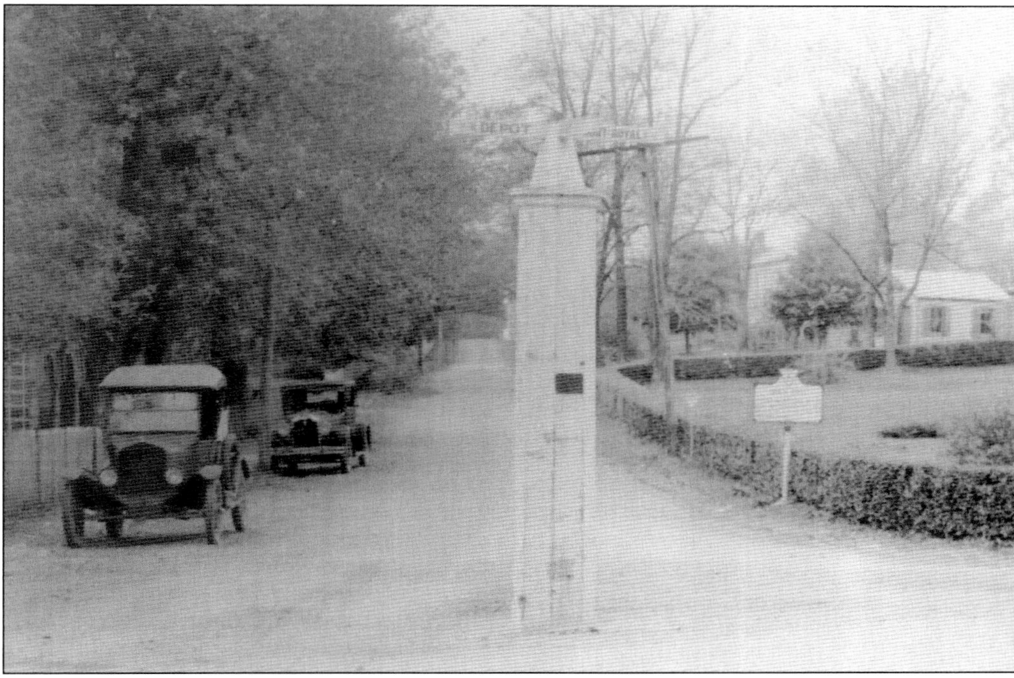

This photograph of the distinctive white post was taken about 1929 looking southward toward Greenway Court. Directional arms extending off the top of the octagonal wooden post point the way to the railroad depot to the east, Front Royal to the west, and Berryville to the north. An early Virginia Historical Highway marker about White Post acknowledges the historic significance of the village, which has a population of about 150. (CCHA.)

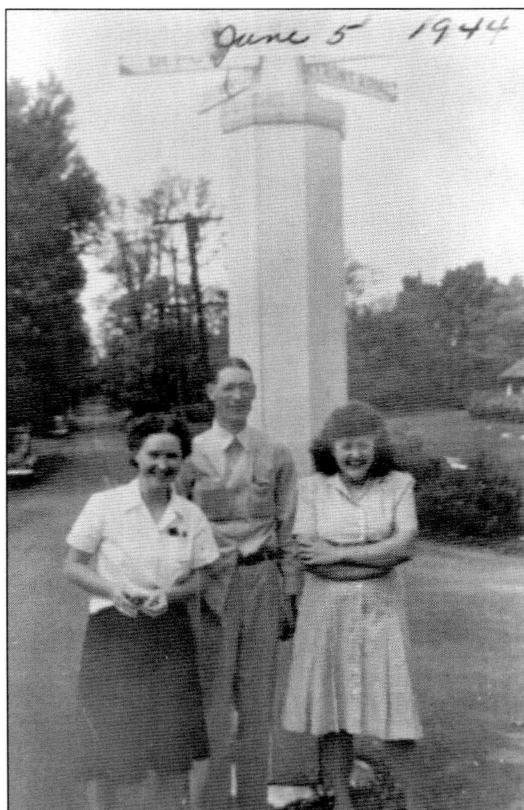

This picture taken on June 5, 1944, the eve of D-Day, shows Mae Lanham (left), who worked at Green's Store; Bill Thompson (center), a local businessman; and Betty Meade Elsea Stuart, who eventually became the owner of a number of buildings in White Post. Replaced on multiple occasions, often due to being damaged by a car, the post remains a tangible symbol of the community's identity. (Billy Thompson.)

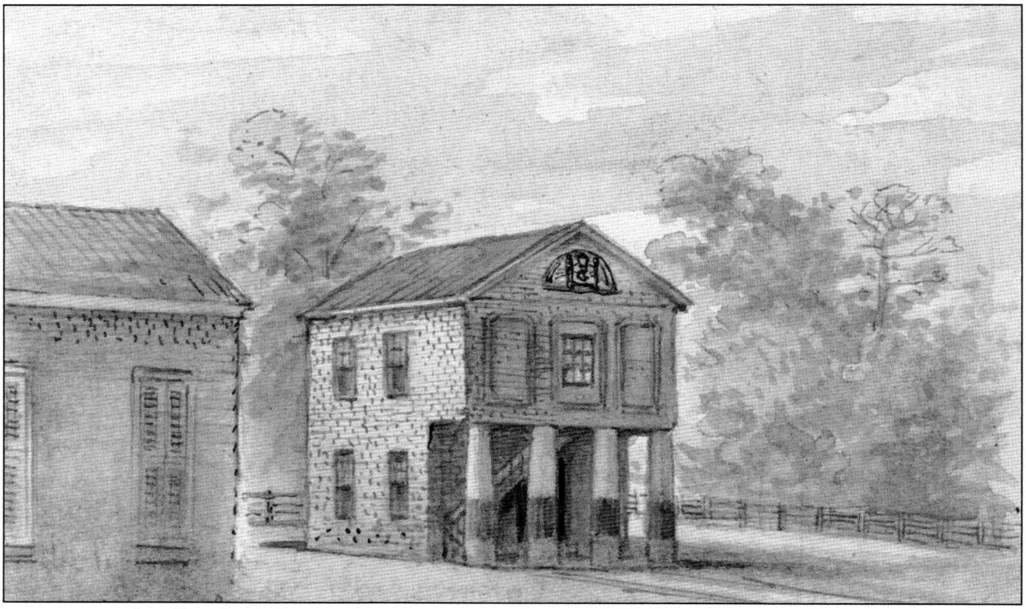

James E. Taylor sketched this "odd contrived" two-story brick with "bulging upper story supported on 4 plastered pillars of brick or stone" because he thought it was so unusual. Constructed in 1844, the building, which stood about 100 yards north of the white post along the east side of the road to Berryville, was a Masonic temple. It no longer stands, although Masons still meet in the village. (Western Reserve Historical Society.)

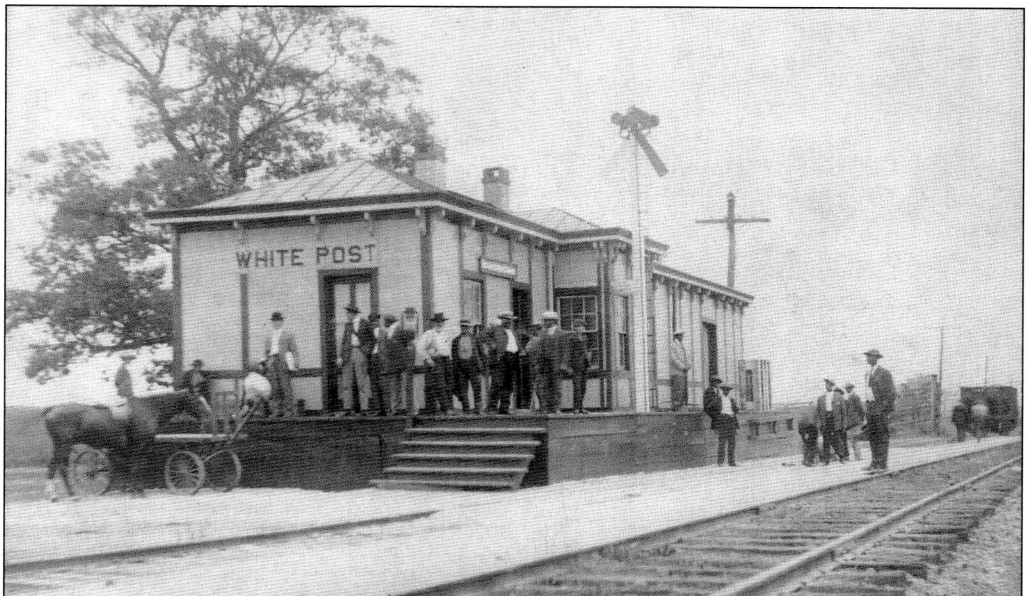

This view of the White Post station from about 1905 shows men congregating and a saddled horse. This station was identical to the original one in Boyce and was a standard design used by the railroad. The push to complete the Shenandoah Valley Railroad through the county was great—to the point that a magistrate in White Post complained of men working on Sundays. The workmen disregarded the protest. (CCHA.)

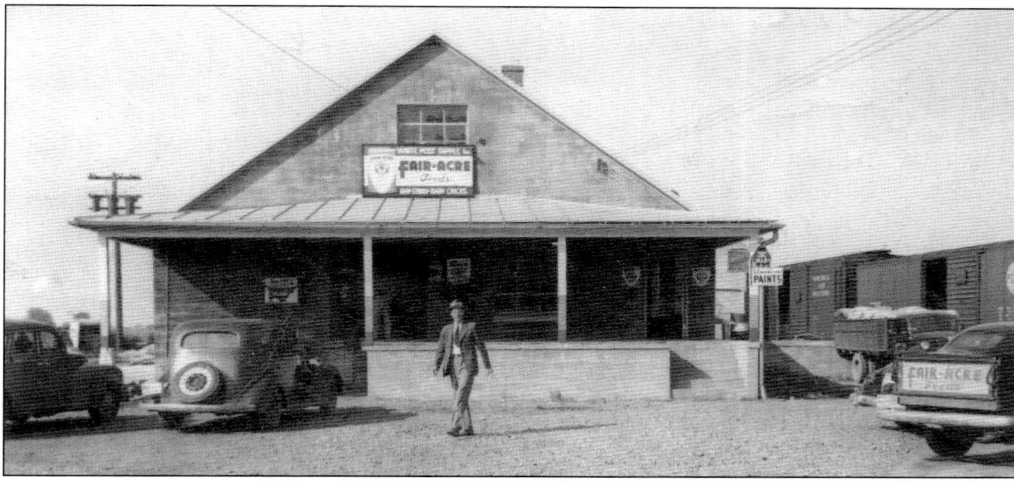

Bill Thompson is shown outside his business, White Post Supply, Inc., which he opened in the early 1940s at the junction of Berry's Ferry Road and the railroad. He constructed the cinder-block building on the site of an old apple packing shed that had burned. When the railroad was opened, the commercial center of White Post shifted to the east, from the crossroads to the rail crossing. (Billy Thompson.)

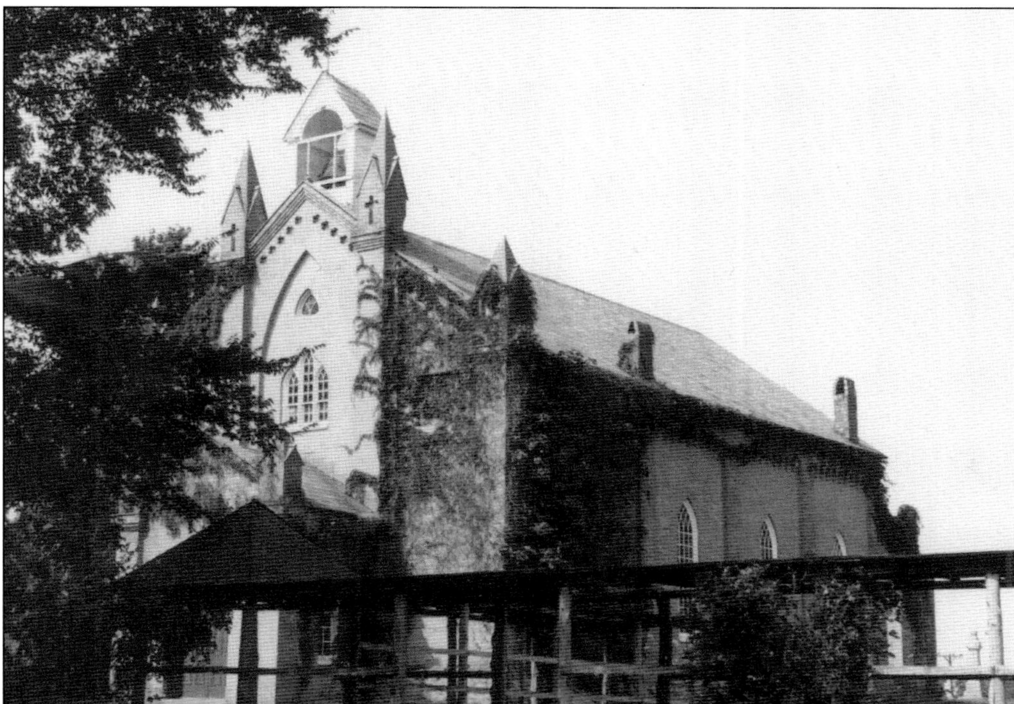

The brick Bishop Meade Memorial Church, pictured in the 1970s, was constructed in 1873 and dedicated two years later. The elegant Gothic Revival–style building was named for White Post's most famous son, Bishop William Meade. A frame parish house has traditionally served as a meeting place for the village, and many local residents and Meade relatives are buried in the cemetery behind the church. (CCHA.)

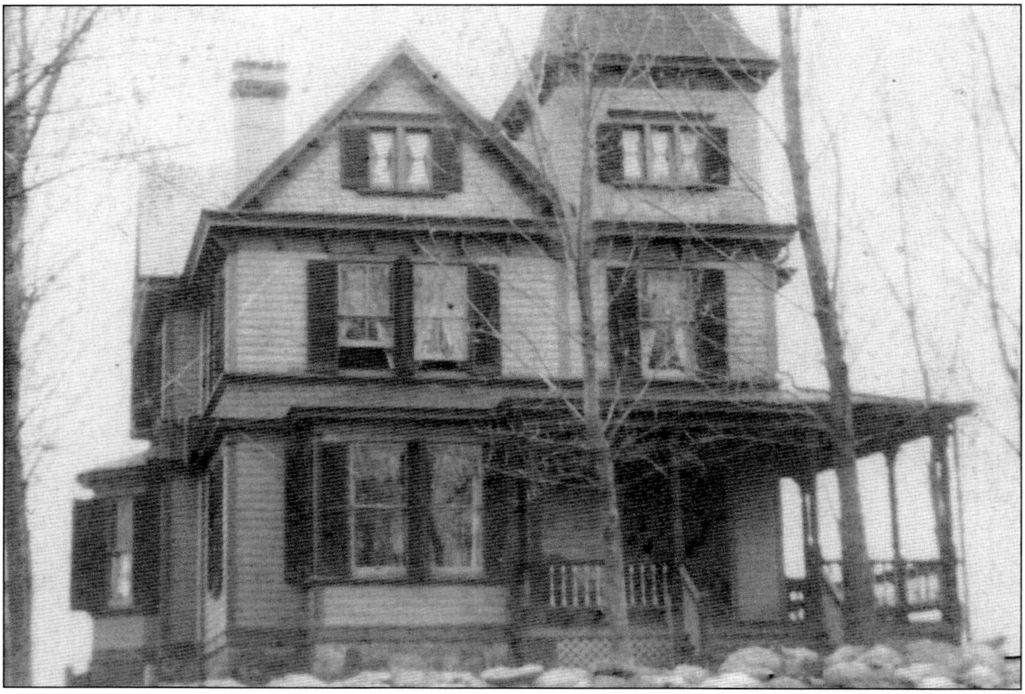

Gunston Hall, constructed around 1893 by Dr. Wilton Rosenberger Stuart, is White Post's most ornate frame dwelling and features a square corner tower topped by a bell-cast roof. In 1900, White Post was home to three other physicians: Thomas Lewis, Robert Randolph, and Henry Sommerville. Writing about the community in the early 1910s, Dr. Sommerville claimed, "White Post always seemed to have an attraction for the doctors." (CCHA.)

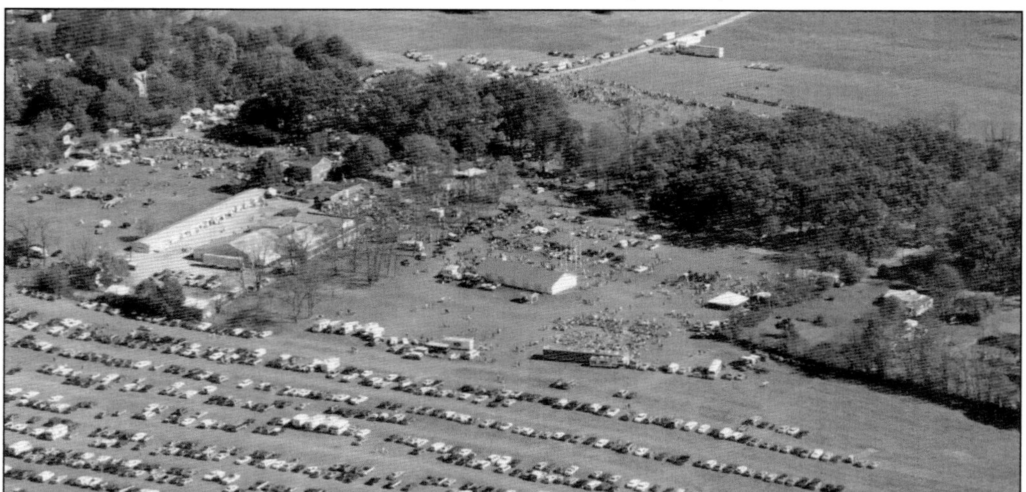

White Post Celebrates was the brainchild of Billy Thompson, owner of White Post Restorations and chairman of the 1986 Clarke County Sesquicentennial Celebration marking the county's founding in 1836. Held annually in White Post for four years, the festival included food, antique car displays, and family activities. This 1989 aerial view shows the last festival, which attracted nearly 75,000 visitors to the village. (Billy Thompson.)

Seven

THE MOUNTAIN

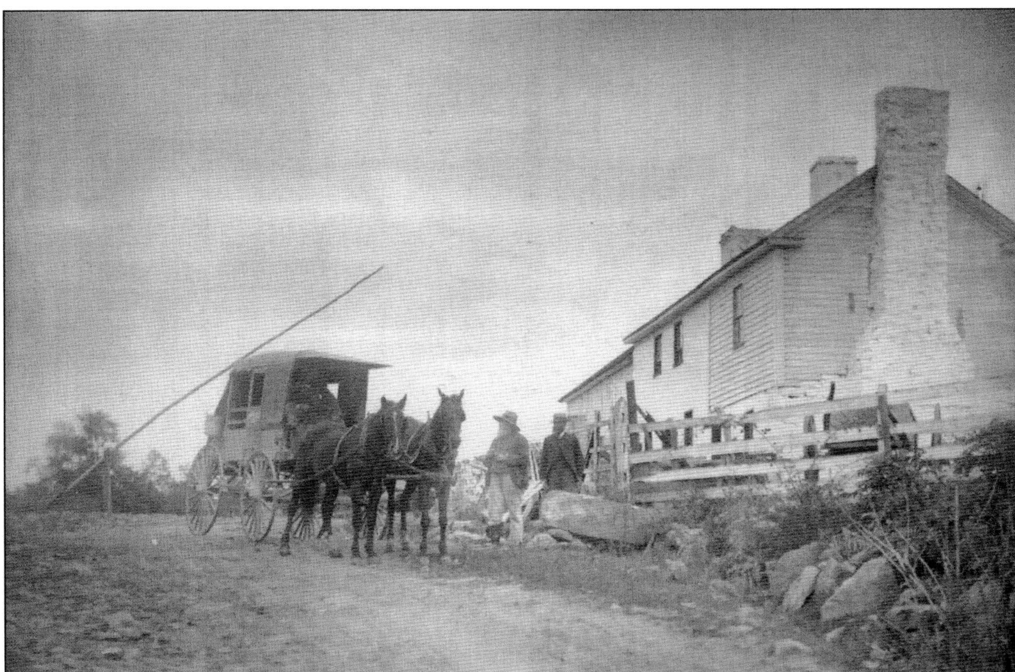

Two natural gaps in the Blue Ridge Mountains have long provided eastern gateways to the Shenandoah Valley. Shown here about 1900 is a tollhouse that once stood along Route 7 west of Snicker's Gap, originally known as Williams Gap. Along with Ashby's Gap at the present Route 50 crossing, these clefts in the mountain are still the primary eastern access points into the county. (Library of Congress.)

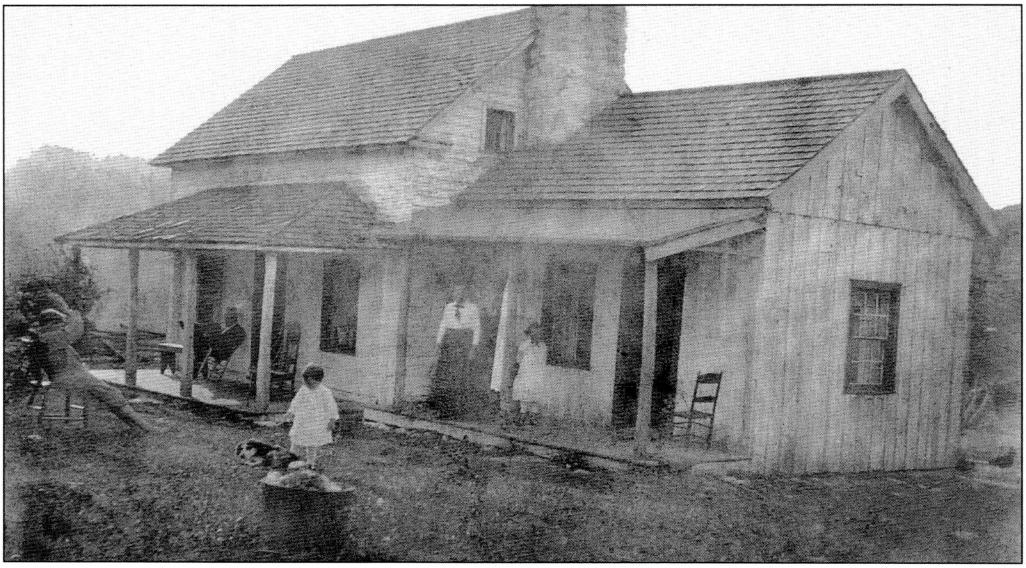

Most of Clarke's mountainous region was part of Lord Fairfax's Leeds Manor. The rugged terrain made it difficult to settle. The earliest houses would have been similar to this one, the John Letcher Lloyd House, a one-story log dwelling with a large exterior-end stone chimney and wood-shingled roof. Lloyd, wife Mary Frances, their children, and a family dog, are shown in this late-1800s image. (CCHA.)

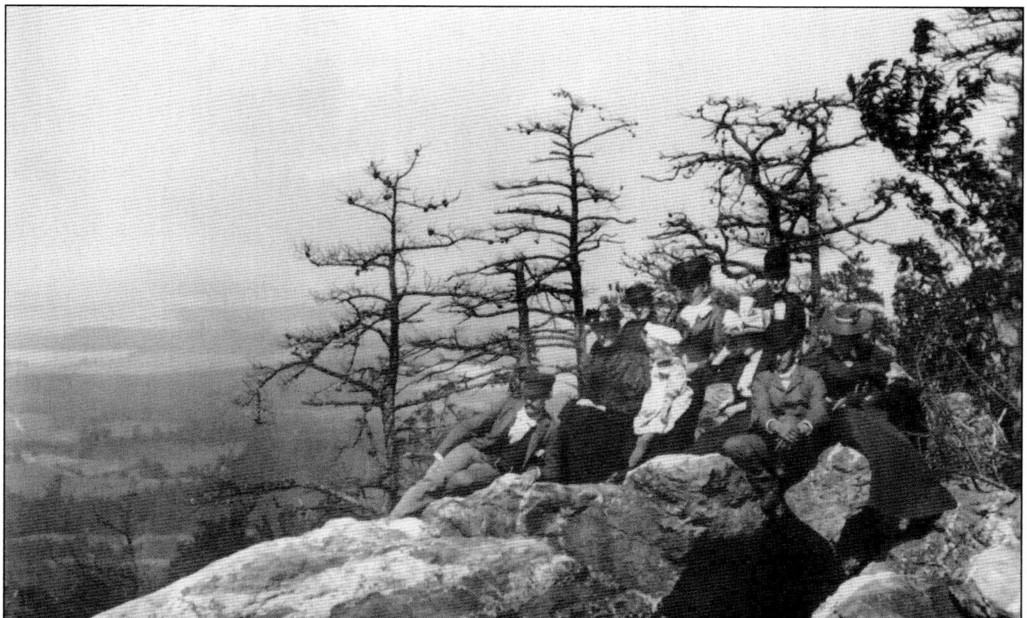

Bear's Den Rocks, located near the top of the Blue Ridge Mountains south of Route 7, have long been recognized as a spectacular observation point from which to view Clarke County and further expanses of the Shenandoah Valley. Shown relaxing at the rocks around 1900 is a group dressed in suits, ties, long dresses, and hats. Bear's Den remains a popular destination for hikers. (Library of Congress.)

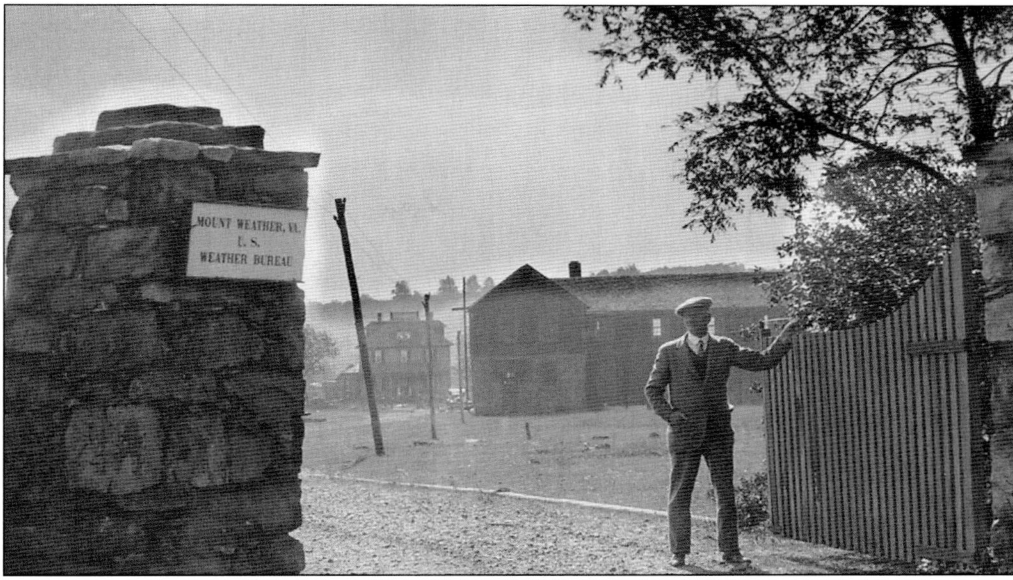

Straddling the Blue Ridge in both Clarke and Loudoun Counties, the Mount Weather Station of the US Weather Bureau was established in 1902–1903. Its location atop the mountain ridge was ideal for taking meteorological readings with kites and balloons launched from the Reel House, shown below. With advances in meteorology, the weather facility became obsolete. Alternative uses for the property were sought, including a summer White House for the president, a tuberculosis hospital, a prison for women, a poetry center, and a resort. During the Cold War years, the US Defense Department took over the property, which continues today as a secure and highly classified installation. Since 2003, it has been part of the US Department of Homeland Security. (Both, National Archives.)

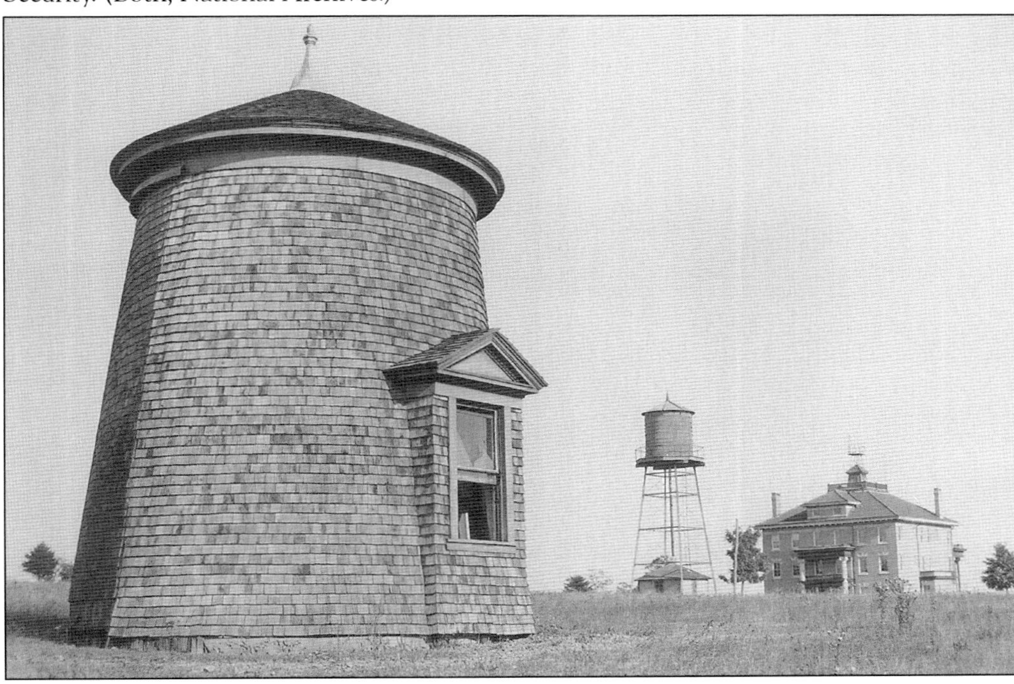

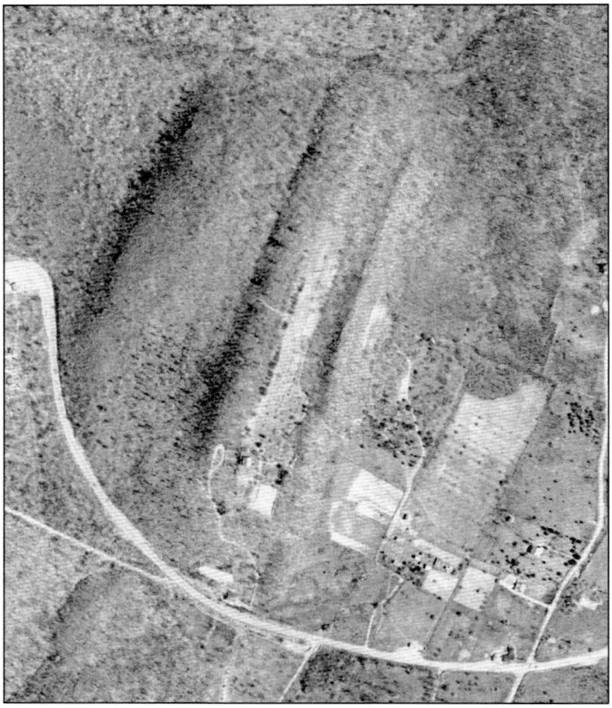

The May 1937 aerial at left shows Route 7 crossing into Clarke County (north is at top) and Route 601, now Raven Rocks and Blue Ridge Mountain Roads. Several late-19th- and early-20th-century dwellings on the ridge, surrounded by large open areas and orchards, are visible at the center of the picture. A comparison image (below) taken in 1985 from the same vantage shows how deeply forested the mountain had become during the intervening 50 years. Small farmsteads stood on the mountain in the early 20th century, and much of the land was logged for commercial or home heating use. The 1985 image also shows, at bottom left, the new road that bypassed the "horseshoe curve" and the widening of Route 7 in the 1960s–1970s. (Both, Les Querry.)

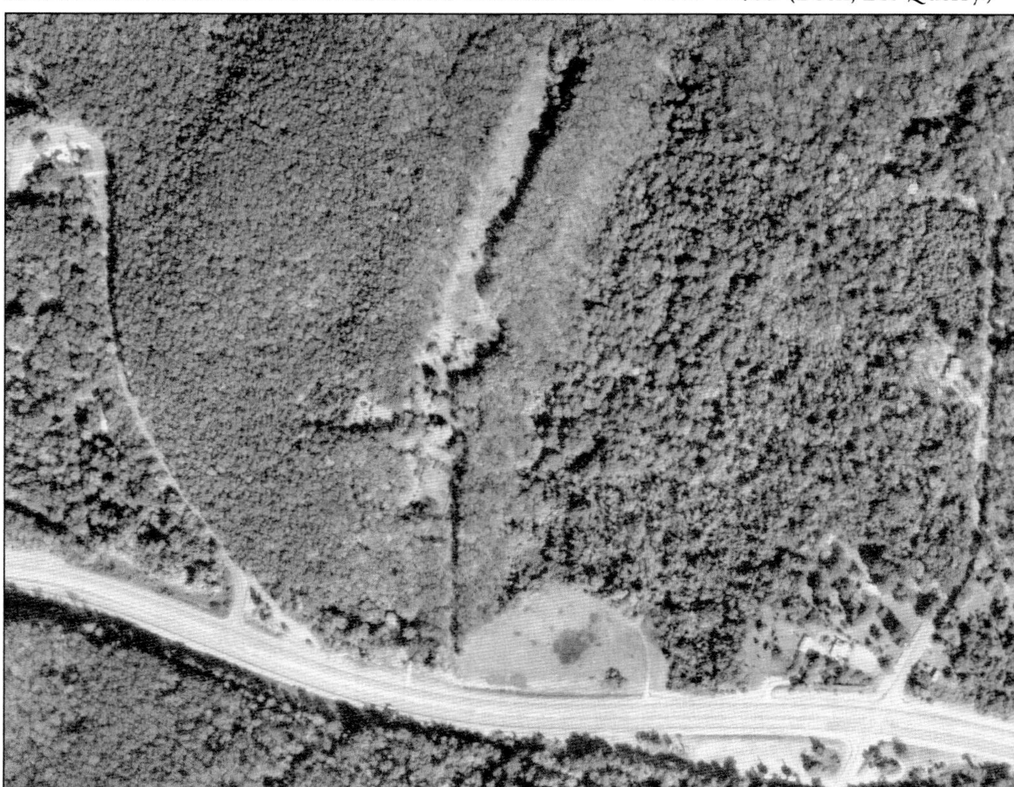

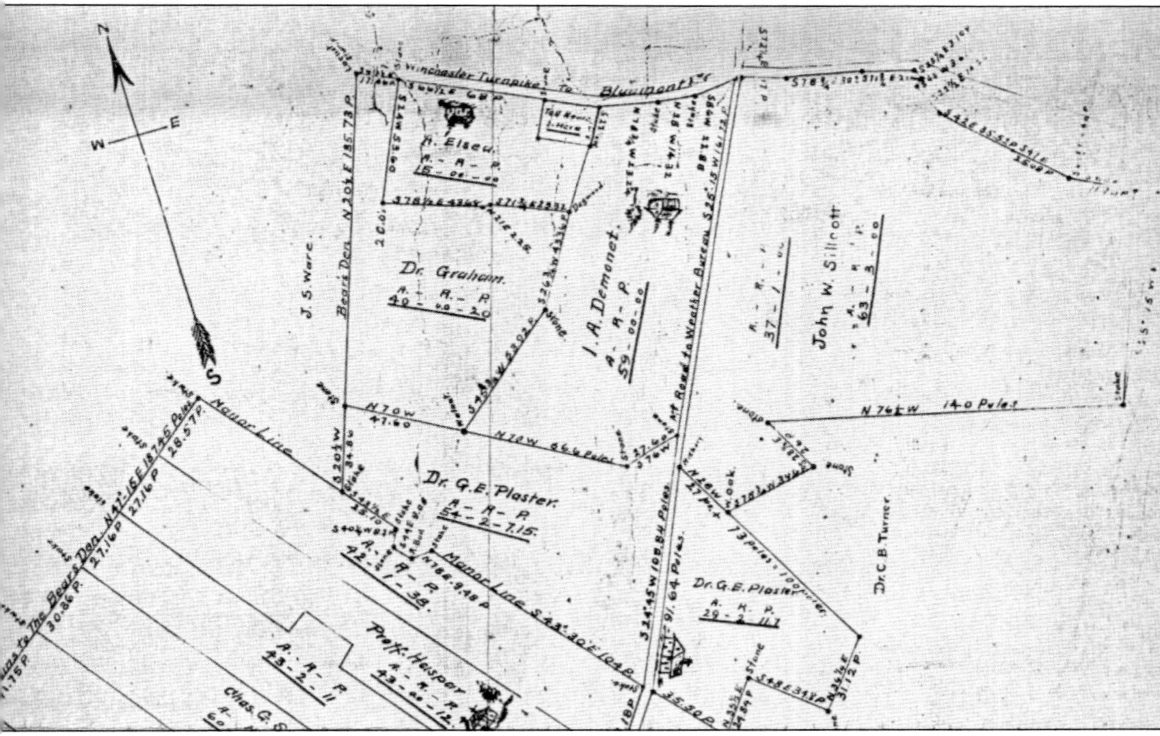

This 1903 map of the junction of Blue Ridge Mountain Road (Route 601) and Route 7 shows how the area along the ridge was being developed by that time. Rail service reached Round Hill in 1874 and was extended to Bluemont in 1900, drawing residents from Washington, DC, who were attracted to the mountain scenery and cooler summer climate. Many built summer homes along the mountain ridge. The new so-called part-timers were an eclectic group that included politicians, diplomats, writers, artists, and musicians. Most of the late-19th- and early-20th-century native stone dwellings they constructed stood on parcels that took advantage of the valley views. Many that survive today are used as year-round residences. This period of growing fascination with unspoiled natural areas led to the creation of the national park system and the building of the Appalachian Trail, which wends its way along the mountain the length of Clarke County. (CCHA.)

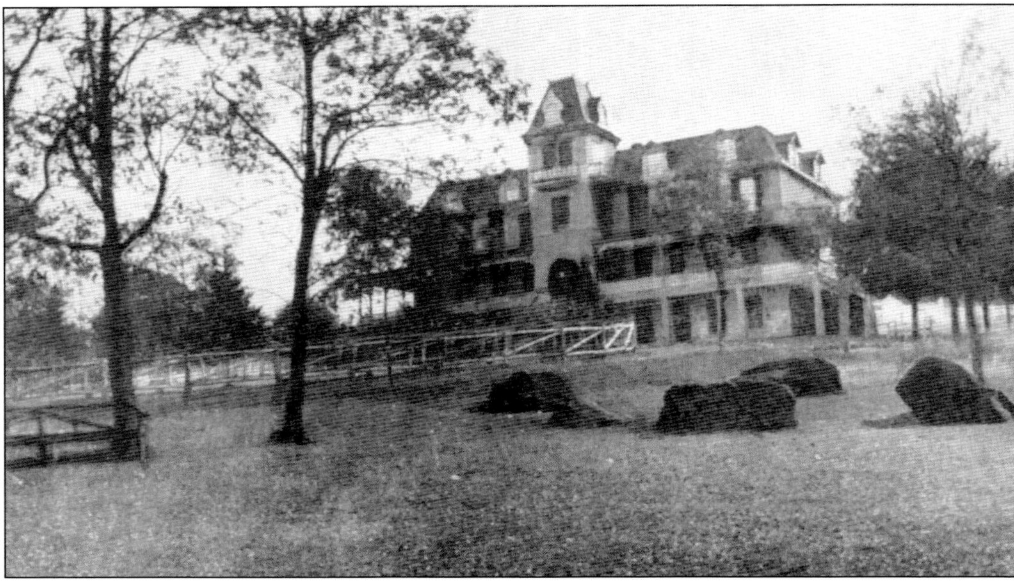

Constructed in 1893 south of Route 7 near Snicker's Gap, the Blue Ridge Inn catered to vacationers who had discovered the area and could now access it by train to Bluemont. The elegant frame structure portrayed on this postcard housed a hostelry run by Jules Demonet, who rose to become chef for the White House. In 1910, a fire originating in the laundry consumed the inn, then valued at $15,000. (CCHA.)

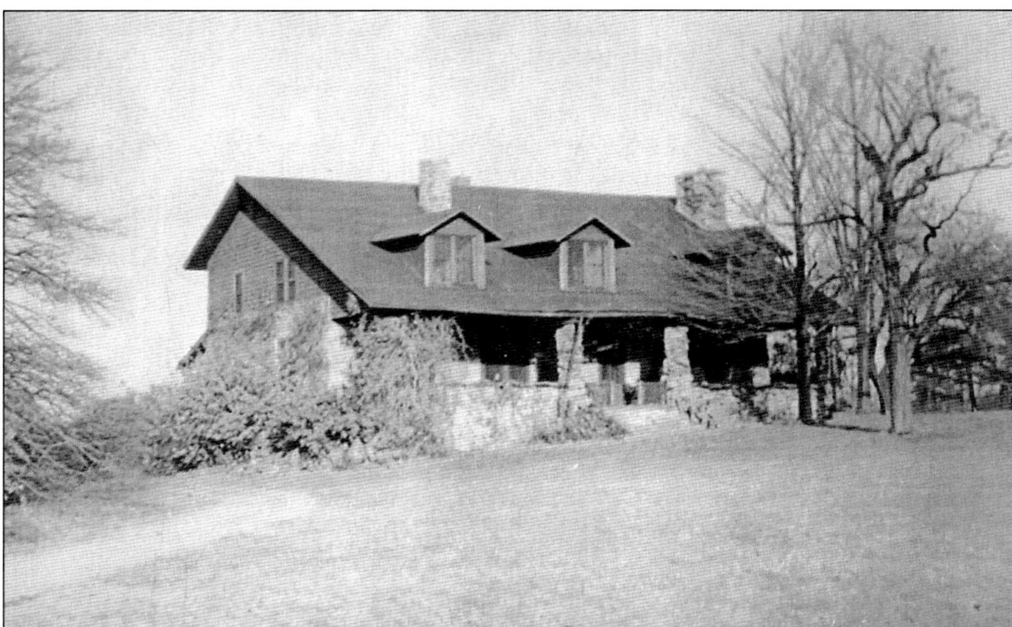

High Meadows was constructed in 1896 as a summer home by Elizabeth Sommers, principal of Mount Vernon Seminary in Washington's Georgetown. During her time on the mountain, she may have operated a local school in a stone building on her property. The stone-and-frame house, shown around 1900, had a long, deep porch from which to enjoy the view and mountain air. The house was enlarged in 1947. (Author.)

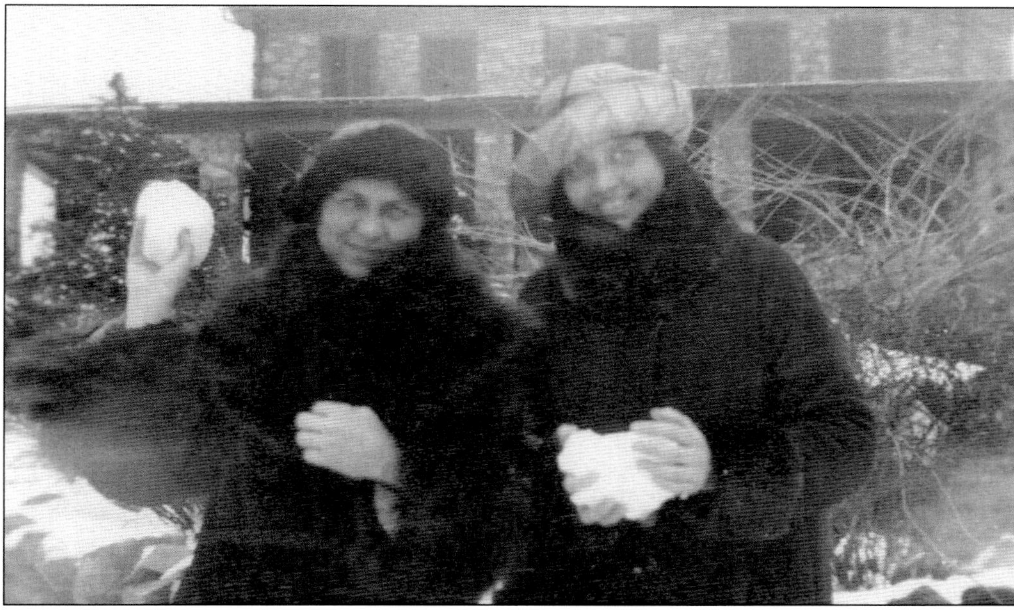

This snowball fight took place on April 15, 1923, in the front yard of Seltenhorst, visible in the background. Constructed in 1903 by Georgetown physician Ernest Sellhausen, the property, whose name means "lofty nest" in German, was inherited by Elfrieda Droop, who owned it through the 1940s. The two women in the photograph are unidentified. The stone house had multiple outbuildings, including one to store potatoes. (Les Querry.)

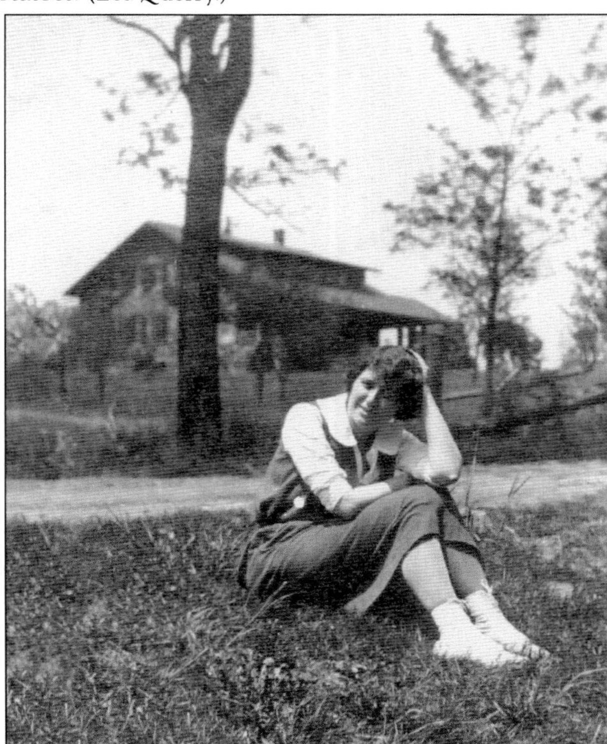

This unidentified woman is relaxing in front of Stonycroft, located near the junction of Raven Rocks Road and Route 7. The house was constructed around 1911 as a summer home by Louise Peters, whose husband was a US Navy commander. An extensive system of stone walls delineating property lines and stone gateposts marking property entrances are part of the mountain's distinctive landscape. (Les Querry.)

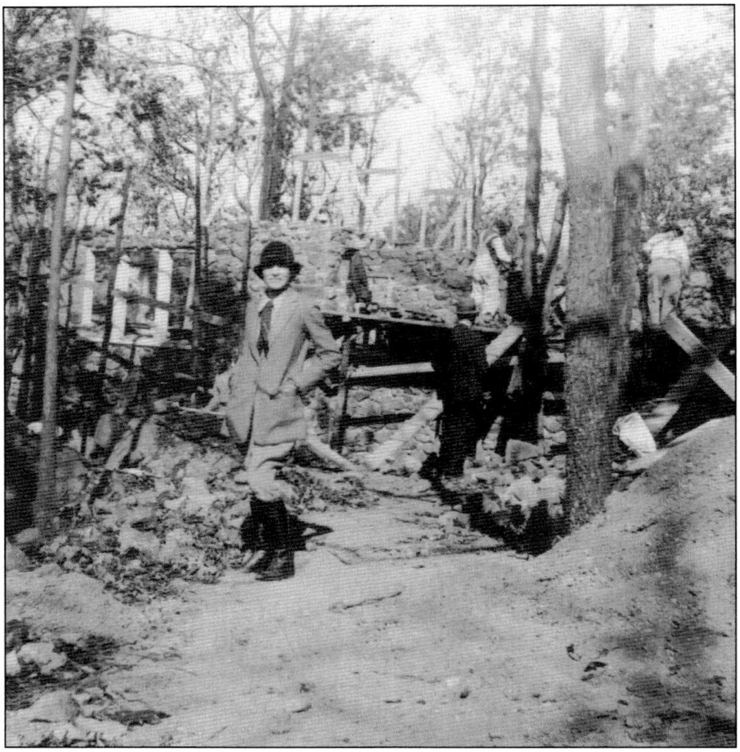

Shown under construction around 1933 is Llanmeath Lodge, located along Raven Rocks Road. The lodge name and the unusual, massive exterior stone chimney and hearth recall a dwelling the Lewises saw on their honeymoon in Wales. Pictured is Mrs. H. Turner Lewis (Madge B.), fashionably dressed in jodhpurs and riding boots. (Ritchie and Elizabeth Thomas.)

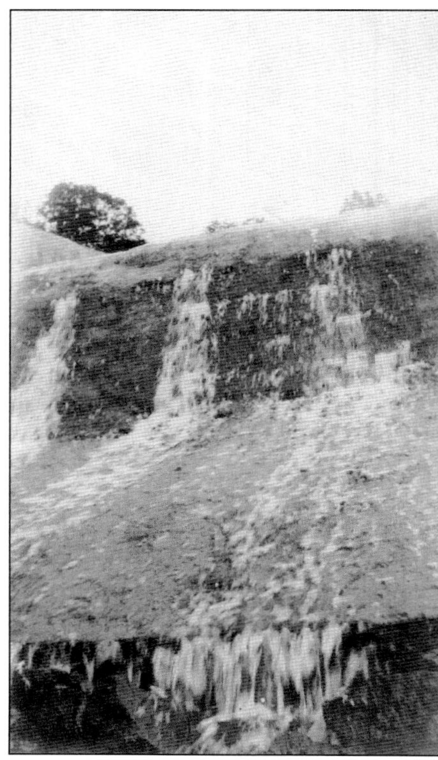

The Berryville Water Company, the first municipal water system for Berryville, was established in 1891 with its water source on the mountain seven miles away. The site contained several earthen and concrete reservoirs and a concrete dam, along with buildings dating from when the property was a farm. All were demolished in the early 1990s after Berryville's water source became the Shenandoah River and the property was sold to the Appalachian Trail. (CCHA.)

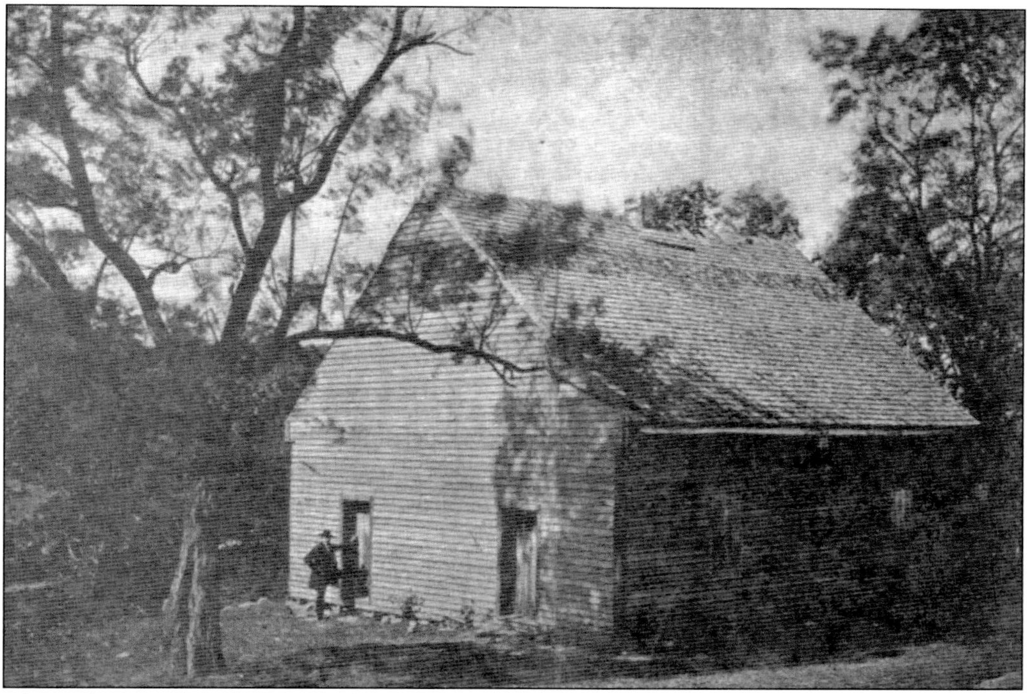

The 18th-century Mount Carmel Church, the oldest log church in the county, stands just north of Route 50, about halfway up the mountain to Ashby's Gap. Methodist bishop Francis Asbury is thought to have preached here. This photograph from about 1900 shows the building with weatherboard siding, wood-shingle roofing, and separate entrances for male and female members of the congregation. Numerous other churches also served the mountain community. (CCHA.)

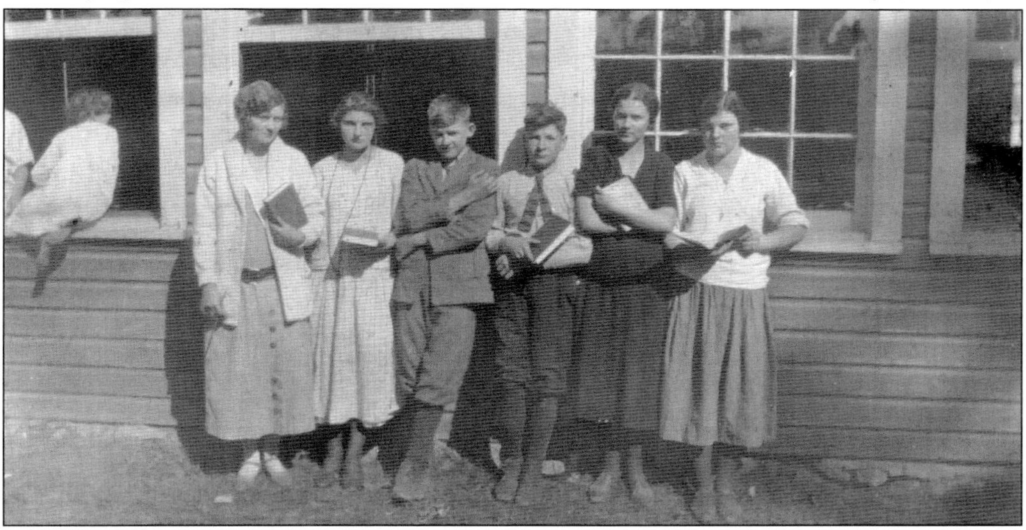

This photograph from about 1925 shows high school students leaning against a frame school in the community of Pine Grove. Others schools on the mountain included Ebenezer, Linsay, Morgan's Mill, Mount Carmel, Mount Weather, Providence Chapel, and Valley View. As transportation methods improved and county school consolidated, most of these one- and two-room schools had closed by the early 1940s. (CCHA.)

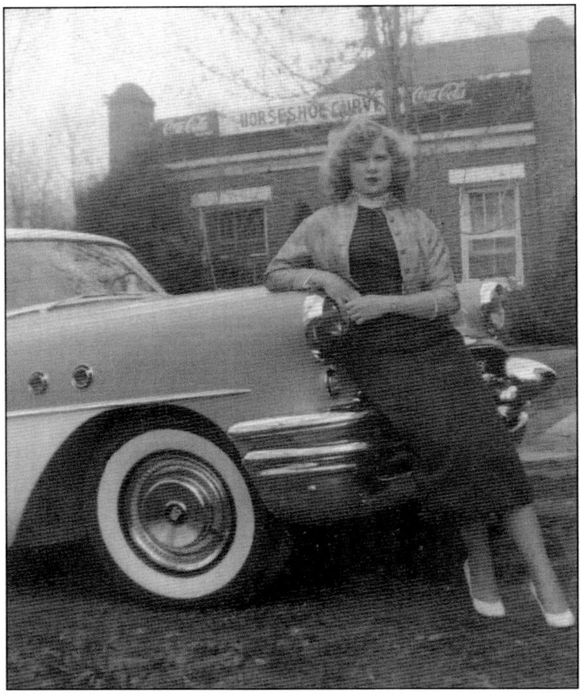

Linda McLaughry leans against a 1950s Buick in front of her father's restaurant, the Horseshoe Curve. Family-operated since 1946, the popular restaurant is located at a horseshoe bend near the village of Pine Grove off Route 7. It was bypassed when the road was realigned in the 1970s. The Horseshoe Curve Benevolent Association supports the local community with an annual fundraiser for the Blue Ridge Fire Department. (Tracee Wink.)

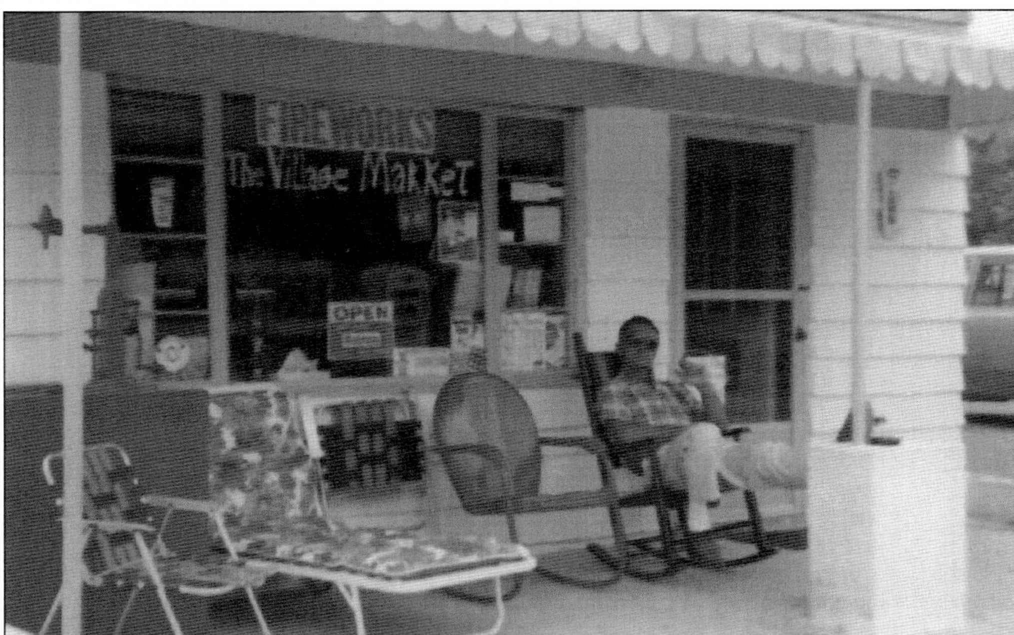

Located just below the crest of the mountain above the Shenandoah River, the village of Pine Grove is a small settlement that dates to the 19th century. A central meeting place for the locals, the Village Market is one of several commercial enterprises in Pine Grove. Ray McLaughry, pictured on the porch of the store, and his wife, Louise, purchased the property in the late 1960s. (Louise McLaughry.)

Eight

Agriculture and the Hunt

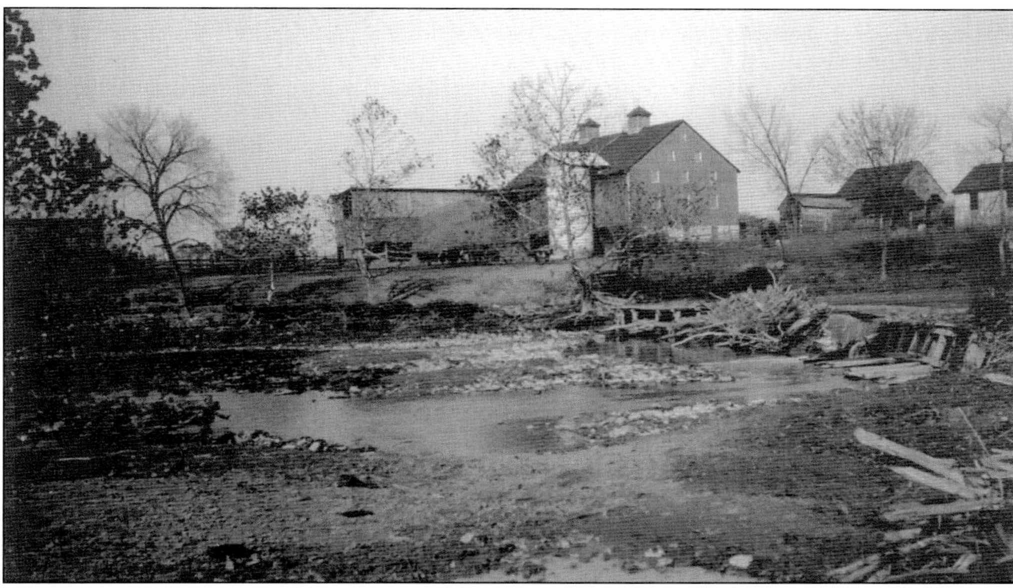

Clarke's well-watered, gently rolling topography and rich limestone soils make it well suited for agriculture. As young George Washington noted during his 1748 surveying expedition into Clarke, "The land [is] exceedingly fertile . . . [and] produces abundance of grain, hemp, [and] tobacco." Pictured around 1900 is Circle Hill Farm. It is located on the Opequon Creek near Wadesville in the northern part of the county. The 1868 brick barn is one of Clarke's few masonry barns. (SBA/HRL.)

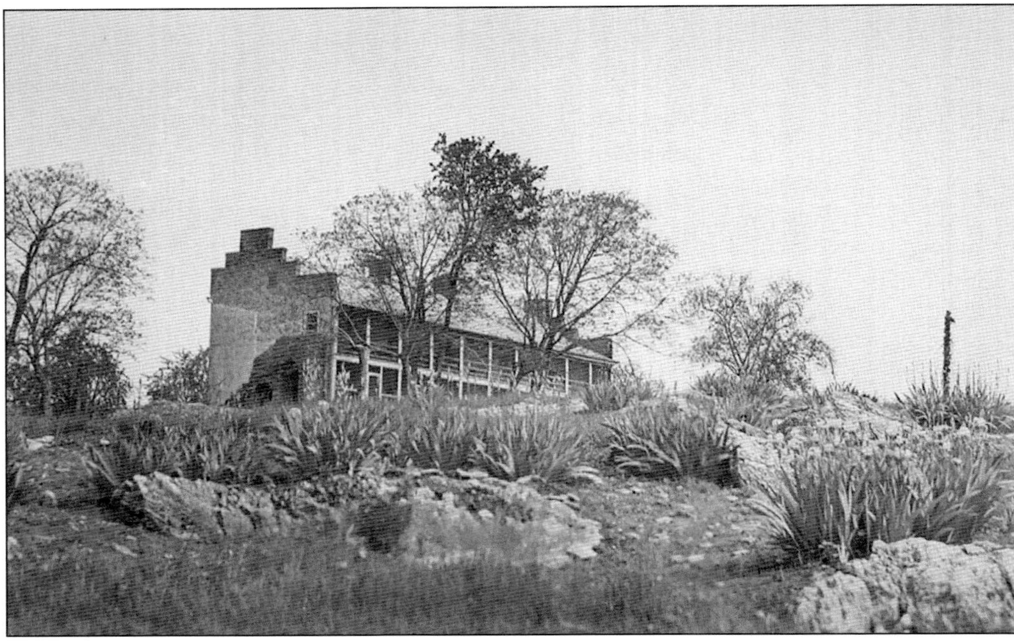

Clarke contained many plantations where slaves labored to produce crops, tend livestock, and maintain buildings. Joseph Tuley owned nearly 1,000 acres and held 73 slaves in 1840. The brick slave quarters (above in 1933) on his estate the Tuleyries was one of the largest such buildings in the county. Graham F. Blandy, a wealthy New York stockbroker, purchased the Tuleyries in 1903 from Col. Upton Boyce, who had purchased it after the Civil War. In 1926, Blandy left 712 acres of his property, including this building, to the University of Virginia (UVA) to "teach boys how to farm." To that end, Blandy Experimental Farm, with a 172-acre arboretum, was developed. The photograph below shows the enlarged slave quarters (right) and its conversion into laboratories and housing in 1941 after a design by UVA architect Stanislaw Makielski. (Both, Blandy Experimental Farm.)

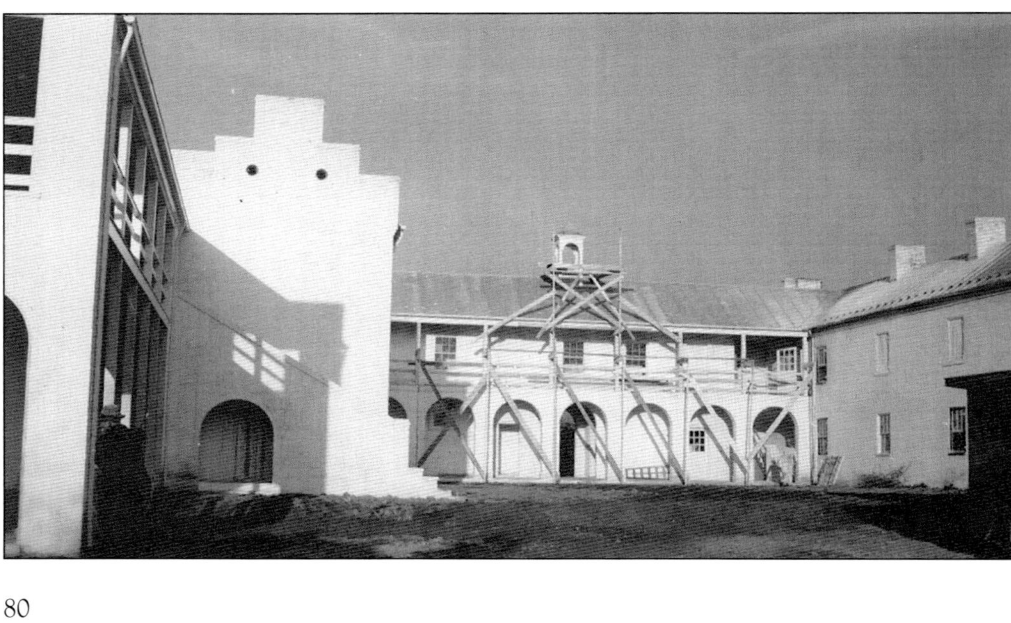

Beyond raising field crops, livestock, and producing dairy products, most farms kept several beehives to provide garden pollination, wax for candles, and honey for sweetening. Beekeeping was sometimes delegated to the women of the family, as at Circle Hill Farm (shown around 1900), where Rebecca Pidgeon tended the hives. The stone-and-brick farmhouse, built around 1800, is visible in the background and remains in the Pidgeon family. (SBA/HRL.)

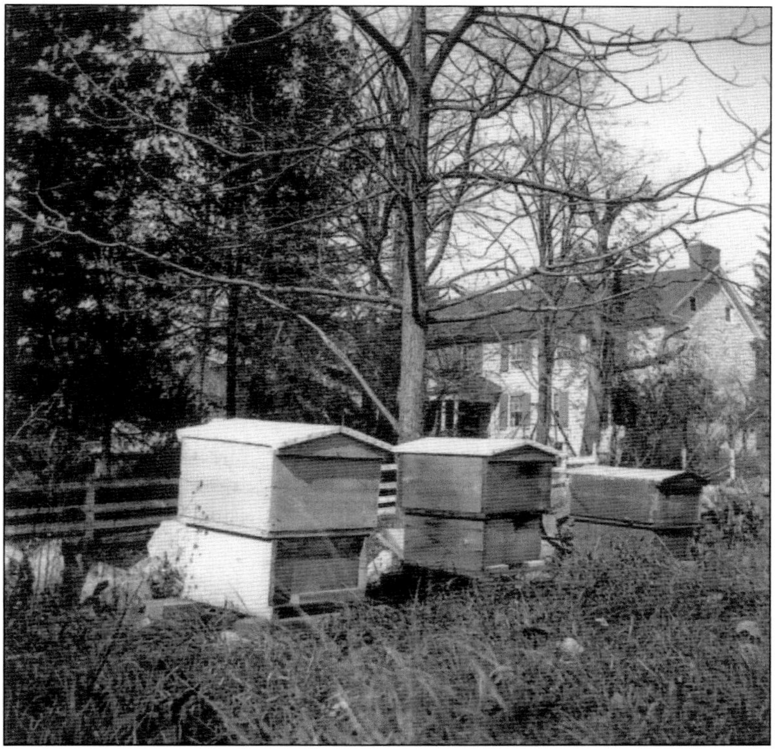

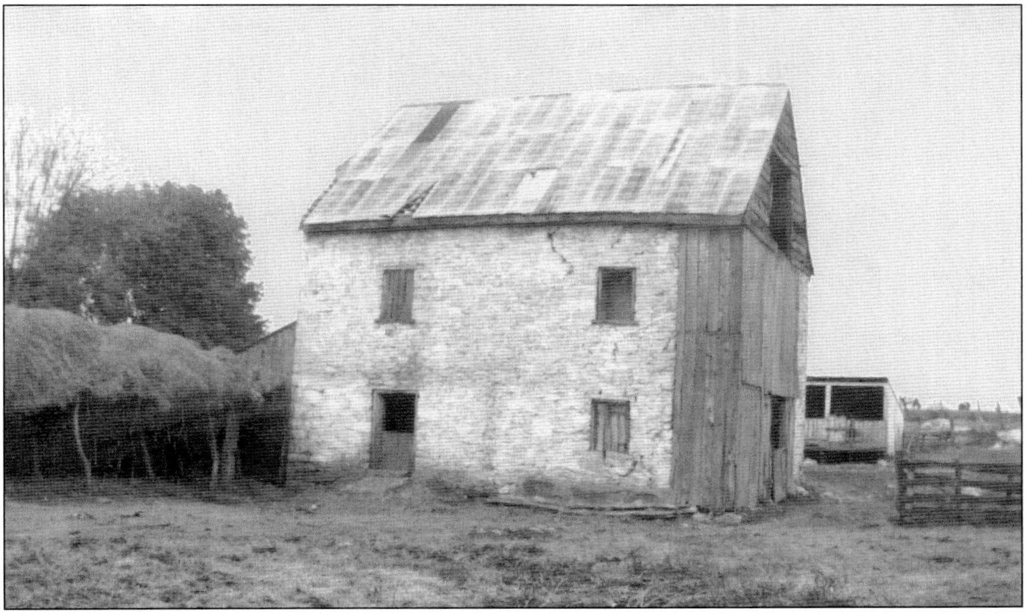

Clarke's plentiful watercourses and the large corn and wheat harvests were the reason for the numerous water-powered mills built in the area to grind wheat flour, cornmeal, and feed. The Larue (Anderson) Mill, later converted into a barn, was one of three mills standing along Long Marsh Run in northern Clarke by 1809. Mills like this were small operations, grinding on a custom basis for farmers in the immediate area. (CCHA.)

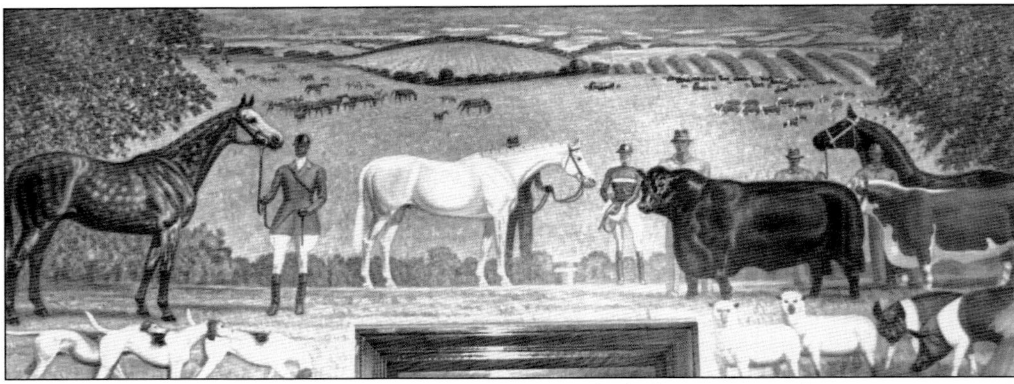

The mural in the lobby of the Berryville post office titled *Clarke County Products, 1939* accurately depicts the county's agricultural character. Local artist and horse portraitist Edwin "Ned" Lewis completed the painting in 1940 as part of the Treasury Department's New Deal Art Project. The foreground depicts fox hunters, groomsmen, farmers, foxhounds, cattle, sheep, and pigs in a setting of mountains, orchards, and crop fields. (CCHA.)

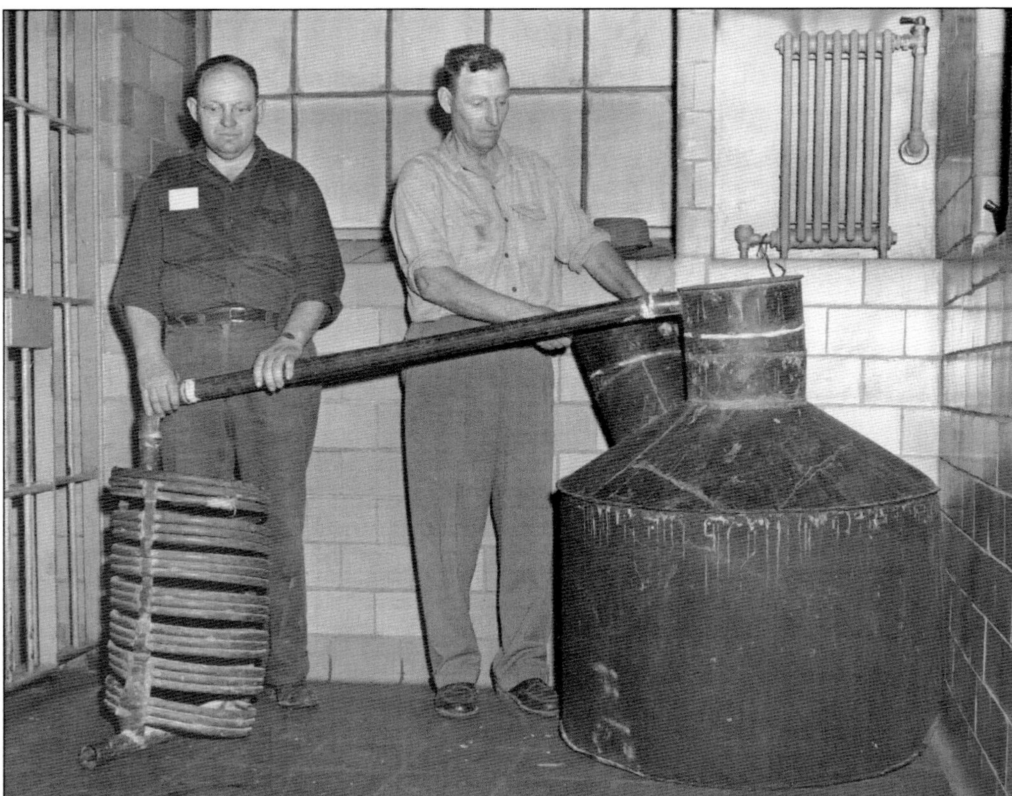

Distilleries evolved as a by-product of corn and rye from local farms, and they proved profitable. In 1850, John Richardson, owner of Fairfield, and his partner and son-in-law Thorton P. Pendleton used horse-powered machinery to produce 16,500 gallons of whiskey valued at $8,250. This activity continued into the 20th century, even after it became illegal. In this 1952 photograph, former sheriff William Smallwood (right) and his deputy are inspecting a confiscated still. (CCHA.)

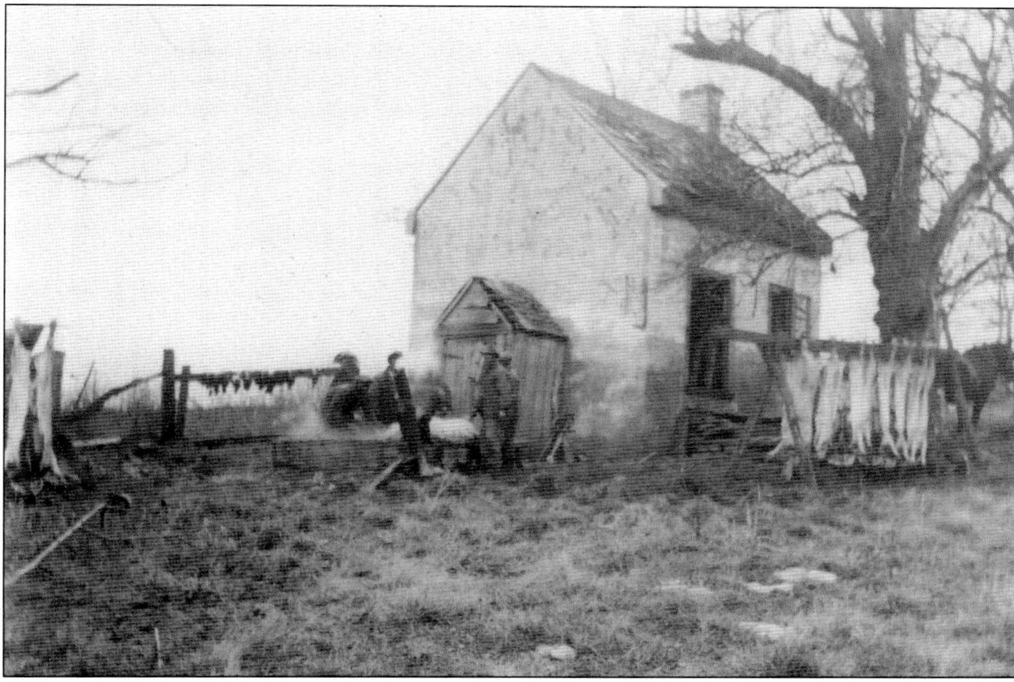

Butchering was conducted in the fall, after the hogs had fattened and the weather turned cold. The activity involved multiple steps that took several days and produced not only hams to cure but also bacon, lard, scrapple (pork scraps combined with cornmeal), and leather. According to old-timers, the only thing not used from a pig was its squeal. This early-20th-century scene is at Springfield Farm. (Barbara Clagett.)

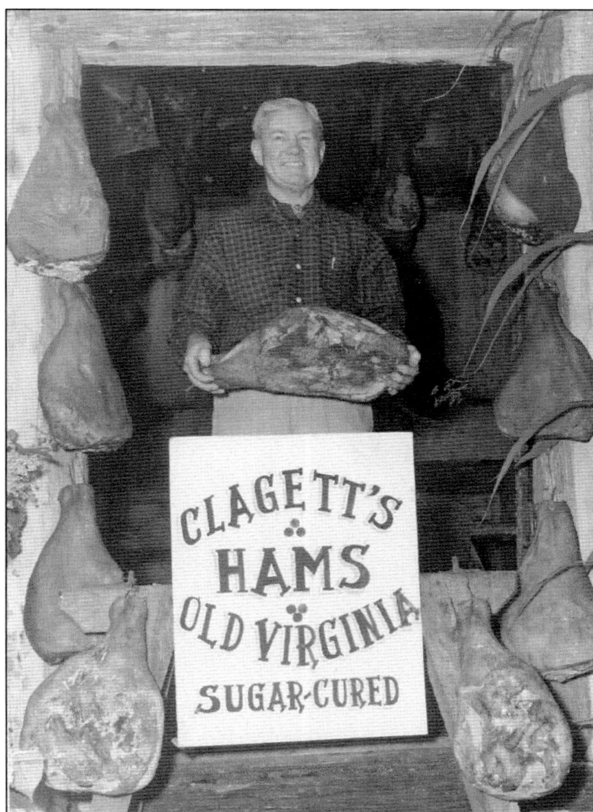

William Branson Clagett Jr. was a successful farmer who sold hams butchered and cured at his Springfield Farm as a sideline. Pictured in the 1960s, Clagett proudly displays his Old Virginia hams in the doorway of the smokehouse. According to his daughters, who retain his recipe for sugar-curing 2,000 pounds of meat, Clagett's hams were especially popular at Christmastime and were sold across the country by mail order. (*Clarke Courier.*)

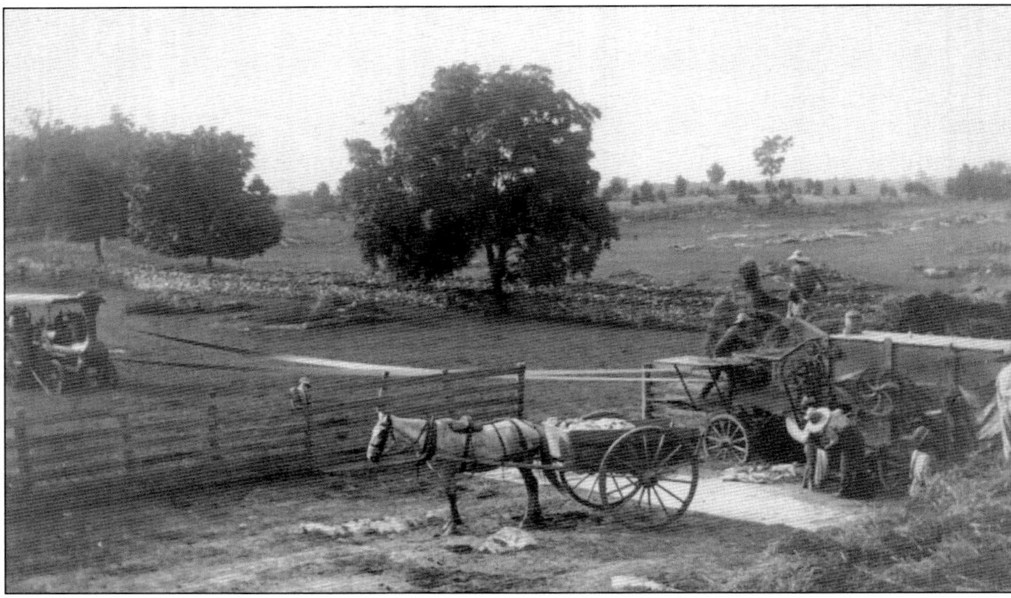

By the turn of the 20th century, steam power began to replace horses for many farming endeavors. The stationary steam engine to the left powered the thrasher to the right by a long, flat belt at the Fishpaw farm in northern Clarke. Stone walls like this one—dry-laid and constructed with native limestone gathered from the fields—are used throughout the county to delineate property lines. (CCHA.)

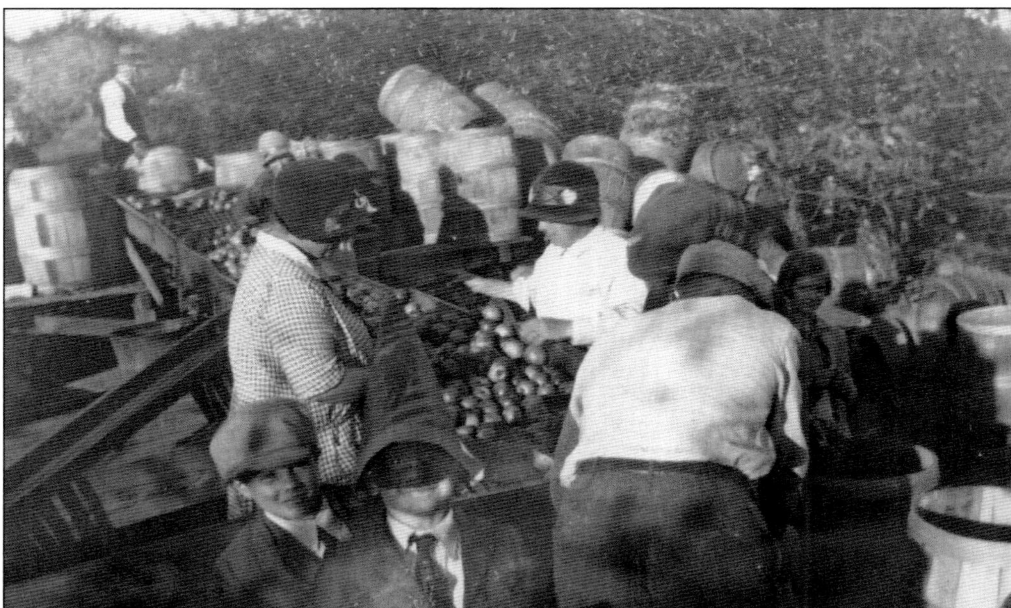

By the 1920s, apple harvesting was a common autumn activity. Apple growing became one of the primary agricultural endeavors in Clarke during the early 1900s, replacing wheat as the main cash crop. From 1890 to 1940, the number of bushels harvested in the county skyrocketed by more than 1,600 percent, outperforming even top producer Frederick County. One of the unidentified boys in the foreground proudly boasts his Halloween mask. (CCHA.)

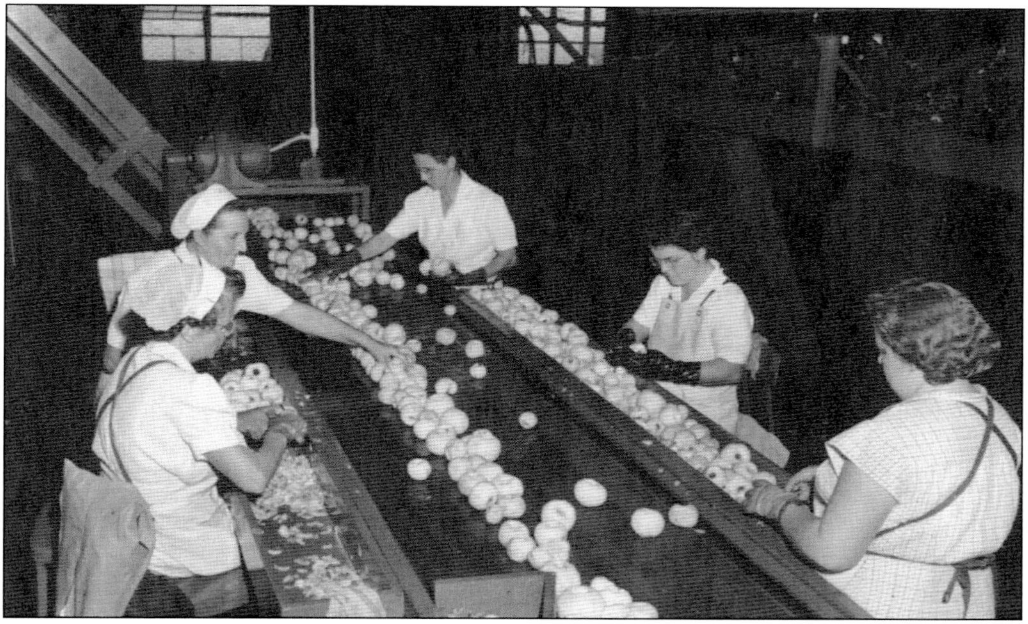

During the closing decades of the 20th century, county apple production dramatically declined, and many orchards reverted to growing corn or soybeans. In the late 1950s, fruit production generated approximately half of Clarke's farm income. These women are shown peeling and coring apples in the Byrd Canning Plant in Berryville. The business closed in the 1970s, and the building converted into a cabinet manufacturing plant. (Virginia Tech ImageBase: Norfolk-Southern.)

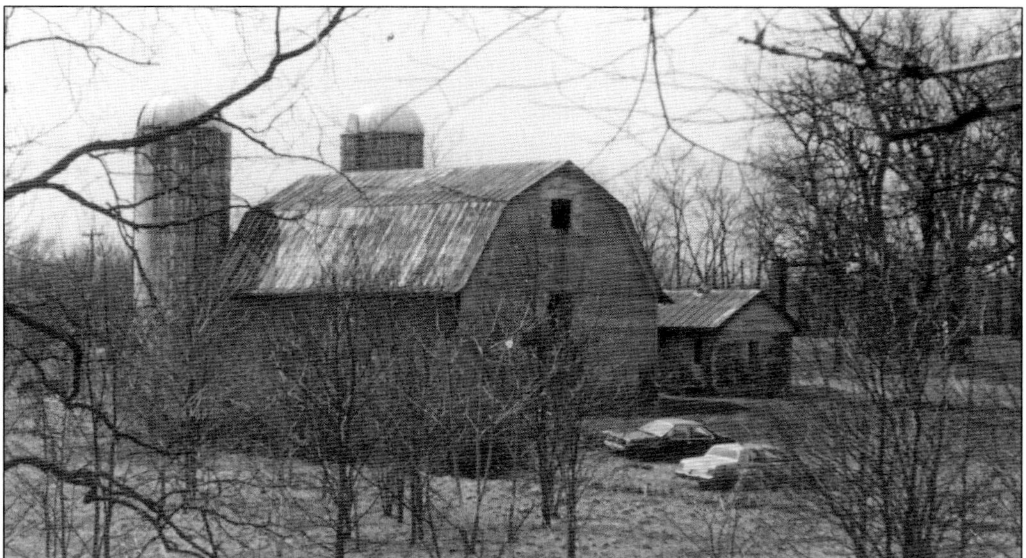

Multiple dairies were established in the county as technological advances made milking and storage operations more efficient. In 1922, Matthew W. Jones Jr. established one of the largest in Clarke at Woodside Farm. Harry Light constructed a state-of-the-art barn for Jones in 1929, and a milk house was added in 1937. With the help of his young children Louise, Harry, and M.W., Jones delivered milk and cream daily to Berryville. (Author.)

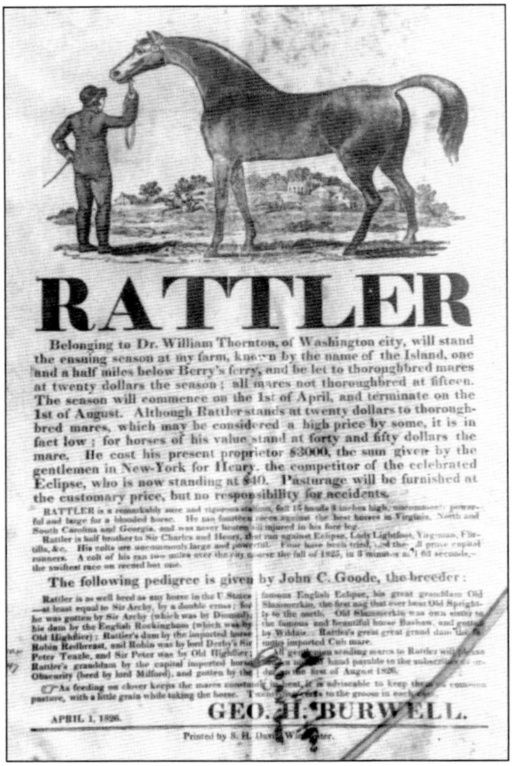

Lord Fairfax is credited with introducing fox hunting to the region. The interest in horses—whether for drafting, racing, or fox hunting—has been a critical part of Clarke's agricultural heritage. This 1826 poster advertises the services of Rattler, a "remarkably sure and vigorous stallion," who stood at Island Farm, owned by George H. Burwell at the time; the farm is now part of the Burwell–Van Lennep Foundation, established in 1967. (CCHA.)

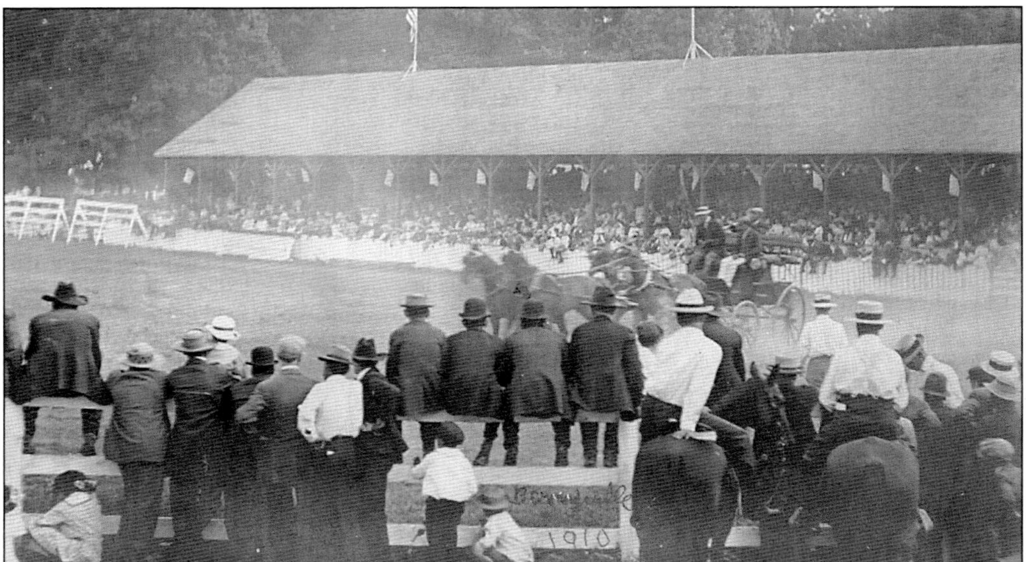

The Berryville Horse Show grounds were located at the current site of the Ruritan Fairgrounds, west of Berryville. Begun in the late 1880s to showcase horse-racing events, the show grew to include riding, harness, steeplechase, and confirmation competitions, and drew large crowds from around the region. The covered grandstand shown in this 1910 photograph collapsed in 1960 under the weight of heavy snow. (CCHA.)

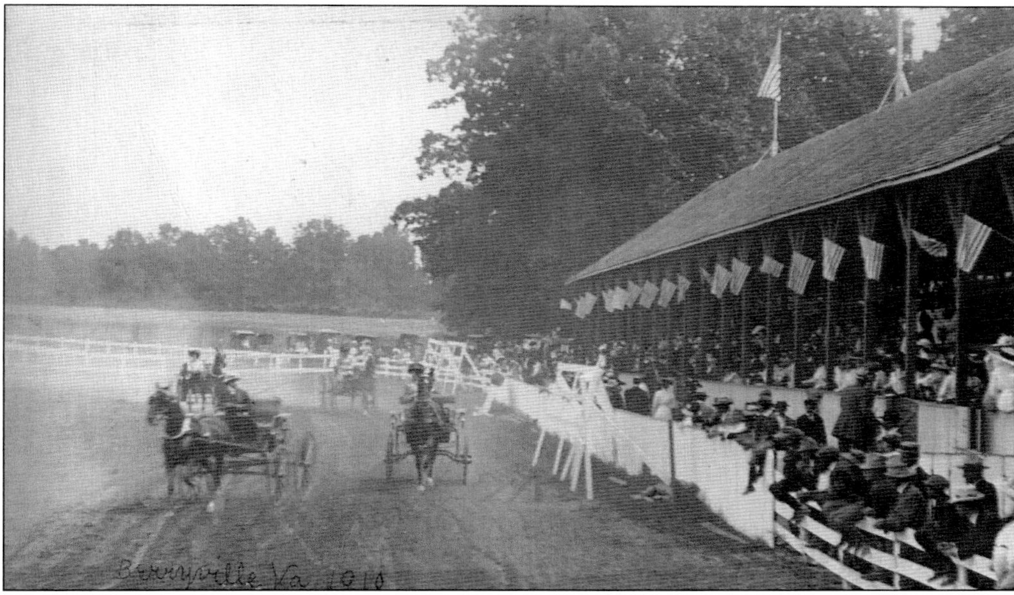

This harness competition at the Berryville Horse Show of 1910 shows male and female drivers watched by a large crowd. The *Clarke Courier* reported that while "very few accidents marred the show," nine attendees were arrested for "peddling liquid cheer." The horseshows, which were held over a three-day period in August, ran until at least 1936 but finally succumbed to the financial downturn of the period. (CCHA.)

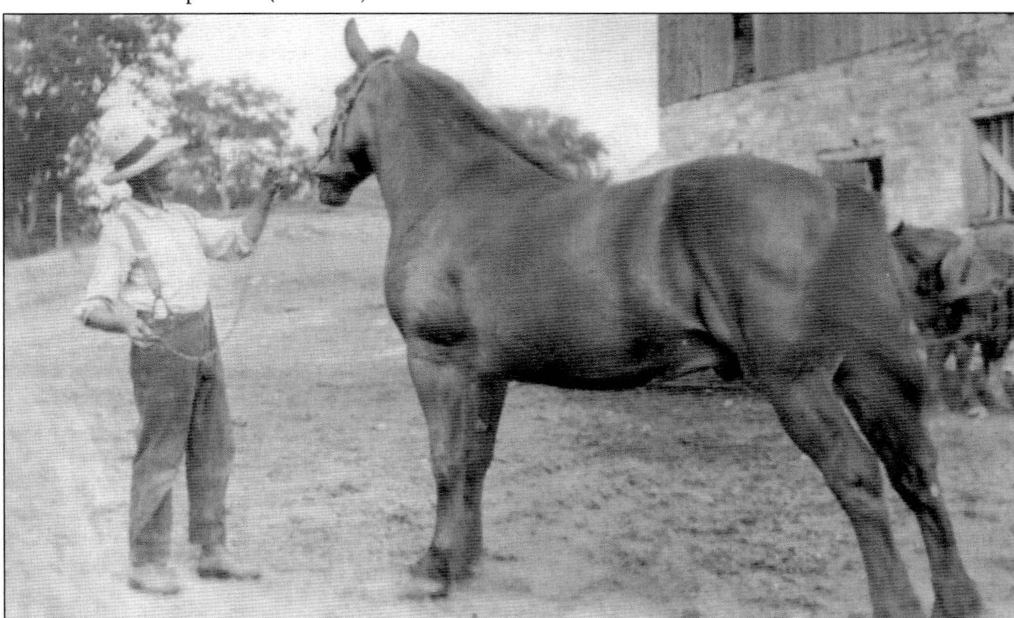

This large draft horse named Dick is shown in the 1920s with his groomsman, Will Rutter. Owned by the Bell brothers, who farmed multiple properties on the south side of Route 7 east of Berryville, Dick was a frequent winner at the horseshow competitions. He apparently knew to turn his head to receive ribbons and to dance when the band played and the audience cheered. (Herman Lloyd.)

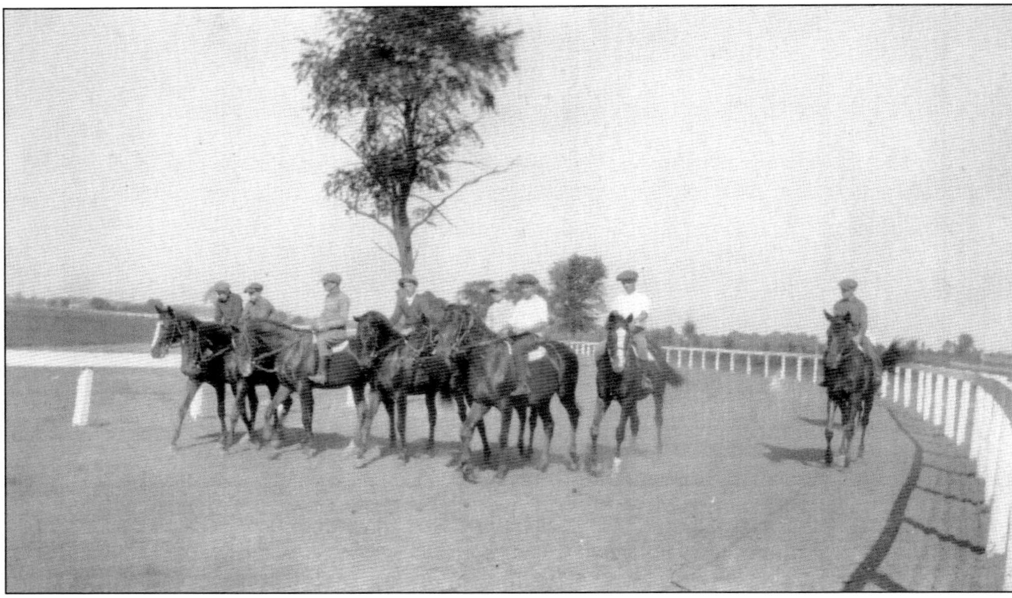

Horse racing in the area dates back to the competitions Lord Fairfax held at Greenway Court. Jousting tournaments were a common social and sporting event in some mid-19th-century Clarke circles. Brothers Montfort and Bernard B. Jones established a major Thoroughbred breeding and training facility at Audley farm in 1921 and attained international acclaim for their success. During the 1920s and 1930s, Audley horses won 838 races, earning owners nearly $1.7 million. One mare alone, Princess Doreen, captured over $170,000, making her the leading money-winner of her day, and Sir Barton was America's first Triple Crown winner. The 1923 image above shows men at the Audley training track. The historic Audley house, home of Nellie Parke Custis, George Washington's ward, appears below. The horse and automobile were two competing modes of transportation at the time. (Both, SBA/HRL.)

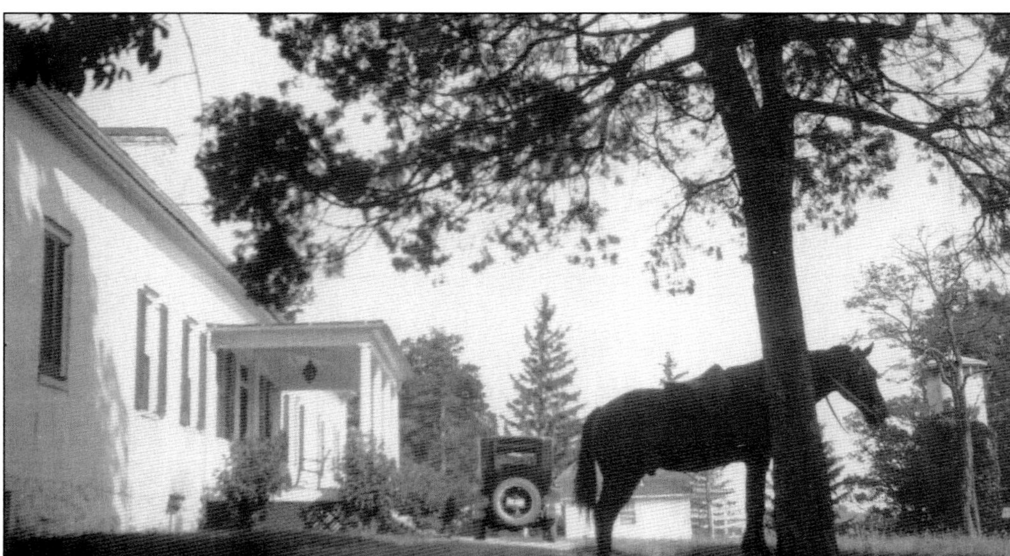

Archibald Bevan was one of the organizers the Blue Ridge Hunt in 1888 and served as its first master until 1896. He was one of several Englishmen who came to America at the turn of the century and formed official fox hunting organizations and subscription hound packs. The Blue Ridge Hunt is still an integral part of Clarke's social and sporting community, offering scheduled meets throughout the year. (CCHA.)

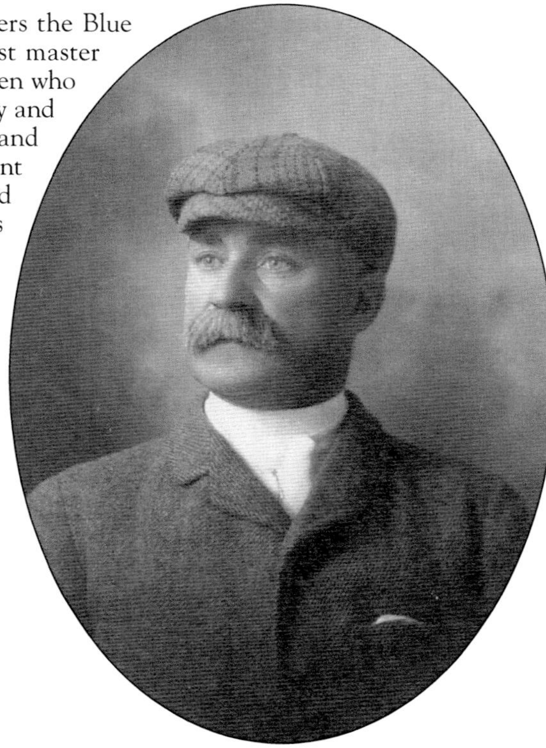

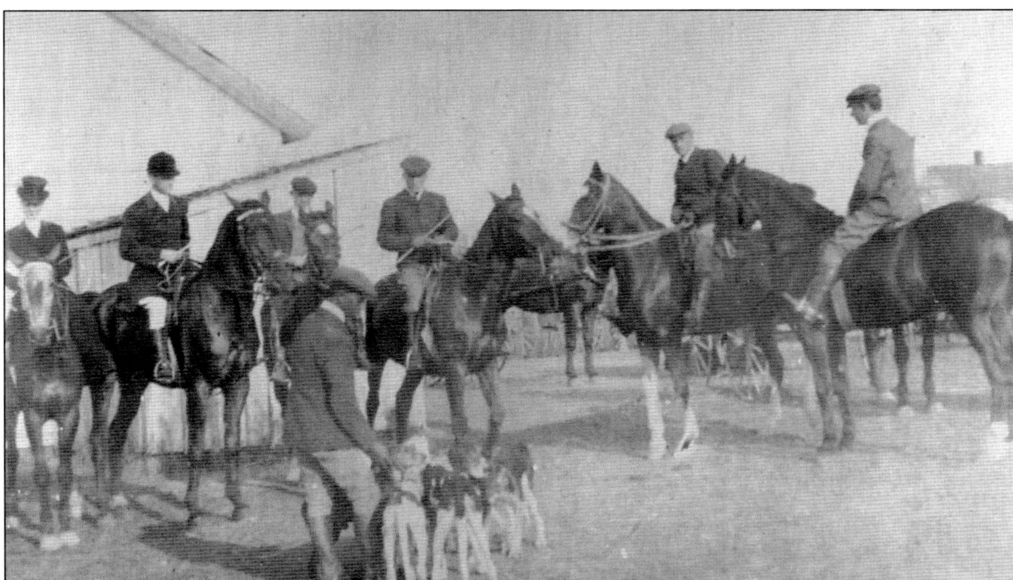

Members of the Blue Ridge Hunt met in 1904. Pictured are, from left to right, Dora Henry (riding sidesaddle), master of foxhounds Edward Butler, Will Dearmont, George Page, Thomas H. Burwell, and William Randolph. Adam Hubbard tends the hounds in the foreground. The organized hunt rides over the countryside, following the hounds on the scent. Clarke's rolling topography enhances the thrill of the chase. (CCHA.)

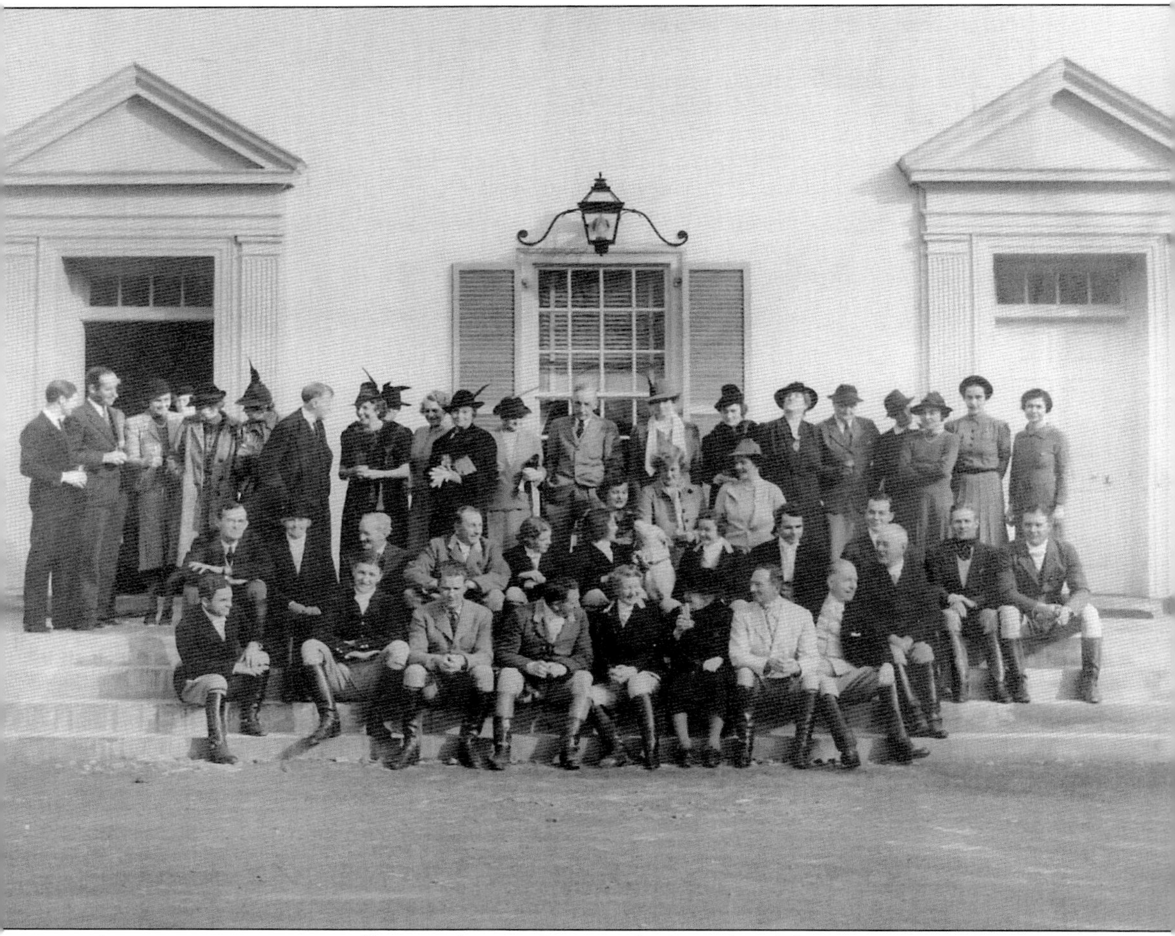

A misnomer, as it is usually served around noon, the hunt breakfast continues to be a popular tradition of the Blue Ridge Hunt. While the horses and hounds are cooling off after the meet, the hunters and guests gather for comradeship. Pictured at this mid-1930s hunt breakfast at Springsbury, the home of Mr. and Mrs. George Greenhalgh Sr., are, from left to right, (first row) Sandy Baldwin, Alexander Mackay-Smith, Bob Randolph, William Watkins (master of foxhounds), Mrs. George Greenhalgh Sr. (Marie), Mrs. George Burwell (Lucy), George Greenhalgh Sr., Mr. Ruthroth, and unidentified; (second row) Ben Randolph, Sybil Jacobs, Edward Butler, Jack Johnson, Floz Ruthroth, Jane Brook, Billy Wetherall, Stacy Lloyd, Rollie Mitchell, Bill Clagett, and Henry Mitchell; (third row) Arnold Seruton, Percy Randolph, Nina Seruton, Mrs. Courtney Jones (Juliet), Mrs. Ewart Johnston (Cecil Jane), Beth Beverley, Richard Whiting, Judy Randolph, Mrs. R.G. Mitchell (Susan), Mrs. Ruthroth, Mrs. Edith Taylor, Mrs. Richard Whiting (Rosa), unidentified, Mrs. William Watkins (Gladys), Etta Williams, Mrs. Ed Butler (Emily), Mary Page, Mrs. Crim Stribling, Mary O'Fallon, Cary Harrison Mitchell, and Marge Willoughby. The three people in the center with the dog are, from left to right, Mary Dougherty, Gertie Dougherty, and Virginia Jacobs. (CCHA.)

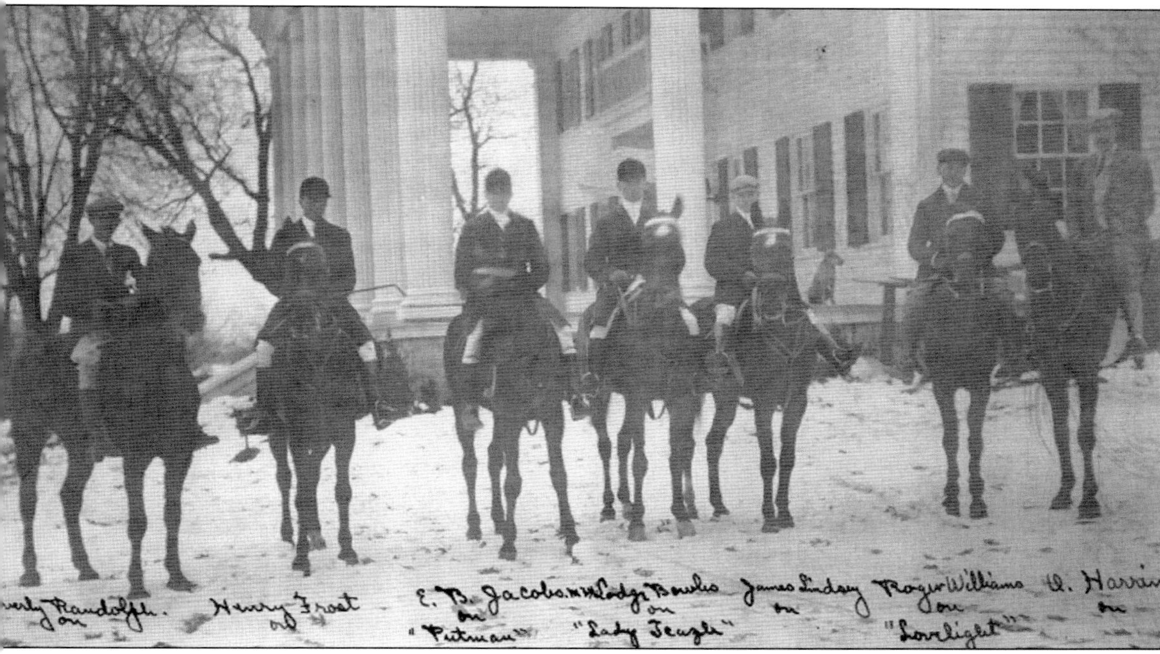

Shown at the 1910 Christmas Eve Hunt are, from left to right, Beverly Randolph, Henry Frost, A.B. Jacobs on the horse Putman, W. Lodge Bowles on Lady Teazle, James Lindsay, Roger Williams on Lovelight, and O. Harriman. Rosemont, home of E.L. Harriman at the time, stands in the background. The original house was constructed around 1811 by George Norris, the first sheriff of Clarke County, but was greatly remodeled (or possibly replaced) with the large Colonial Revival–style frame house by the next owners. Mr. and Mrs. Charles Clapp (Cornelia) purchased the property in 1902, and the Harrimans, a wealthy New York family, held the property in the 1910s. Harry F. Byrd Sr., then governor of Virginia, purchased the estate in 1929. With its park-like setting and expansive acreage, Rosemont was a hub of social and political activity. Byrd entertained many luminaries there, including Presidents Kennedy and Johnson. Surrounded by family apple orchards and located on the outskirts of Berryville, Rosemont left Byrd ownership in 1997. The manor house and surrounding 60 acres are now a bed-and-breakfast. (CCHA.)

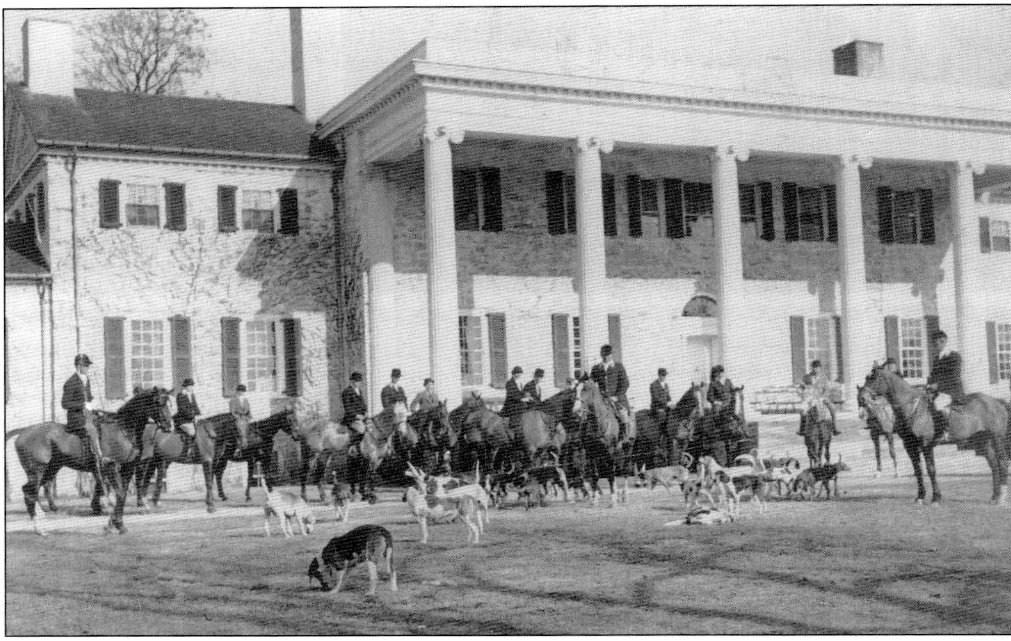

Col. Nathaniel Burwell built Carter Hall in the late 1790s as the centerpiece of his 5,000-acre estate. Updated in the 1930s by pharmaceutical magnate Gerard Lambert, of Listerine fame, the residence often served as the starting point for the Blue Ridge Hunt, drawing huge crowds. Since 1977, Carter Hall has been the headquarters for Project HOPE, a global health foundation. (CCHA.)

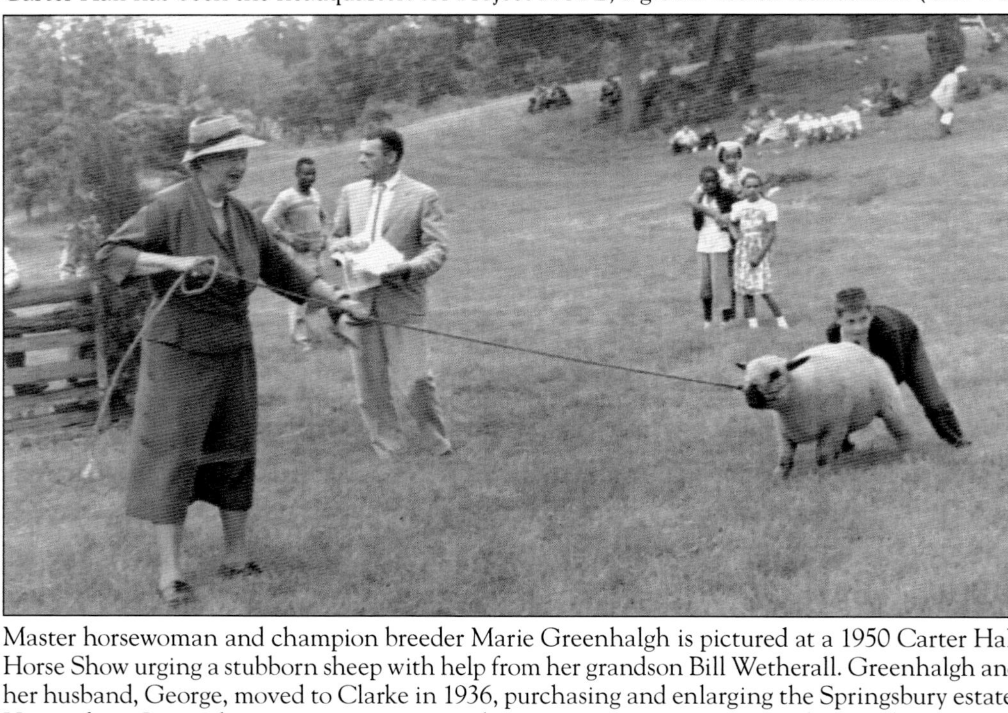

Master horsewoman and champion breeder Marie Greenhalgh is pictured at a 1950 Carter Hall Horse Show urging a stubborn sheep with help from her grandson Bill Wetherall. Greenhalgh and her husband, George, moved to Clarke in 1936, purchasing and enlarging the Springsbury estate. Horses from Springsbury were winners at such prestigious competitions as the North American Horse Breeders Association at Madison Square Garden. (CCHA.)

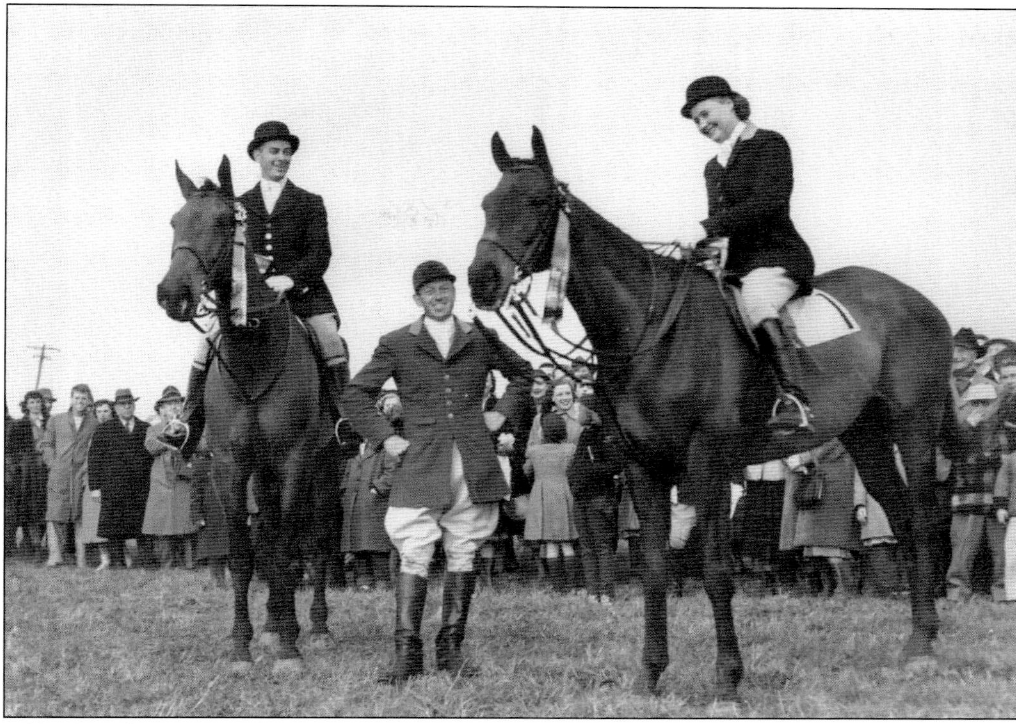

Billie (Sybilla) Greenhalgh is pictured after earning first place at the 1948 Virginia Field Hunter Championship. To the left is reserve champion Roland Mitchell, and standing between them is an unidentified huntsman. The Blue Ridge Hunt offers a variety of activities other than hunting, including point-to-point races, begun in 1949, which provide young and seasoned horses an opportunity to compete and prepare for sanctioned races. (Gin Mitchell.)

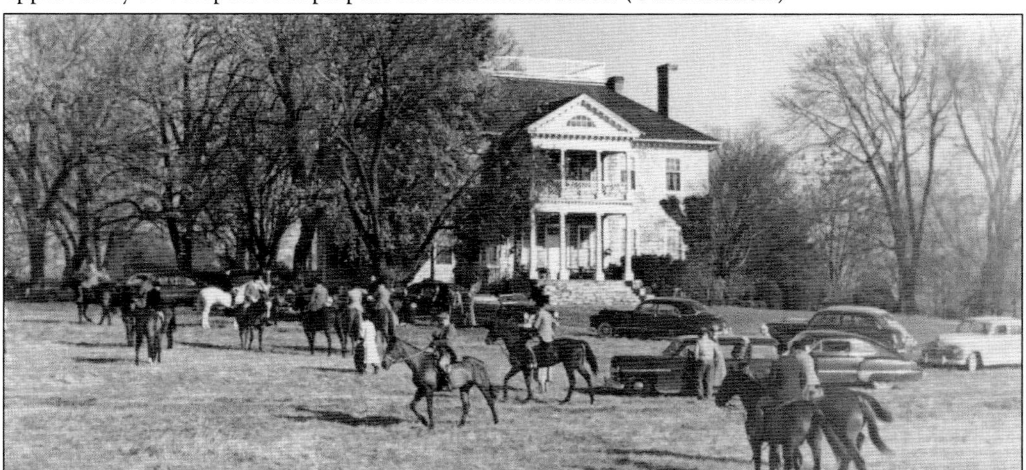

Annfield, home of William Bell Watkins, who was master and huntsman during the 1930s, is the setting for this 1950 Blue Ridge Hunt meet. Annfield was constructed in the 1790s by Mathew Page and named for his wife, Ann, sister of Bishop William Meade. Mary Custis, Robert E. Lee's wife, was born here in 1808. According to the Virginia Department of Historic Resources, Annfield is "one of Virginia's grandest works of Federal architecture." (SBA/HRL.)

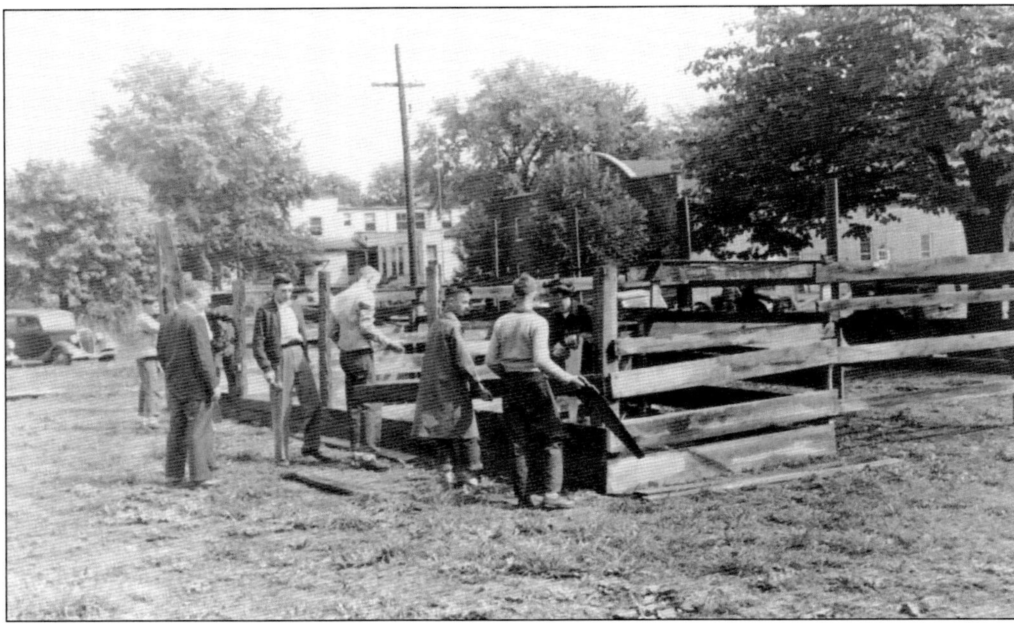

This picture, taken at the corner of South Church and Crow Streets in Berryville, shows pens being set up for the first Clarke County Fair, held in 1949 by the Future Farmers of America (FFA). After receiving its charter in 1952, the Clarke County Ruritan Club, a rural civic organization, held its Fall Festival at the same location until moving to the old Berryville Horse Show grounds in 1955. The Ruritan Club subsequently purchased the grounds in 1960 for $24,500. Held in August, the annual week-long Clarke County Fair showcases the agricultural heritage of the county and is a huge draw for the community. Activities at the fair include livestock, farm, homemaking, and garden exhibits as well as competitions such as the pig scramble, the truck-and-tractor pull, and, as shown below, the horse pull. (Both, CCHA.)

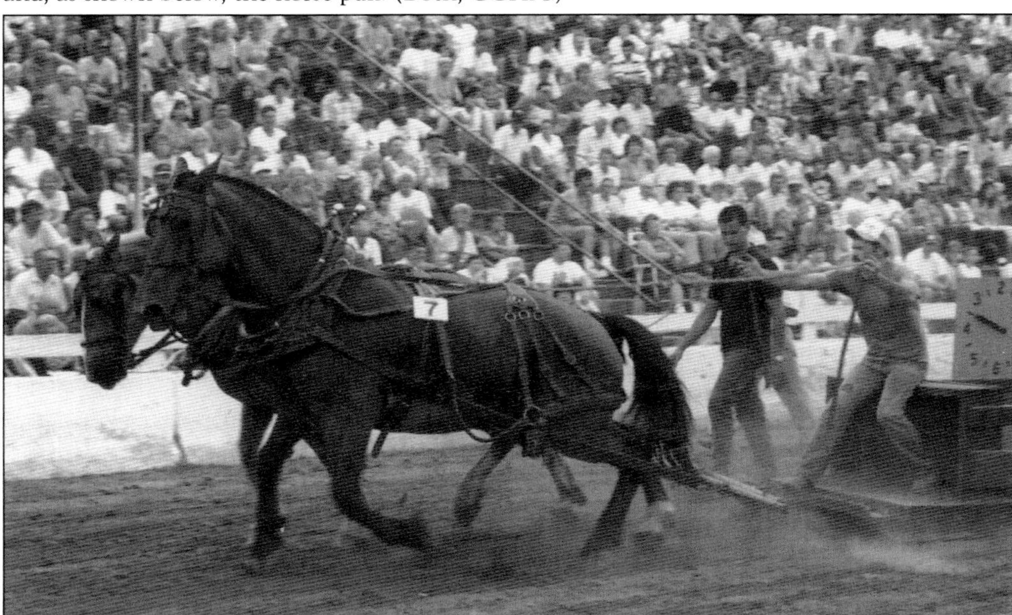

Nine

TRANSPORTATION

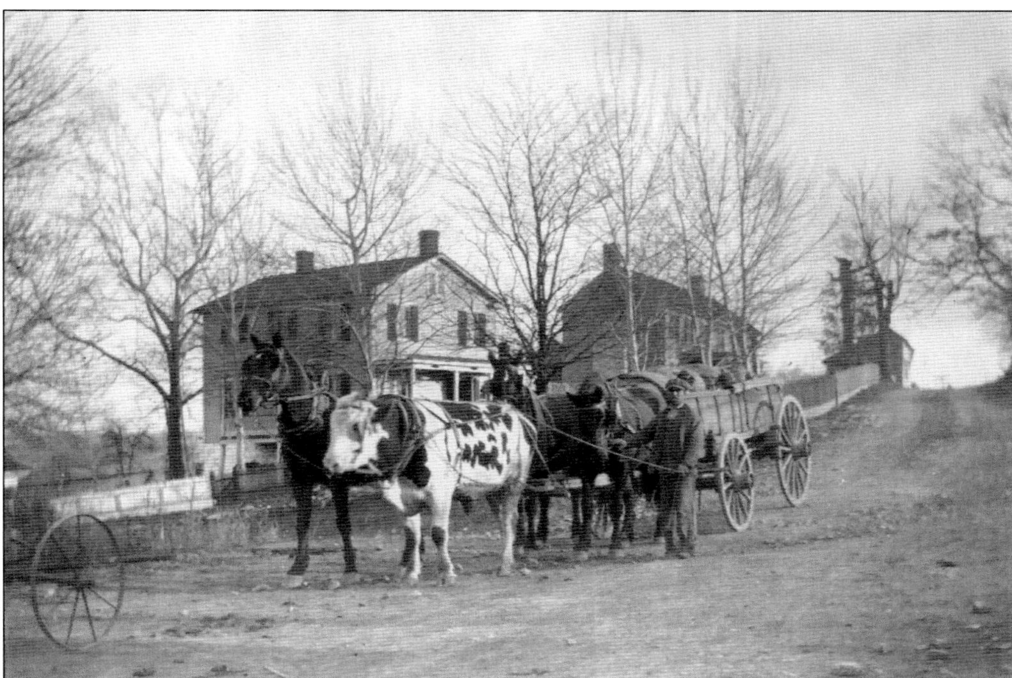

By the time Clarke was formed in 1836, it had a complex network of roads that linked settlements, farms, mills, residences, and churches to one another. This scene in northwestern Clarke from about 1900 shows a wagon being hauled by three horses and an ox, suggesting a heavy load. Clarke County still maintains a number of unpaved public roads such as the one shown, adding to the county's rural character. (SBA/HRL.)

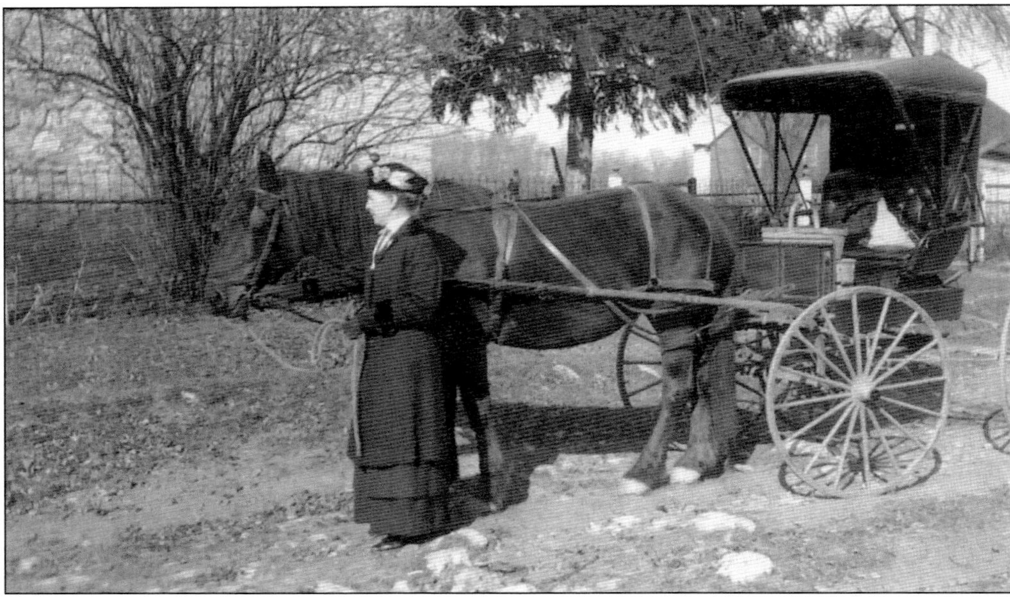

This photograph, taken around 1900, when vehicles had real horsepower, shows Rebecca Pidgeon with horse Captain, who is hitched to a shay. These types of light carriages with a folding top were also called whiskys, a reference to their use for whisking about and running errands. Pidgeon, an active member of Quaker Hopewell Meeting, was a lifelong member of the Women's Christian Temperance Union. (SBA/HRL.)

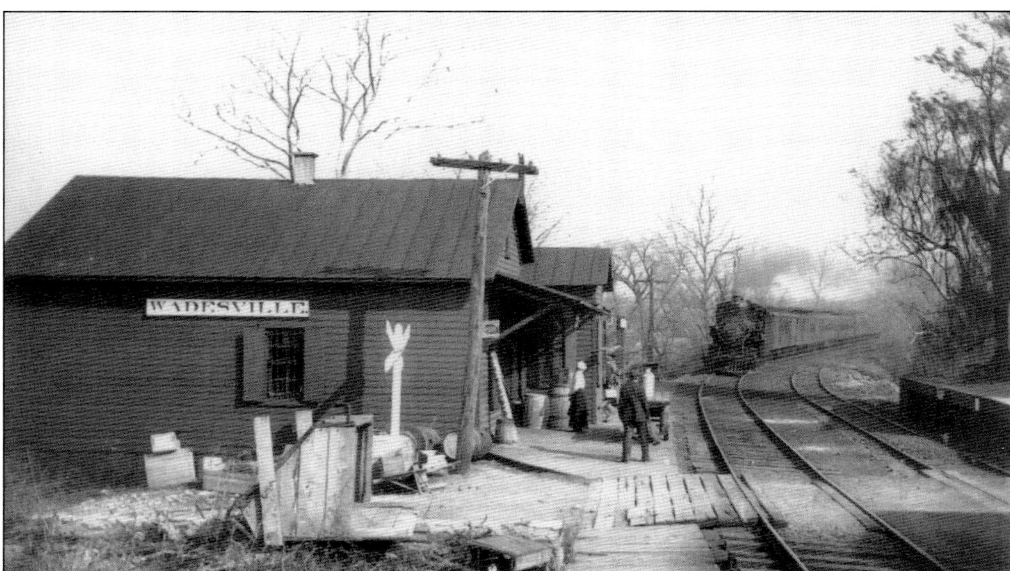

A steam engine pulls into Wadesville, located in the northwesternmost part of Clarke along the Opequon Creek. The community developed at the junction of a busy road and the Winchester & Potomac Railroad, which was completed in the mid-1830s. It later became part of the Baltimore & Ohio Railroad (B&O). Although now off the beaten path, Wadesville and nearby Swimley Station were bustling communities when they were the only train stops in the county. (SBA/HRL.)

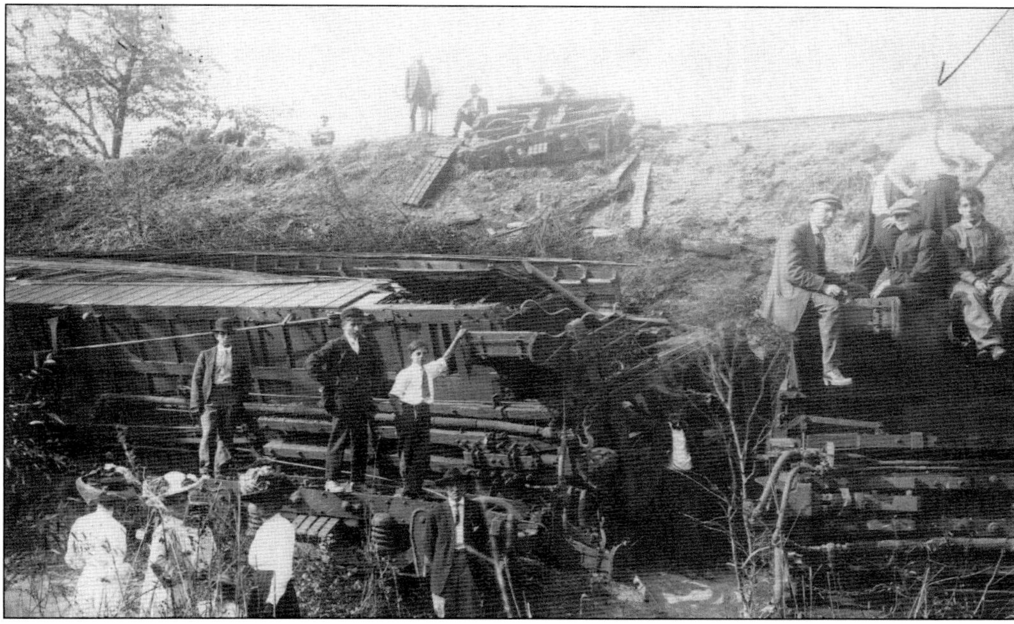

On the evening of Saturday, October 15, 1910, southbound passenger train No. 1 heading from Baltimore to Winchester on the Valley Branch of the B&O derailed at the Opequon Creek bridge near Wadesville. Two cars jumped the tracks and rolled down a 50-foot embankment. Miraculously, no one was killed or seriously injured. The newspaper reported the wreck was caused by "spreading rails," while suggesting speed also could have been a factor. A large number of spectators along with crewmen were at the scene the following day, some sporting their Sunday best. The mangled wreckage of the metal undercarriages was eventually removed and the ruined wooden cars burned, another spectacle that attracted a crowd. (Both, SBA/HRL.)

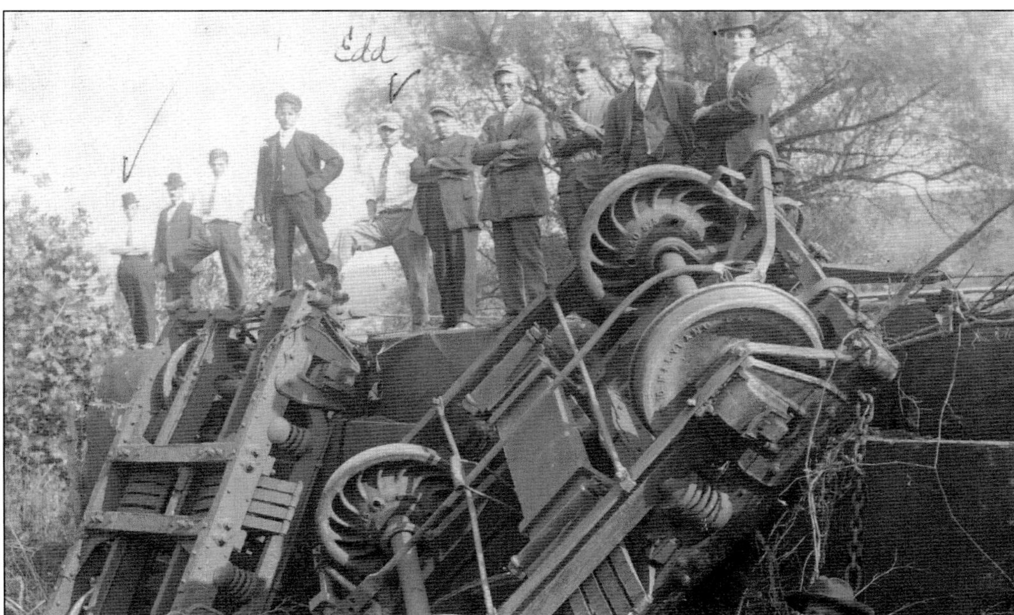

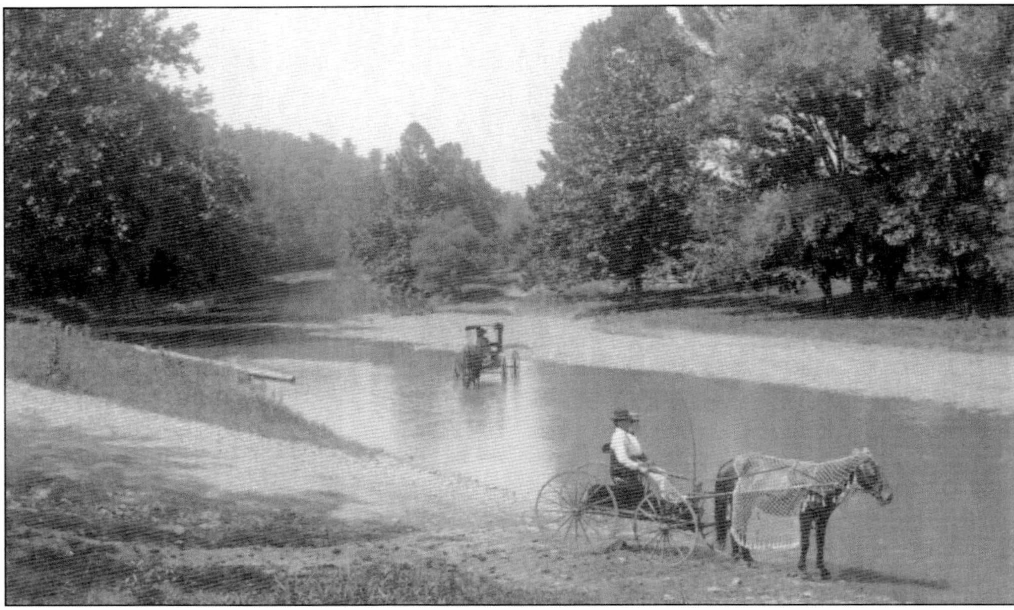

Taken before the construction of any bridges, this 1901 image of Leslie Jordan with an unidentified gentleman in a carriage shows the ford where Route 7 once crossed the Opequon. The decorative net on the horse has tassels whose movement discouraged flies and mosquitoes from landing and biting. In the background is a woman driving a covered buggy and allowing her horse to fill up as they negotiate the creek. (SBA/HRL.)

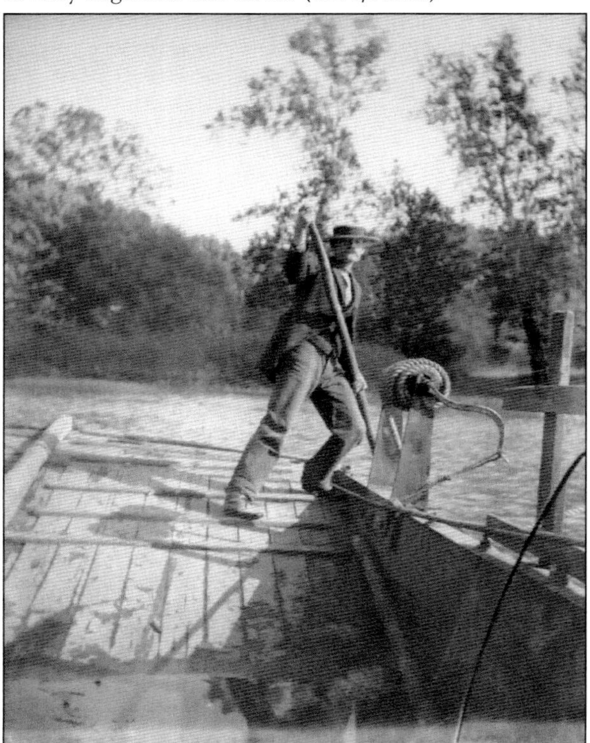

The Shenandoah River flows along the base of the Blue Ridge Mountains, defining Clarke's eastern boundary. The earliest river crossings were made at natural fords where the water was shallower. By the mid-18th century, commercial ferries were established at the base of Snicker's Gap (Route 7) and Ashby's Gap (Route 50), the two main east-west routes. Pictured is a ferryman guiding a boat across the Shenandoah around 1900. (Library of Congress.)

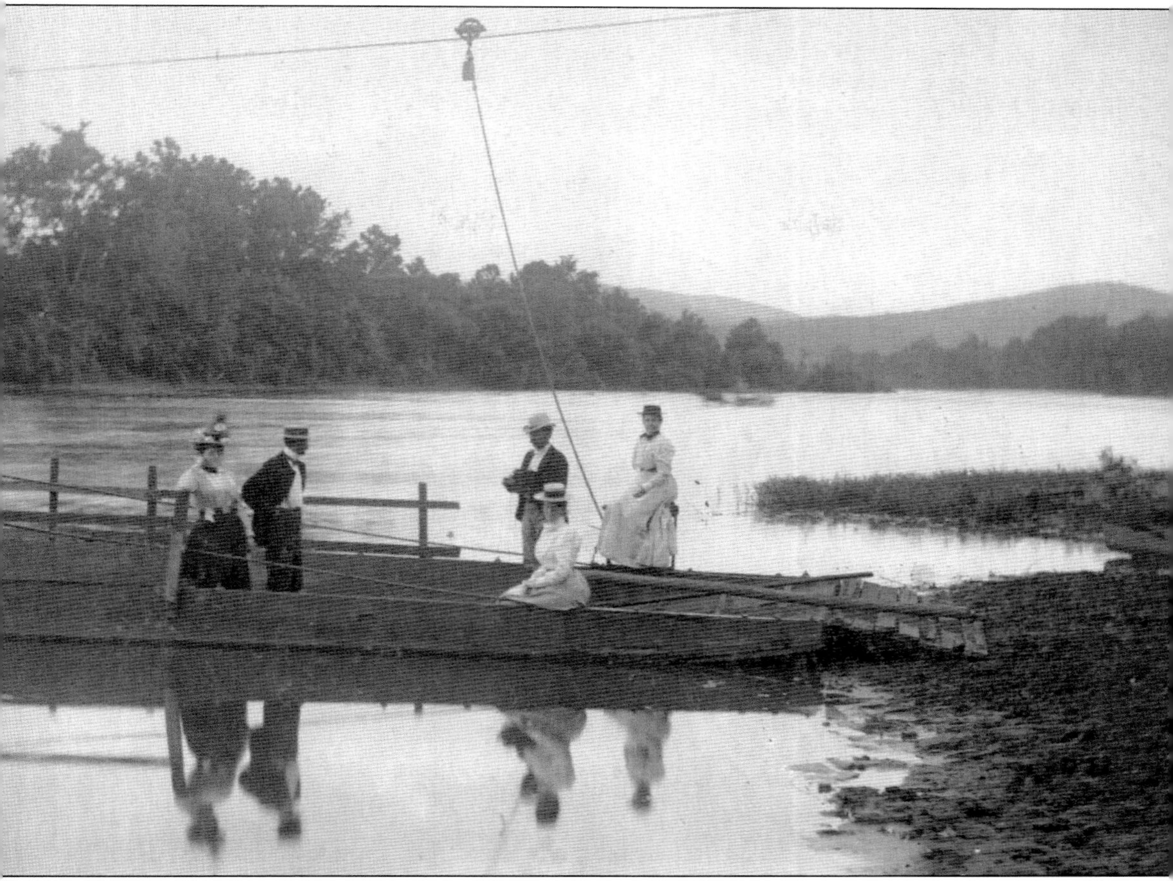

This unidentified group of well-dressed men and women are posed on the east side of the Shenandoah River at Castleman's Ferry around 1910 as they prepare to be transported to the other side. The man in the center may be holding a camera. In the background, a horse-drawn cart fords the river, possibly to avoid paying the ferryman. An overhead rope with a pulley and a winch guided the flat-bottomed boat across the river. Overloading was always a consideration, although the boat was large enough to carry a four-horse team. A ferry known as Snicker's was established at this location near present-day Route 7 and appears on Charles Varle's 1809 map of the county. This ferry did a thriving business, as it served the primary route from Winchester to Alexandria. Flat-bottomed boats also carried grain from local mills down the Shenandoah River to Harper's Ferry, where it was shipped to other markets. An 1831 plan to construct a canal along the Shenandoah met with great opposition and was ultimately abandoned. (CCHA.)

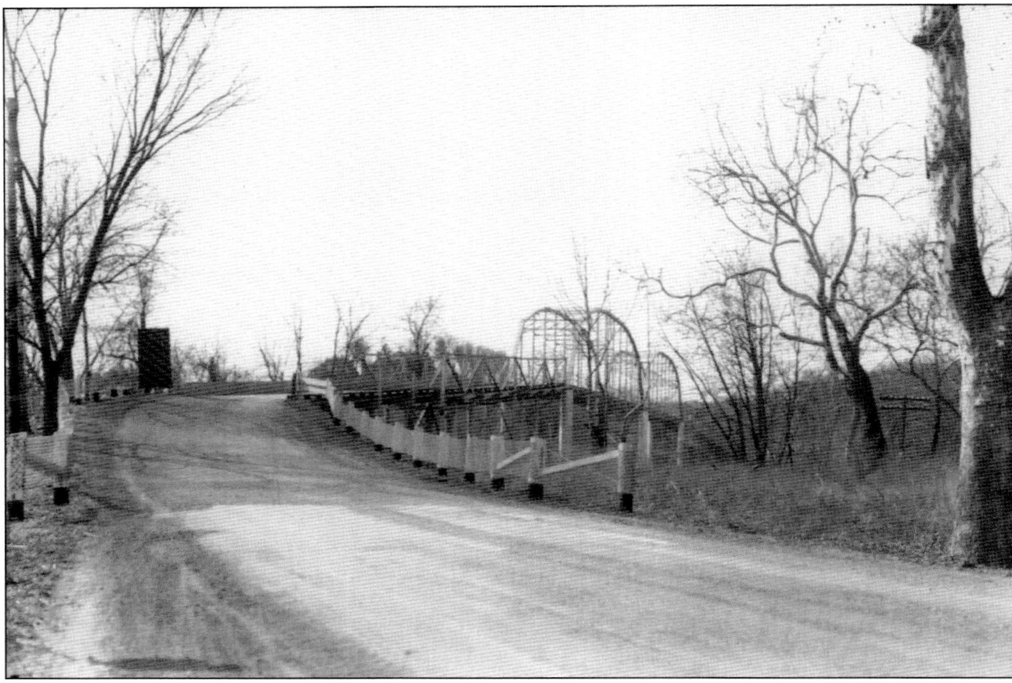

Several bridges have been constructed over the Shenandoah River at Route 7 near the original location of Castleman's Ferry. The first was this steel-truss, two-span bridge from the early 1900s. The view above is from the east approach, where the road steeply rises to the level of the bridge. The image below, taken a year before the bridge was replaced with a more modern one in 1939, is from the western approach and shows the pylons supporting the relatively level roadbed leading to the bridge. An early billboard advertising Coca-Cola stands to the left near the white building known as Riverside Rendezvous. To preserve the Clarke's rural character, no new billboards have been allowed in the county since the 1980s. (Both, SBA/HRL.)

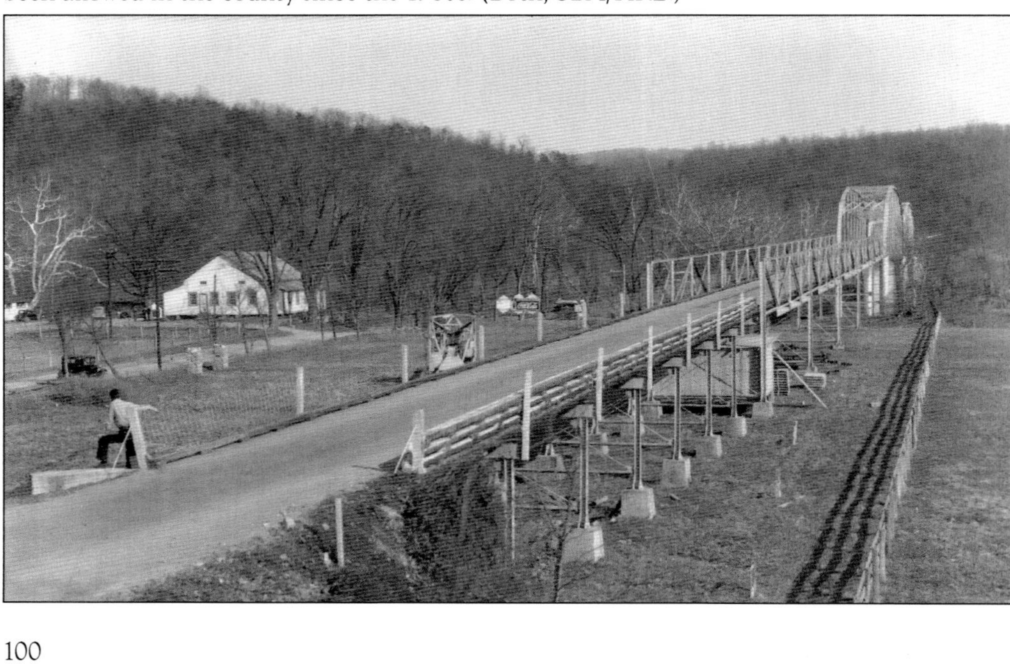

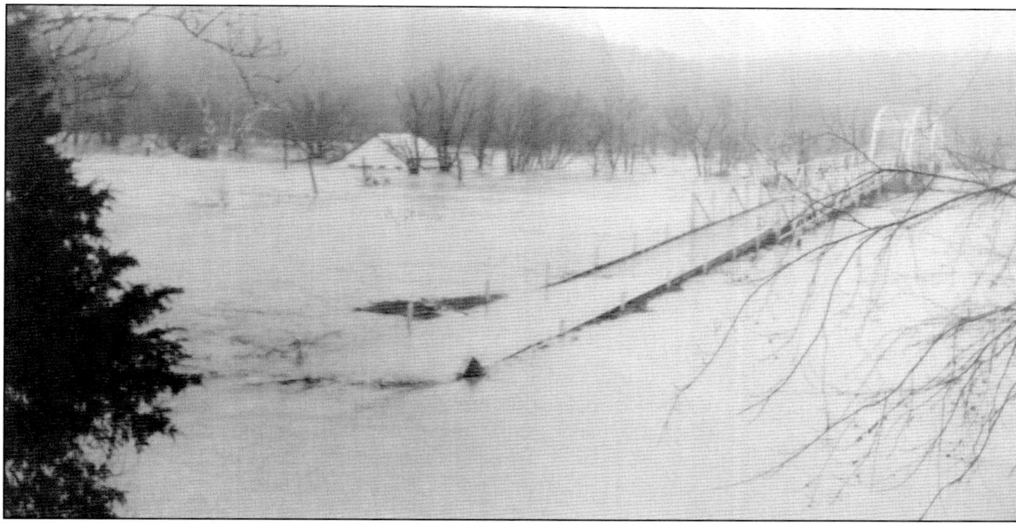

Floods along the Shenandoah River are an integral part of Clarke's story. The view above of the Castleman's Ferry bridge over Route 7 was taken in March 1936 during one of the worst floods of the century. Unlike most floods, which are caused by tropical storms, this one resulted from a combination of multiple heavy snowfalls and successive heavy early spring rainstorms. Another massive flood came through the Shenandoah River in October 1942, breaking the 1936 record by 12 feet. The September 1996 flood caused by Hurricane Fran was the third worst in Virginia history. Its wrath and Route 7 are pictured below. Another memorable Clarke flood was in October 1870, when several mills and houses along the river were carried away. (Top, CCHA; bottom, *Clarke Courier.*)

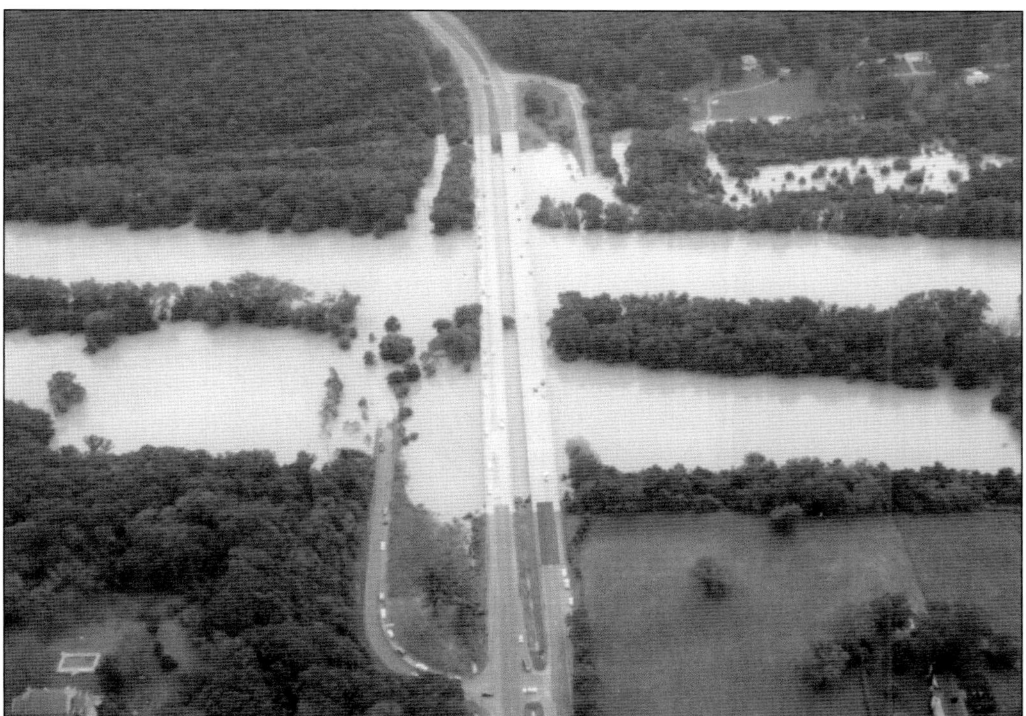

North Hill, which stands on a promontory with a commanding view of the Shenandoah River to the east, is Clarke's earliest summer resort. Shown around 1920, when it was also known as Castleman's Inn, North Hill catered to tourists who journeyed there by car, bus, or train. The complex evolved over time, with the earliest section being the one-and-a-half-story log cabin shown in the center of the photograph with an ivy-covered wooden roof. Located near the ferry at present-day Route 7, North Hill promoted numerous nearby historic sites in its 1930s brochure, including the Shenandoah National Park, Endless and Luray Caverns, Greenway Court, Mount Weather, Harper's Ferry, and Winchester. Extolling the virtues of its location, the advertisement touts the "dryness of the atmosphere and wonderful moon and starlit nights, no mosquitoes, millions of fireflies with the musical twittering of the nightingale and whippoorwill and the call of the hoot owl with the glorious moonlight glittering over the rippling cold waters of the Shenandoah." (CCHA.)

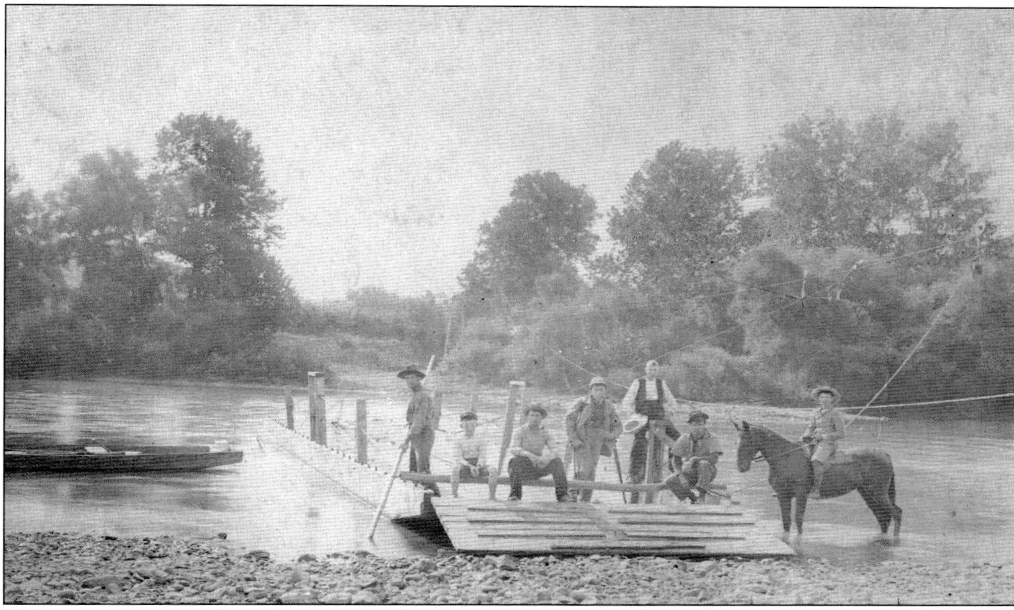

Taken at a site noted on the 1809 Varle Map as Berry's Ferry and earlier known as Kersey's Ferry, this picture shows a group of men gathered on the shore with a flat-bottomed boat being guided with poles and ropes across the Shenandoah River. The ferry ceased operation in 1904, replaced by the first metal truss bridge at the site. Two concrete-and-steel-girder bridges dating from the 1970s now carry present-day Route 50. (CCHA.)

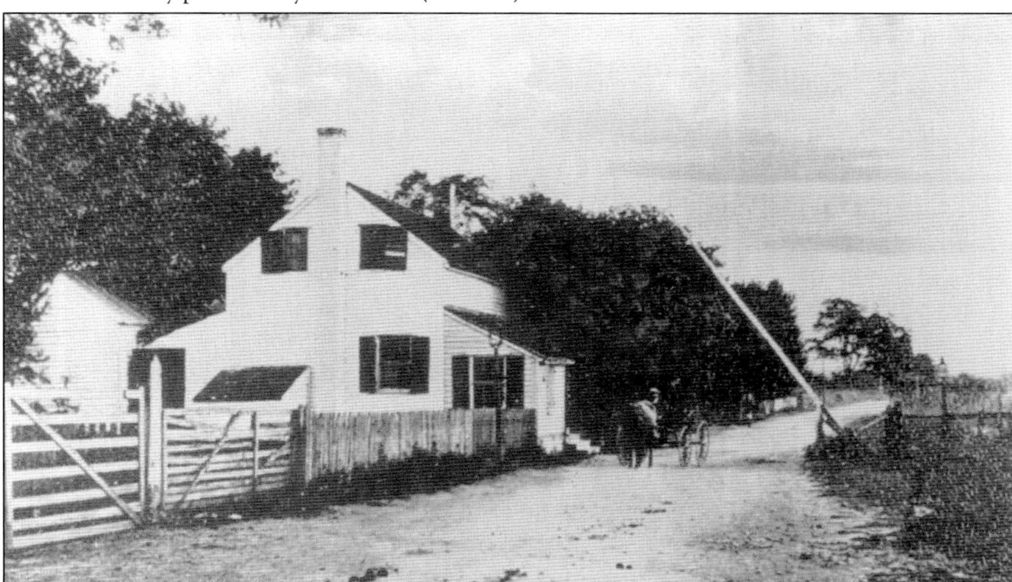

Tollhouses were built to help defray the maintenance costs to those who used the roads. This early-20th-century view taken along South Church Street in Berryville shows the tollhouse for the Berryville-Millwood Turnpike and its tollgate. The county had multiple tollhouses, most of which have since been demolished. This rare resource, along with a few others, still stands and is a private residence. (CCHA.)

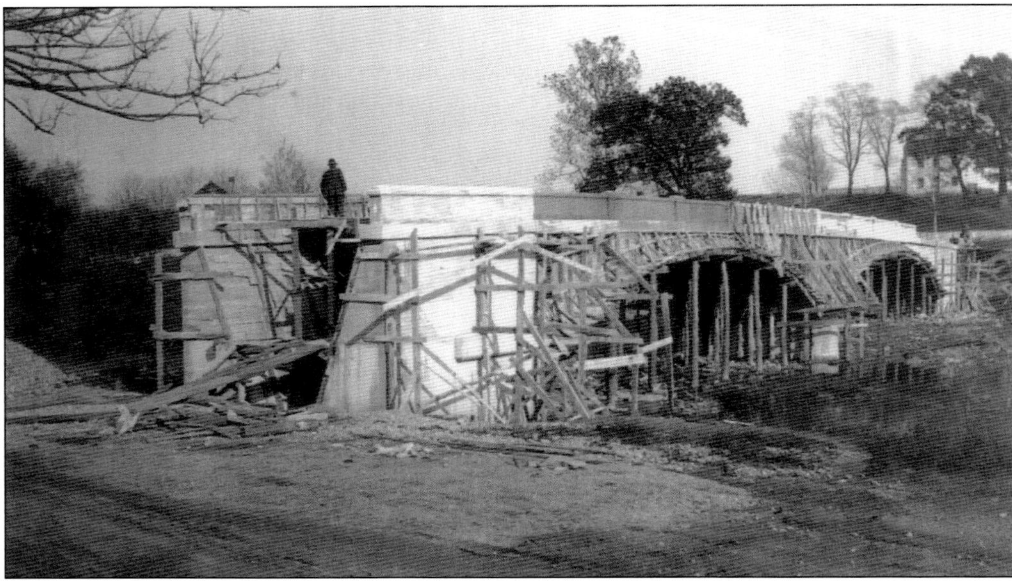

Shown both under construction in 1917 and later completed, the Wadesville bridge crossing Opequon Creek was described by the highway department as "an ornament to the neighborhood and a profitable investment of public funds." Constructed by the Monongahela Valley Engineering Company, the elegant two-span, closed-spandrel concrete bridge is significant in its use of the Thacher reinforcing system, in which a double row of steel reinforcement is employed. A metal truss bridge was originally planned for this location in 1915, but after Edwin Thacher's patent entered the public domain in 1916, a bridge utilizing his system was chosen instead. Still in use for Route 672 between Clarke and Frederick Counties, it is the only bridge in the county that has been determined individually eligible for the National Register of Historic Places for its significance in the area of engineering history. (Both, SBA/HRL.)

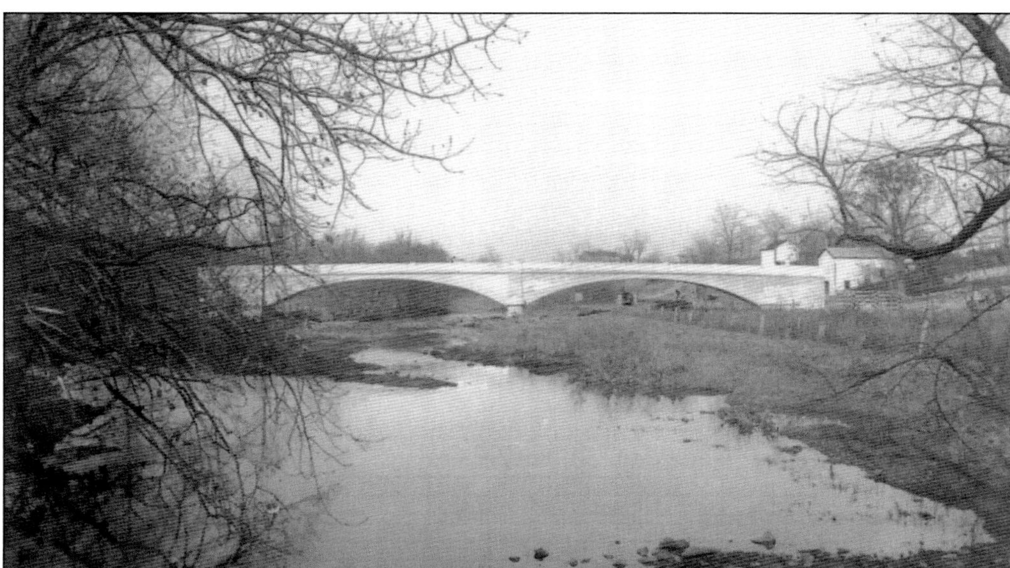

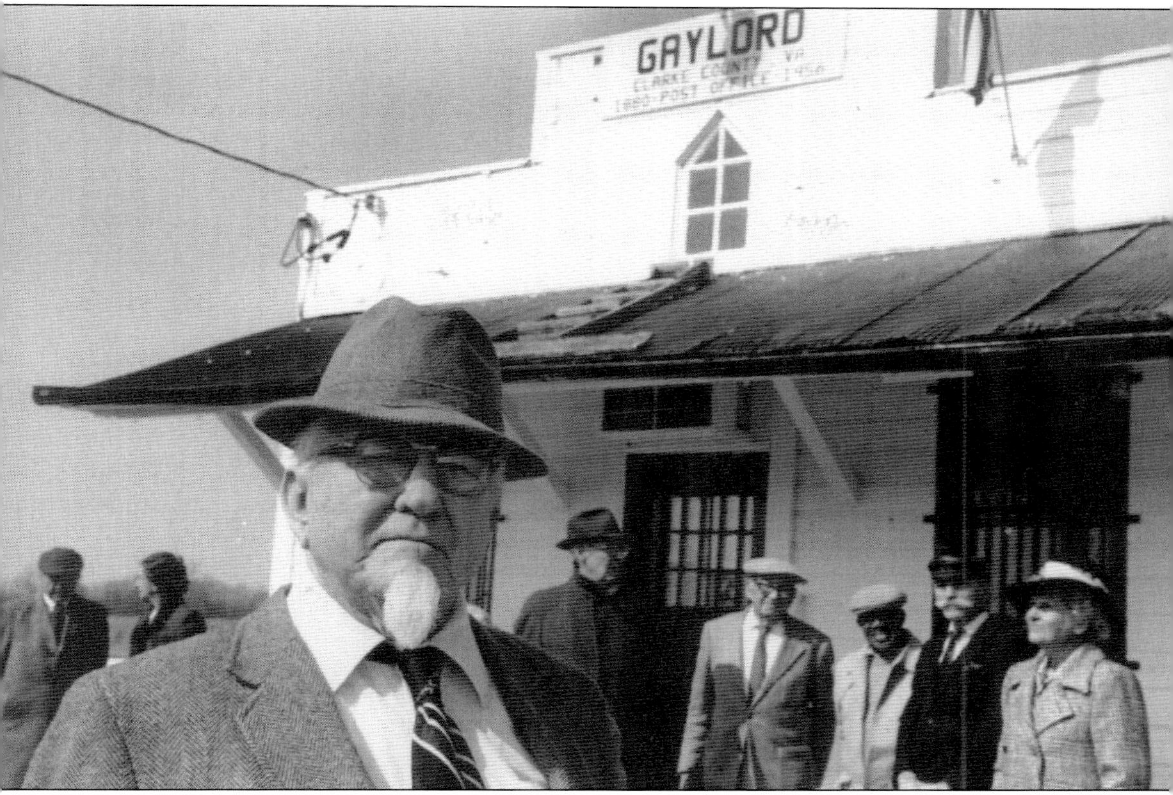

Harry Hayslett, shown in 1988, was the postmaster at the small community of Gaylord for 32 years. Located about five miles north of Berryville, Gaylord developed around 1880 at the intersection of the newly created Shenandoah Valley Railroad (now Norfolk Southern) and the Berryville & Charles Town Turnpike (Route 340). Originally known as Fairfield Crossing for its proximity to the Fairfield estate, the community had its own post office by 1880 and 26 residents by 1917. In the early 1950s, after the new bridge over the tracks cut off most traffic from the post office building (shown in the background), Hayslett had it moved from its original location to his land nearby. Hayslett's wife, Elizabeth, served her acclaimed chicken and waffle dinner at the Gaylord Inn and Tearoom nearby. Another small rail stop along the Shenandoah Valley Railroad in Clarke was Briggs, located near Old Chapel. (*Clarke Courier.*)

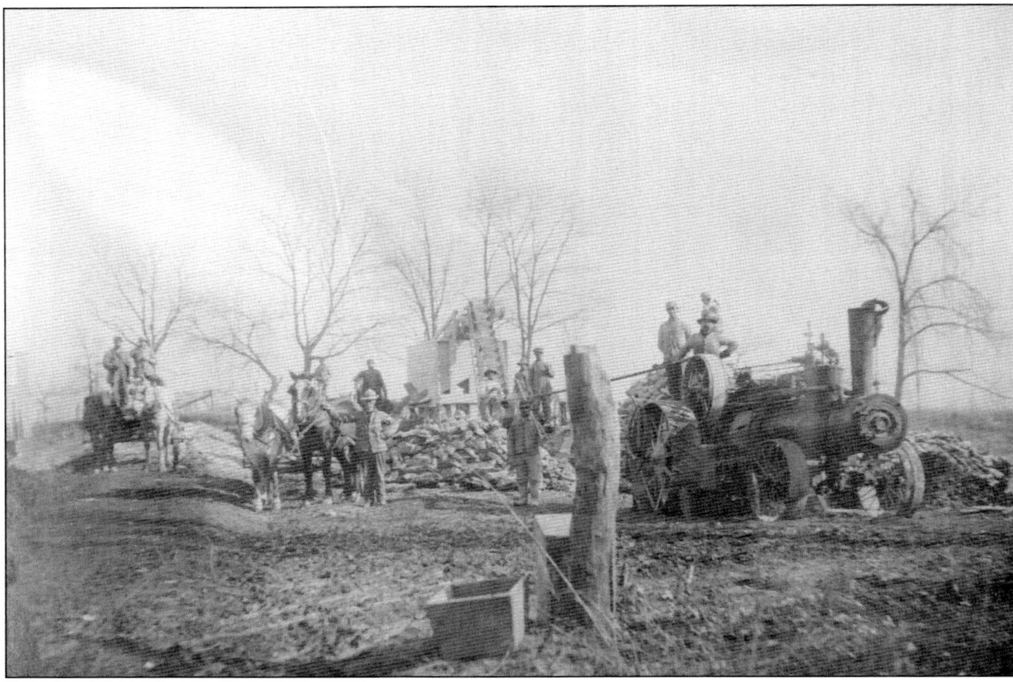

This photograph showing a road maintenance crew was taken on January 16, 1911. The stone crusher in the background was powered by a steam engine. While draft horses were used to move stone and clear paths, much of the road construction was done by hand. Many of Clarke's old roads are still in use today, 19 of which—totaling 80 miles—are designated as Virginia Scenic Byways. (CCHA.)

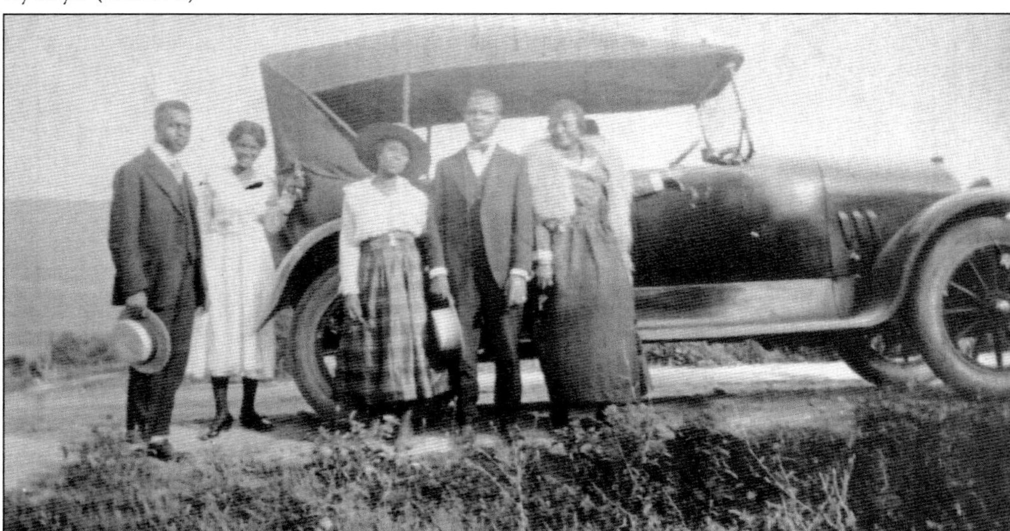

This elegant group of men and women are posed in front of a canvas-roofed roadster around 1918. To the right is Fanny Jenkins, a schoolteacher in Josephine City, and next to her is Robert Jenkins. The others are unidentified. Both men carry straw hats, and Fanny sports a fox shawl. With the advent of assembly-line production of automobiles, more and more people could afford the convenience and prestige provided by an automobile. (CCHA.)

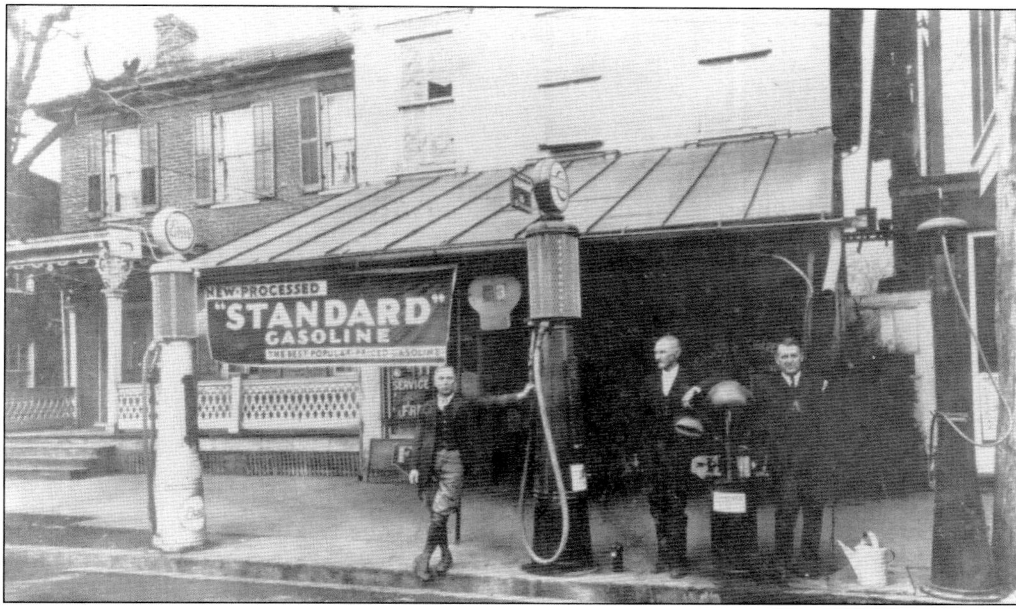

The automobile's dominance impacted the county's landscape, not only with the construction and improvement of roads, but also with the development of new building types that catered to the car, such as filling stations. Pictured in 1927 is Walter Wisecarver's station, which stood at 28 West Main Street in Berryville, probably one of the earliest in the county. From left to right are Wisecarver, W.H. Mesmer, and A.B. Hummer. (CCHA.)

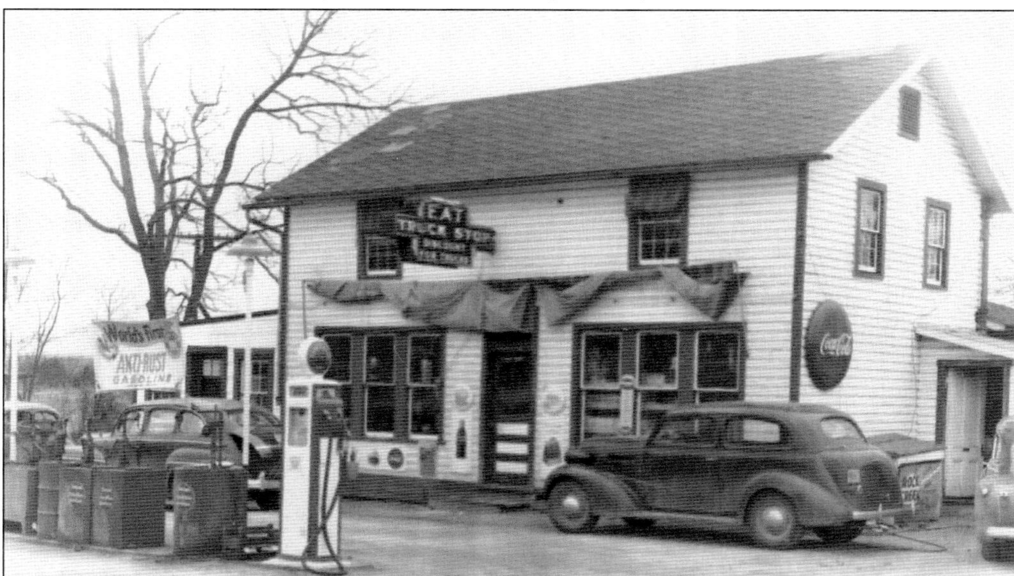

When the road carrying Route 50 bypassed Millwood and Boyce, the intersection known as Waterloo was created at its junction with Route 340. This prompted the establishment of several commercial enterprises that catered to vehicular traffic. One of the earliest was the Waterloo Truck Stop, which stood on the northeast corner of the intersection. Waterloo, with multiple convenience stores and fast-food stops, is still a bustling commercial crossroads. (Les Querry.)

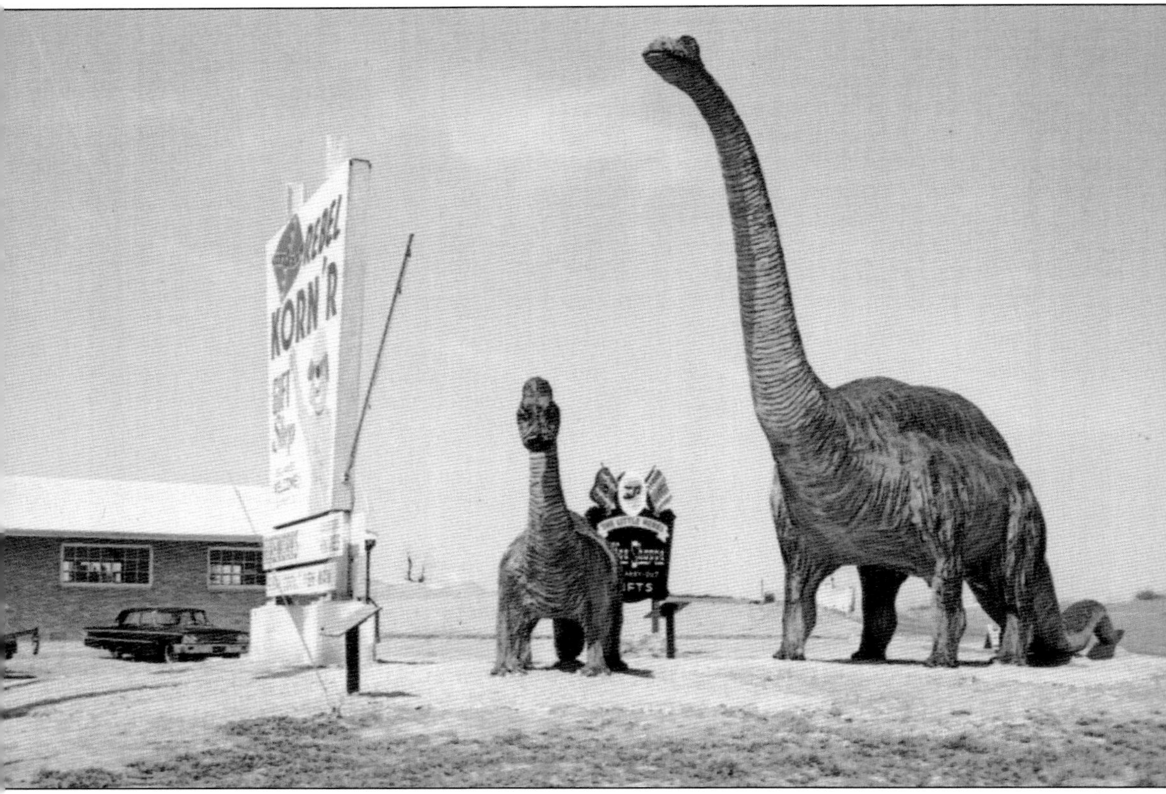

Illustrated on a postcard is Double Tollgate's best-known landmark, Dinosaur Land, an "educational" mini-theme park. Originally known as the Rebel Korn'r, the business opened in the late 1950s and catered to motorists at the junction of Routes 340 and 522—the midpoint between Winchester and Front Royal and on the road to Stephens City. This postcard, taken shortly after opening, shows a mature and baby brontosaurus located out front; a tyrannosaurus rex has since been added. Built in the mid-1960s and a popular location for children's birthday parties, the Dinosaur Land park behind the gift shop contains over 40 replicas of dinosaurs. It is not unusual to pass this busy intersection and see people, both young and old alike, posing with the dinosaurs. The name Double Tollgate dates from the days when both roads were turnpikes. Tolls were collected at the old meeting of the highways, known as Highland Cross Roads, just to the north of the current intersection. (Doug Bartley.)

Ten

Everyday Life

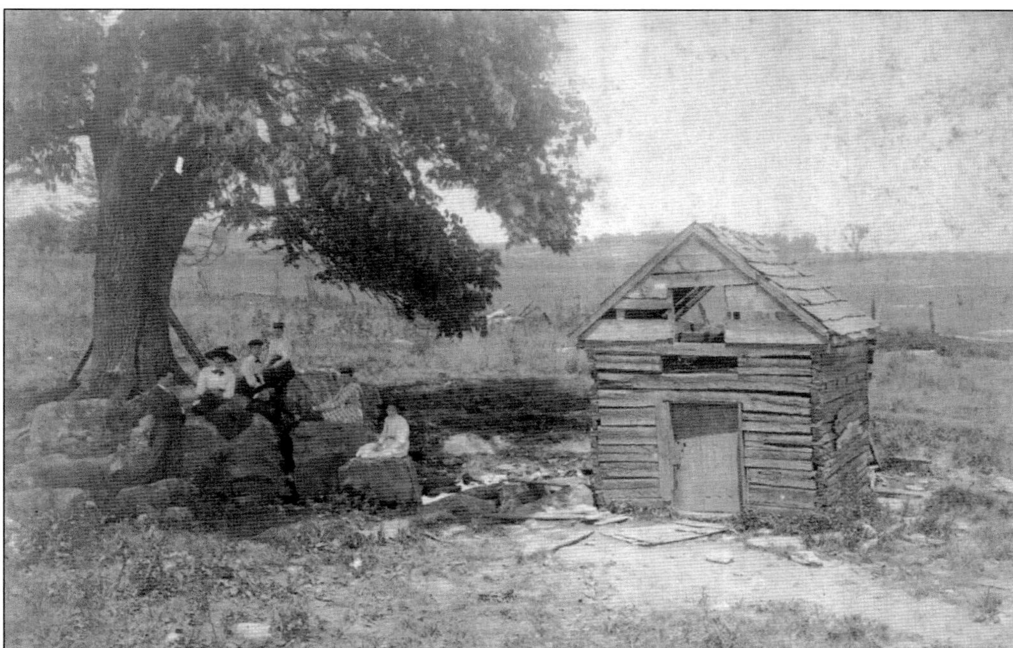

George Washington was said to have slept in the loft of the log springhouse at Soldiers Rest while surveying in the area. This group is posed around 1900 near the hut, a popular 19th-century tourist destination that was even visited by illustrator James E. Taylor in 1864. There are conflicting stories of whether the structure was exhibited at a World's Fair or dismantled and rebuilt as a chicken coop. (CCHA.)

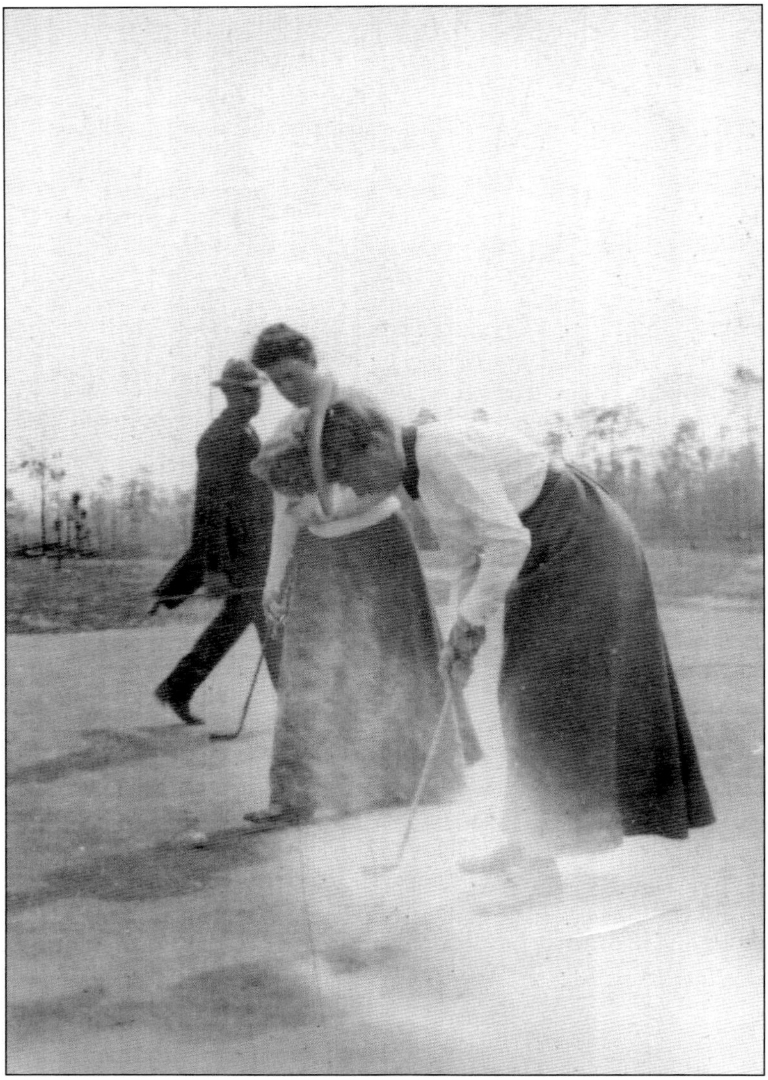

Mary Page and Emily Butler are playing golf in the 1910s with an unidentified man at what is now the Millwood Country Club. The golf course was built on land carved from the Glen and Powhatan properties. The private club features the golf course, a 1920s clubhouse, a swimming pool, and two clay tennis courts. The 54-acre golf course was placed under a protective scenic easement in 2010. (CCHA.)

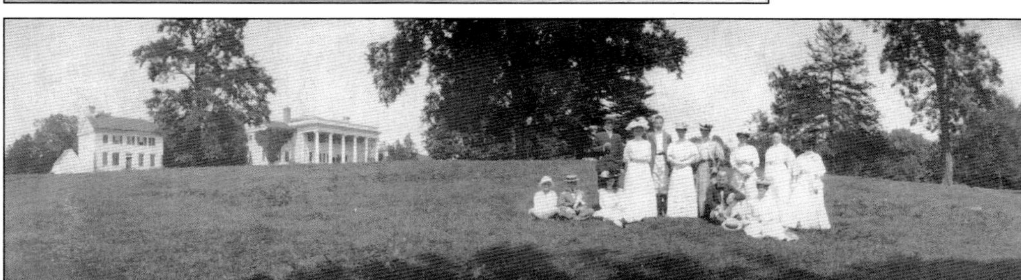

This panorama of the front lawn of Carter Hall documents a 1905 visit by the Smithey family. In October 1862, Gen. Stonewall Jackson headquartered here and used the park-like grounds as a troop camp. Carter Hall was remodeled in the 1930s under the direction of New York architect Harrie Lindeburg, who removed the cupola and the original plaster finish of the stone mansion walls and those of its dependencies. (CCHA.)

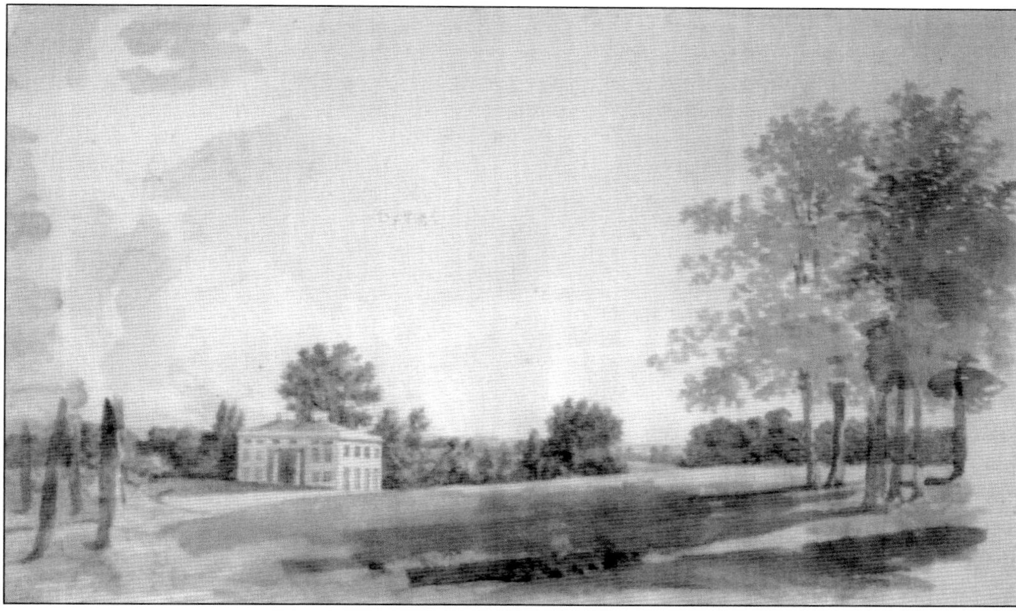

For the design of his home, Long Branch, Capt. Robert Carter Burwell sought assistance from British-born American architect Benjamin Henry Latrobe (best known for his work on the US Capitol building). The Latrobe watercolor above is believed to be a rendering of the house, which was not completed by the time Burwell died in 1813. The porticos, illustrated on the postcard below from about 1900, and elaborate Greek Revival–style interior woodwork were added in the 1840s by Maj. Hugh Mortimer Nelson, a Burwell descendant, using trim from Minard Lafever's pattern book, *The Beauties of Modern Architecture* (1835). Light from the belvedere naturally illuminated the dramatic central curved staircase. The property was purchased in 1986 by a Baltimore textile executive who restored the mansion and established it as a house museum and working farm. (Top, Library of Congress; bottom, CCHA.)

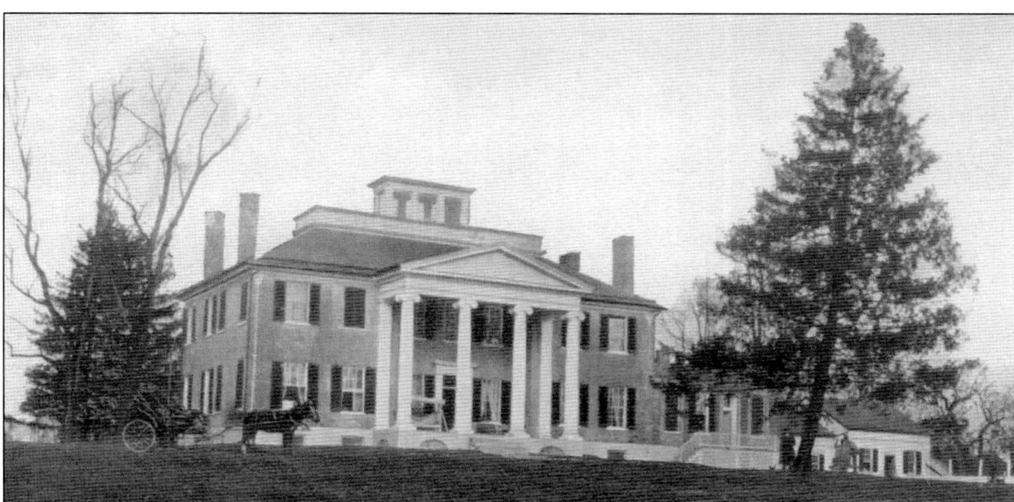

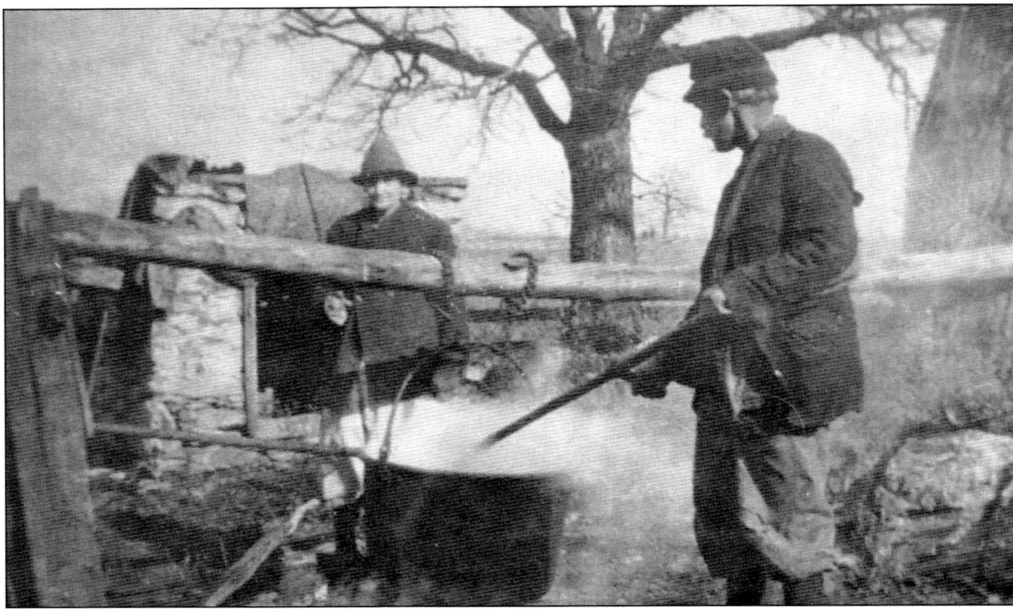

Making apple butter was an annual autumn tradition for many Clarke County families during the early and mid-20th century. In this 1915 photograph, a member of the Huyett family uses a long wooden paddle to stir the large copper-lined pot hung over an open wood fire. Family and friends would gather to take a stir, converse around the kettle, and later share the finished product. (CCHA.)

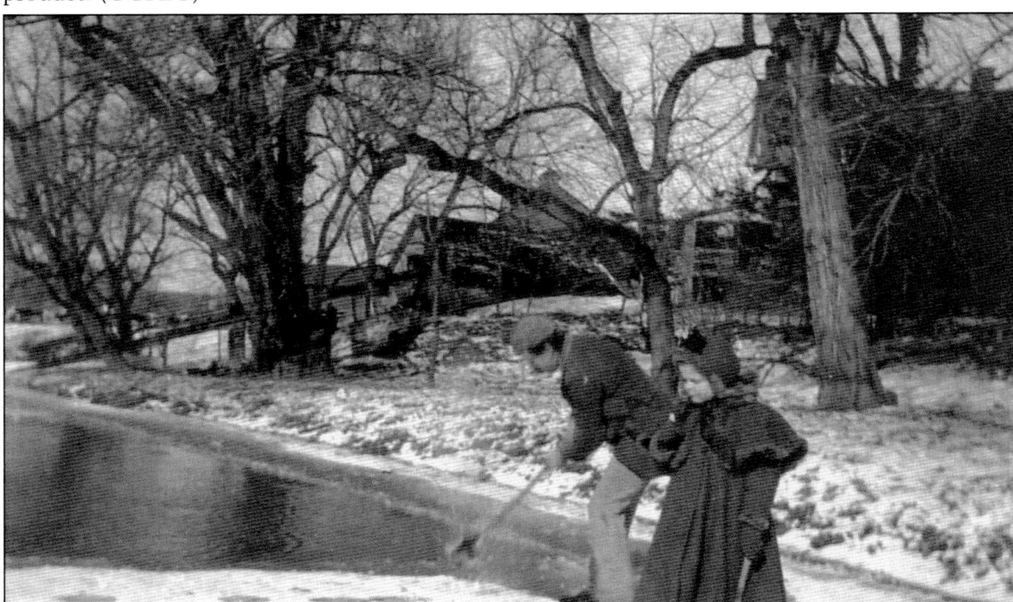

Before the invention of refrigerators and freezers, ice production was a seasonal task that often involved a large group of neighbors. Pictured around 1900, Lewis Pidgeon's daughter watches him cutting ice on the Opequon Creek. During the winter, many would help with the work of cutting and loading ice into the icehouse, where it was stored under sawdust for use the following summer. (SBA/HRL.)

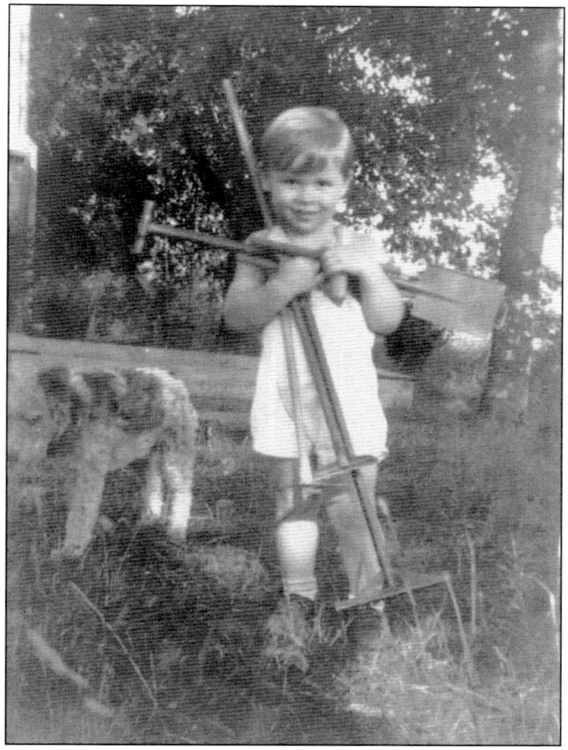

Wilson Lodge Bowles Jr. (right) is carrying his garden tools and is accompanied by his dog at Rockledge, the family farm, around 1940. Children were expected to help with chores such as milking cows, feeding animals, and working the garden. Below, about 1955, youngster Fred Alger is seated on the new family McCormick baler. Standing nearby is his mother, Thelma, and his grandfather E.C. Helvestine. The baler was used to make hay from the grass in the front yard. Pictured in the background is the late-18th-century, two-story house known as both Blakemore and Woodlawn with its side, one-story service wing and large exterior-end stone chimney. (Right, Lyn Bowles; bottom, Fred Alger.)

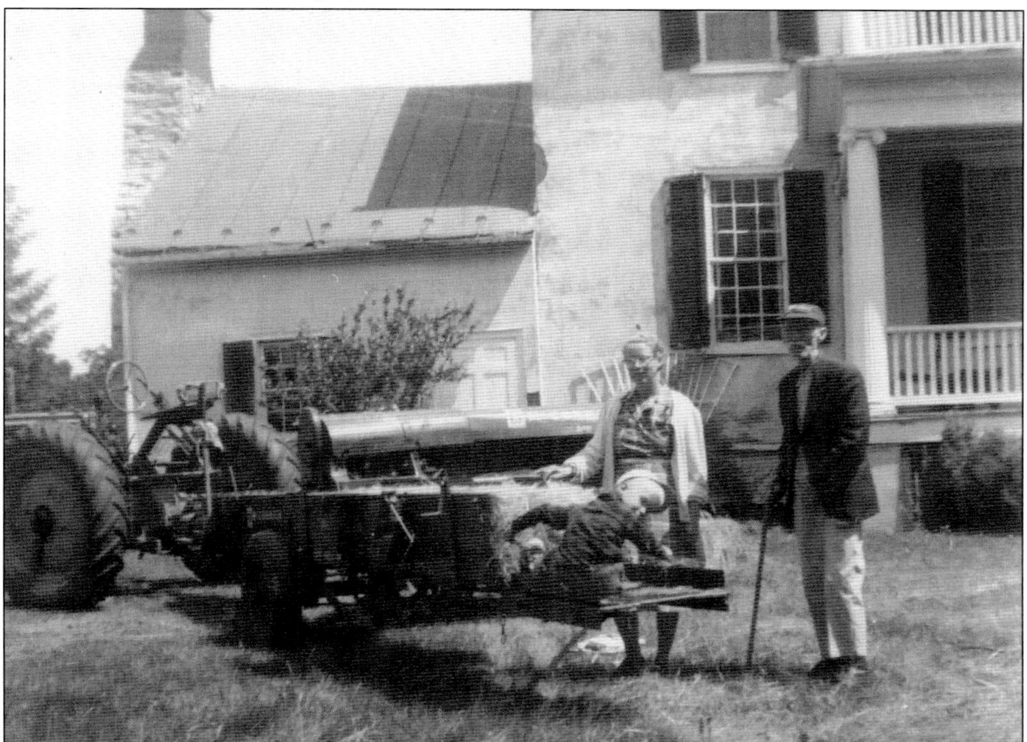

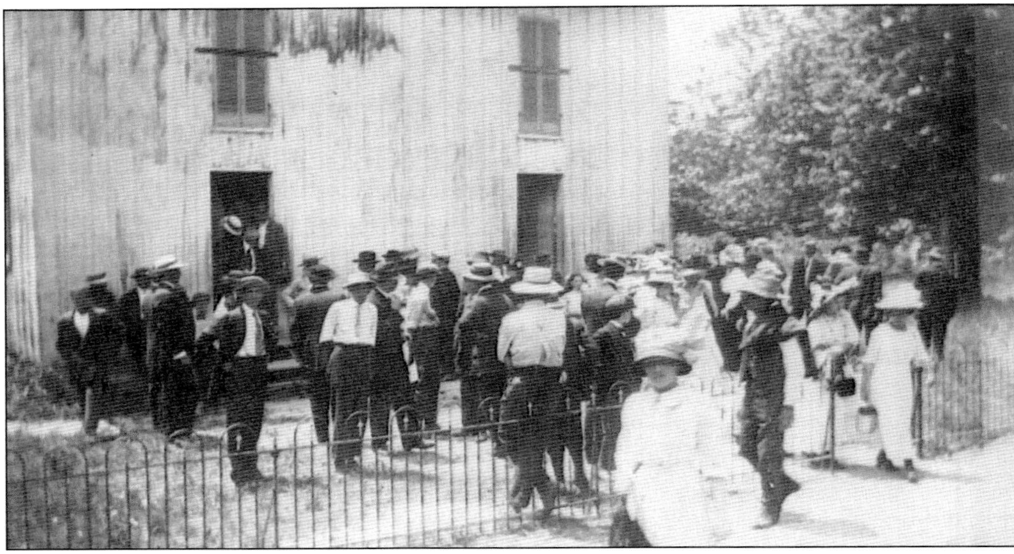

Mountain Baptist Church, located along Frogtown Road on the mountain, was founded in the 1850s. The church was built on land donated by Benjamin and Martha Ann Castleman Morgan. Photographed here around 1910, the frame building is distinguished for its use of board-and-batten wood siding with its overhanging front pediment and two front doors corresponding to the separate entrances for men and women. (CCHA.)

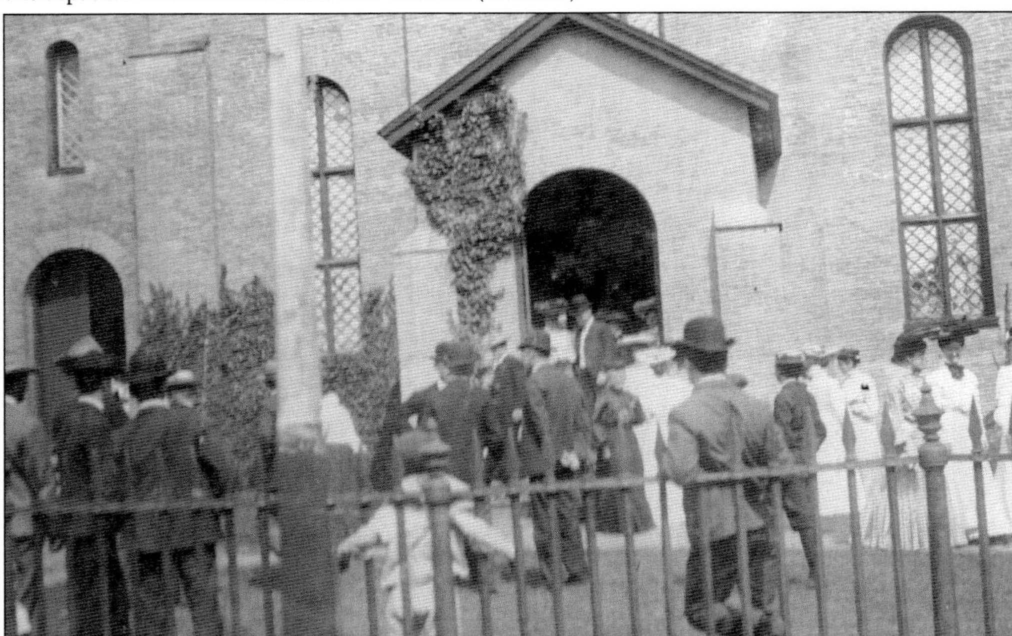

Attending church was a spiritual and social affair greatly anticipated at a time when Sundays were considered a day of rest. This 1910 scene shows church letting out at Grace Episcopal in Berryville. The present building was constructed in 1857 and was remodeled in 1926. From the 1970 to 2002, Grace also served the local Catholics until they built their own church, St. Bridget's Chapel in the Field. (CCHA.)

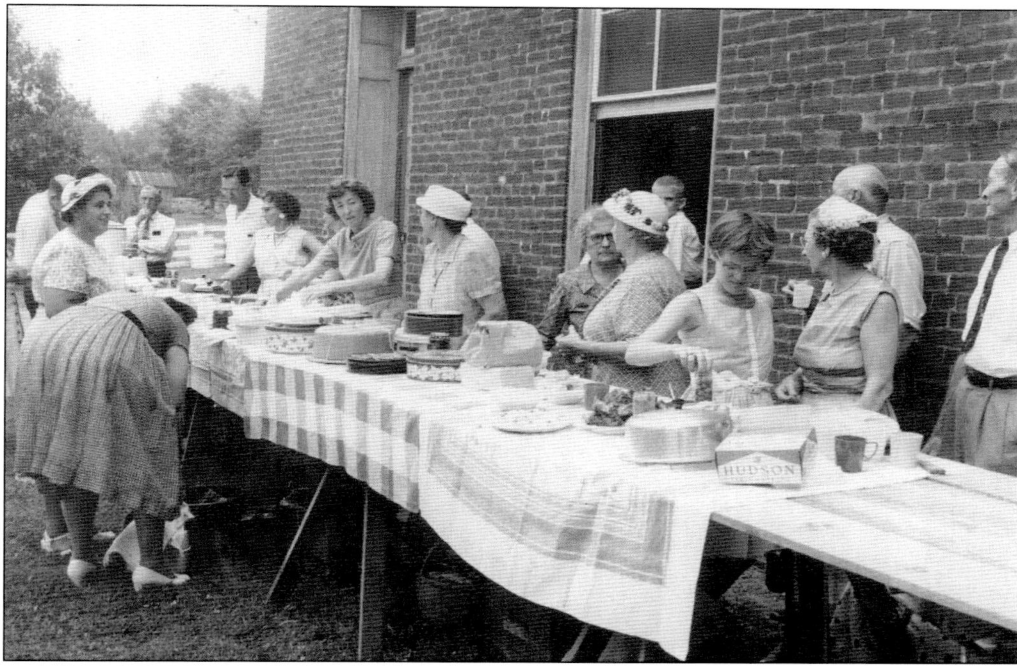

Annual Services with picnics were a common occurrence at many of the local churches, as shown at Old Bethel (above) around 1950 and at Old Salem Regular Baptist Church (below) in 1931. Held during the summertime, these all-day events offered a time for socialization as well as an opportunity for the women to showcase their cooking skills. Frances B. McKay (center with flowered hat) and other churchwomen prepared a memorable lunch at Bethel, an 1830s brick church that McKay's husband, B.B., helped restore in the 1940s. Salem Baptist, constructed around 1802, is one of the county's few stone churches. (Top, *Clarke Courier*; bottom, DeadFred.com.)

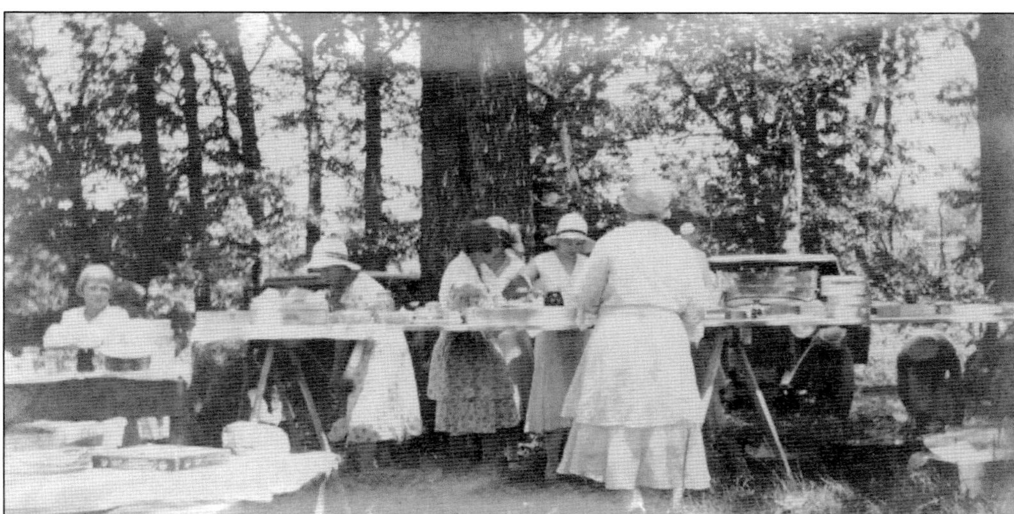

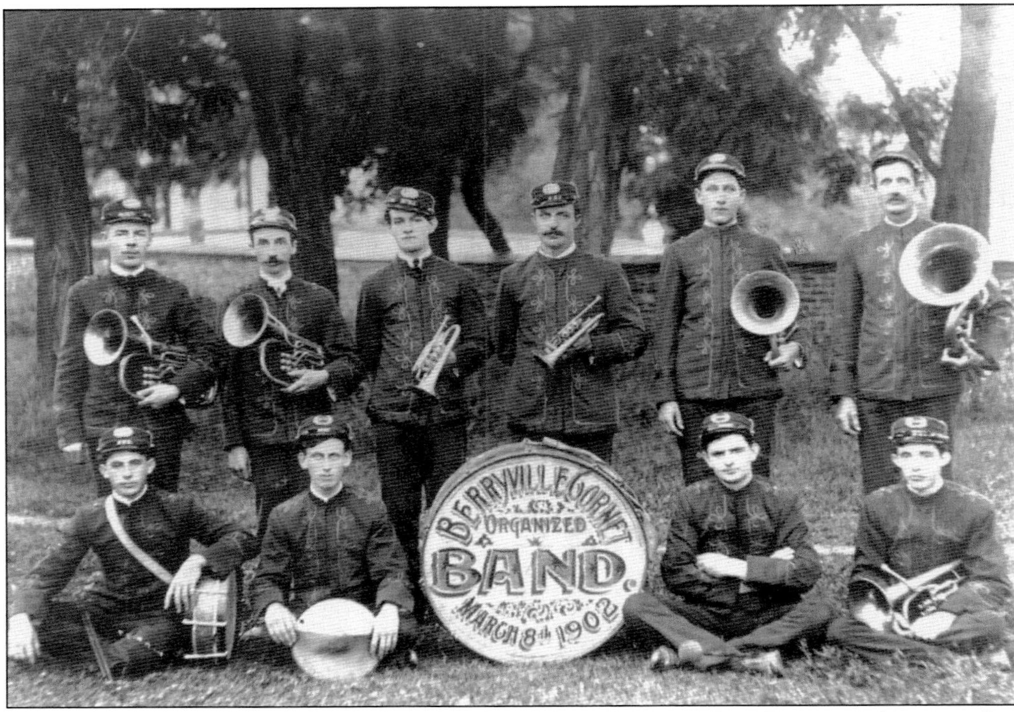

Pictured on the lawn of Grace Episcopal is the Berryville Cornet band, organized on March 8, 1902. Holding their instruments and posed around the bass drum is the 10-man band composed of, from left to right, (first row) Jim Dakeman, Willie Huffman, Preston Kercheval, and Henry Littleton; (second row) Ellis Jackson, Charles Putnam, Herbert Marks, Clayton Young, Charlie Willingham, and Enos Stolle. (CCHA.)

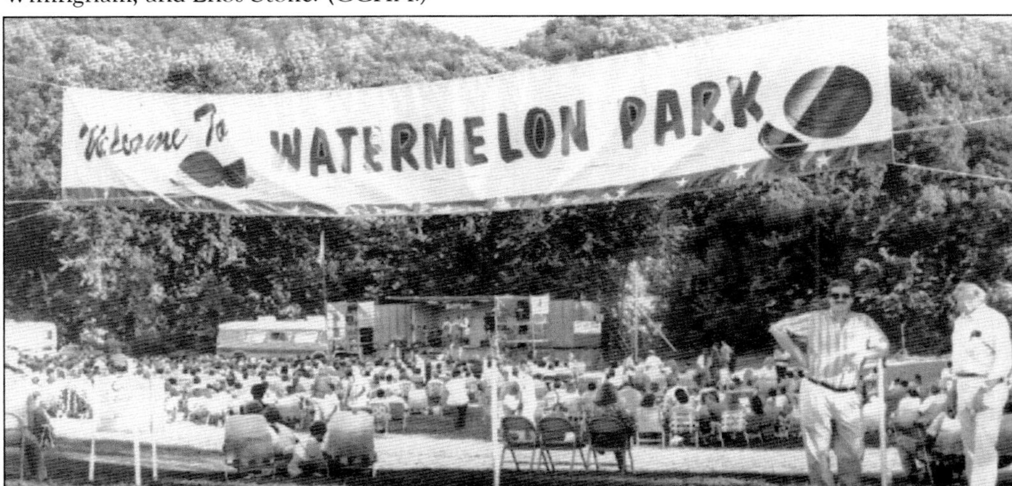

Named for its former use as a watermelon patch, Watermelon Park, pictured in 1993, is located along the Shenandoah River and offers camping as well as recreational access to the Shenandoah. Primarily a family campground and recreation center, the park is also home to the annual Watermelon Park Fest, a Bluegrass festival begun in 1943 as a single-day event and now a hugely successful multi-day affair held each September. (*Clarke Courier.*)

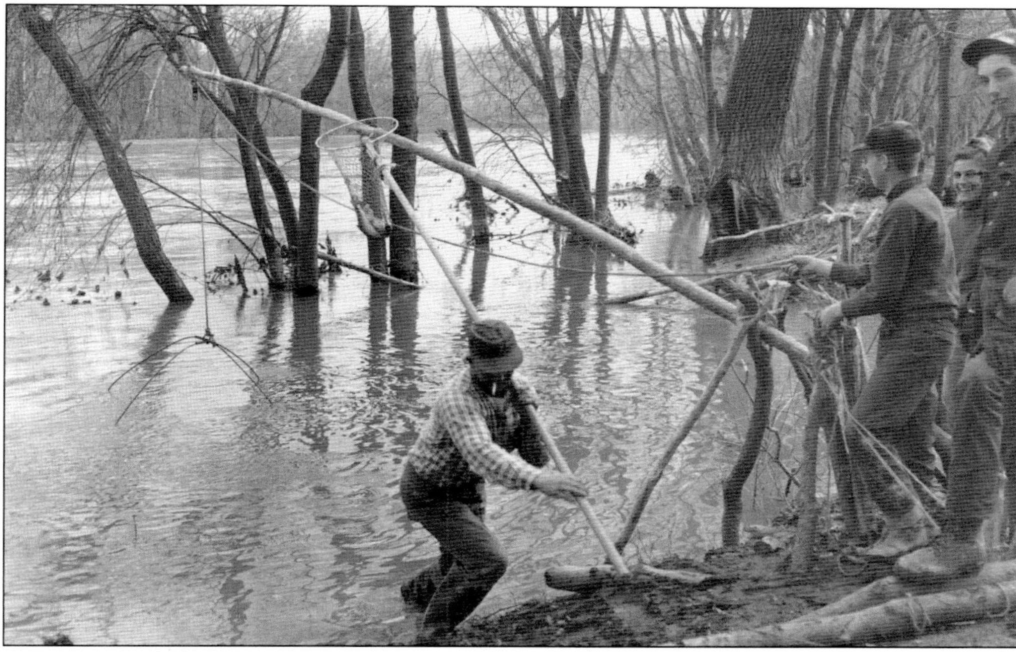

During its early history, the Shenandoah River was primarily a means of transportation and a resource for food. In recent years, it has also become a source of recreation and the water source and sewage output site for Berryville. Above, Sam Pearson, Bill Brown, Jack Ashford, and Margaret Ashford are dipping for suckers along a flooded Shenandoah River in March 1964. A large dip net at the end of a long pole would be lowered into the river using a rope. It would be periodically raised, and the man in waders would venture out and gather the catch, as is evidenced in the net he holds over his shoulder. Pictured below in the 1920s are, from left to right, Anise Lloyd, J.M. Anderson, Lillian Lloyd, and John Lloyd enjoying a day of fishing on the Shenandoah. (Top, *Clarke Courier*; bottom, CCHA.)

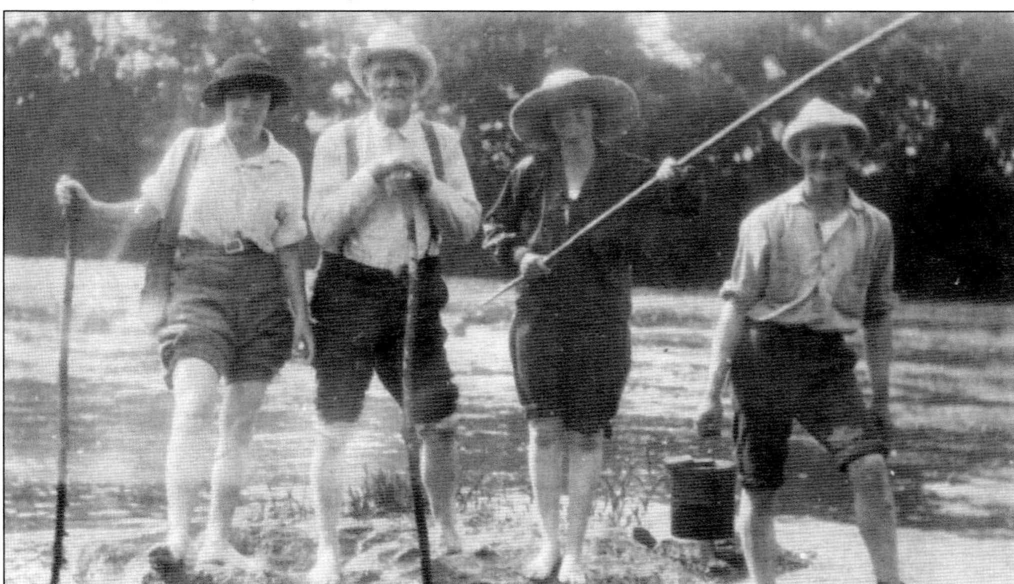

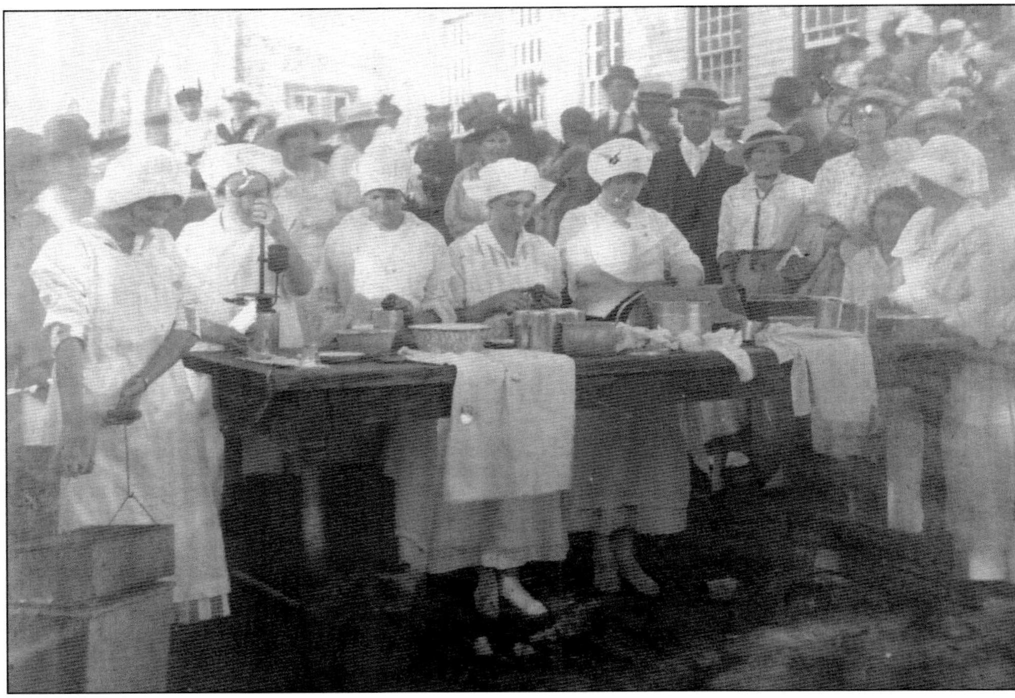

The Tomato Club, which later became part of the 4-H Youth Development Organization, shown in about 1919, is demonstrating how to can tomatoes in front of a large outdoor crowd. Wearing white hats and pinafores, the unidentified young women also took cooking classes in the basement of the old Battletown Inn. (CCHA.)

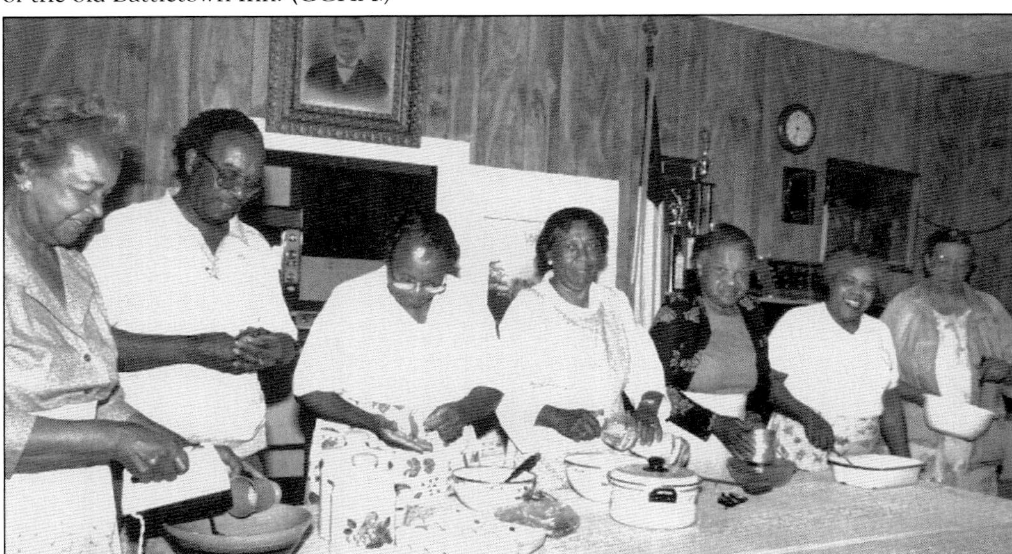

Civic organizations have always played a huge role in Clarke County life. Shown in 1992, members of the Josephine Improvement Association work to prepare for the bake sale at the Berryville Days celebration. From left to right are Florence Paige, Marcellus Harper, Mazie Harper, Rosetta Clay, Annie Brown, Frances Liggins, and Bettie Edwards. (*Clarke Courier.*)

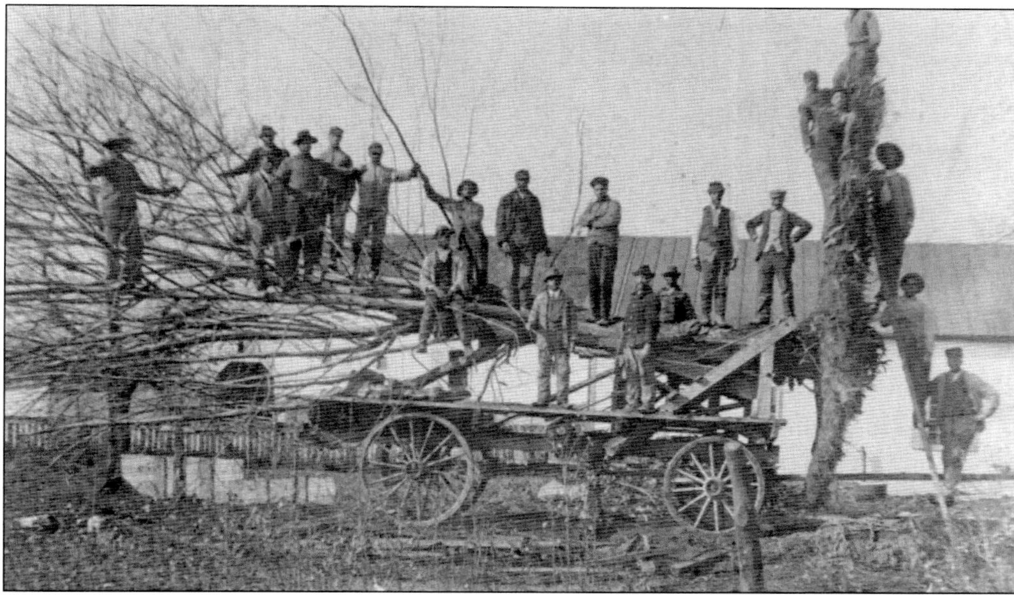

One can only wonder if this tree, which was moved in the early 20th century, lived after it was transplanted. The photograph was taken at Rosemont when it was under Harriman ownership and shows 21 men standing on the tree, complete with shallow root system, as it lay on a wagon supported by wooden scaffolding. (CCHA.)

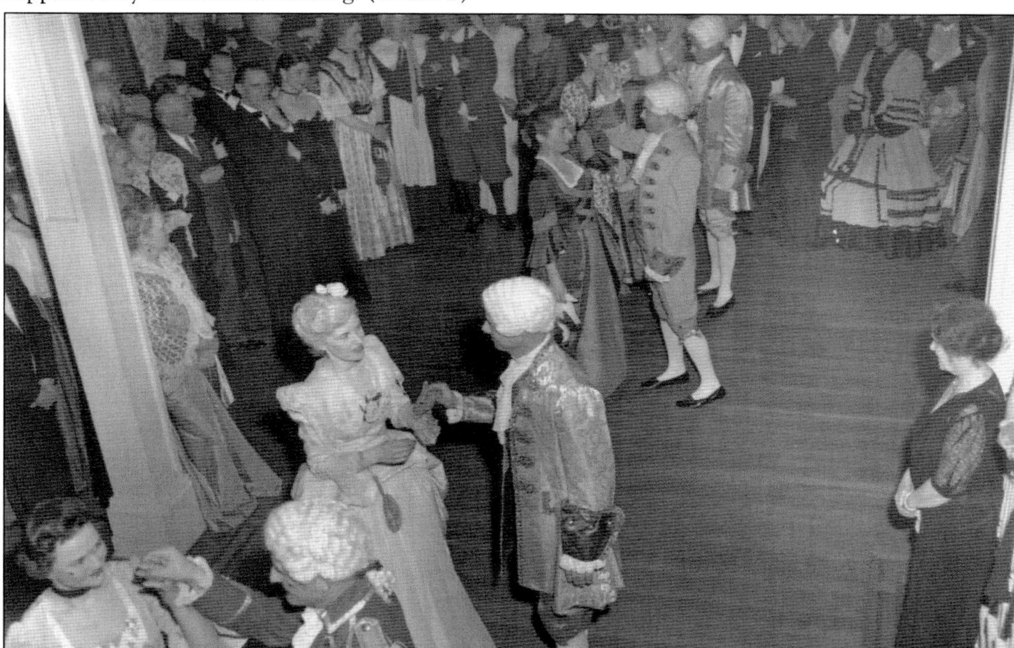

This photograph shows a 1949 fundraiser hosted by Senator Harry F. Byrd Sr. and his wife at their home, Rosemont. The period costume ball, called the Ancestor Ball, was a fundraiser for the Clarke County Historical Association. The tradition of holding lavish events in large Clarke estates is still a popular way of raising money for nonprofit organizations. (CCHA.)

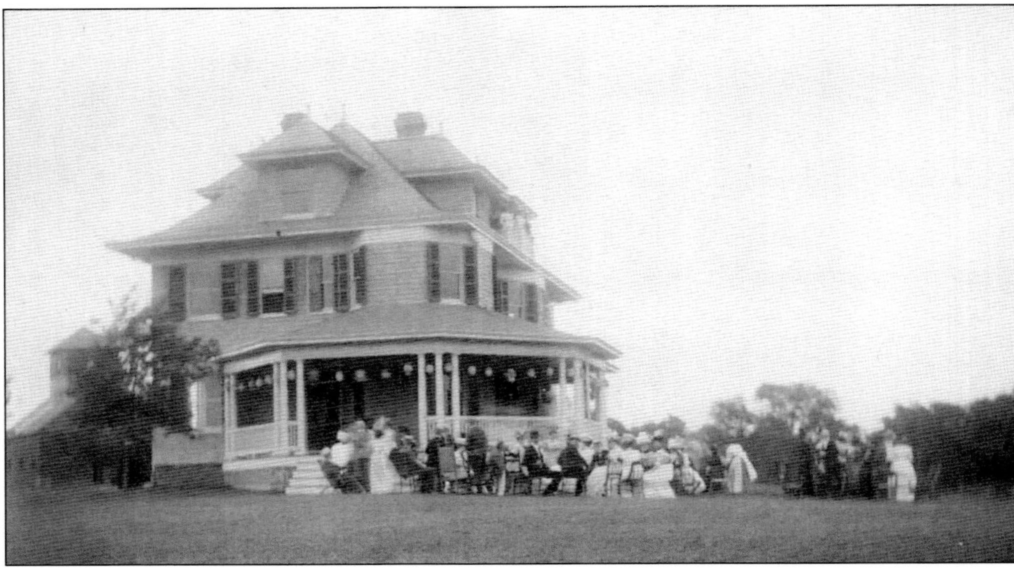

The Knoll is a fine Queen Anne–style frame dwelling located along the north side of Taylor Street between Church and Buckmarsh Streets in Berryville. Constructed about 1895 by Englishman Herbert B. Warde and his Swiss wife, Freda, the house is the perfect backdrop for this 1899 meeting of the Village Improvement Association on the front lawn. Strings of lanterns decorate the porch. (CCHA.)

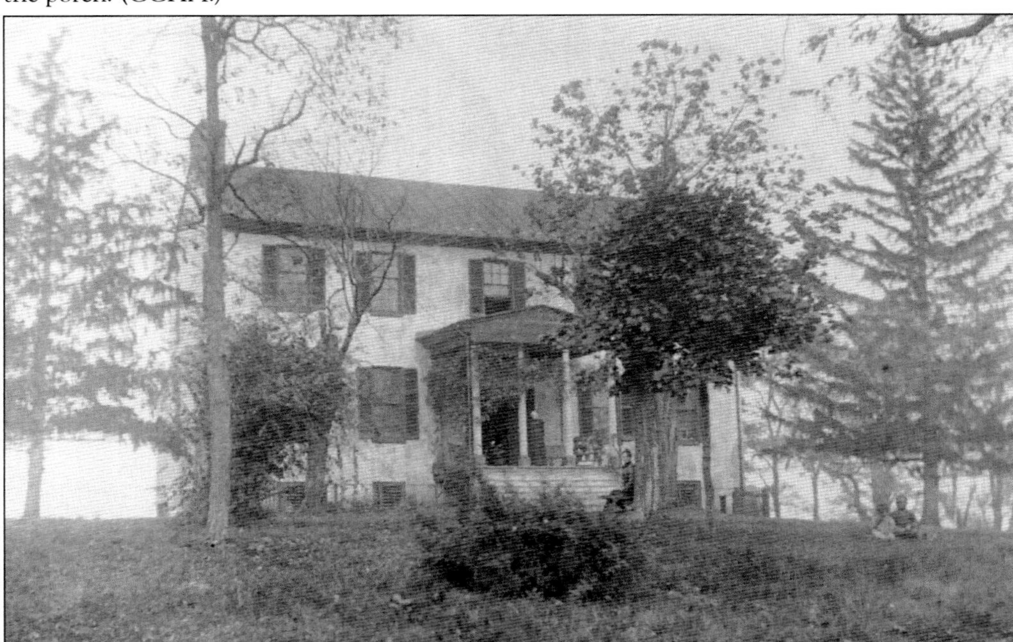

Built about 1816 as a plastered stone house, Clay Hill was doubling as a school when this photograph was taken in 1899. The Clay Hill Academy opened on October 1, 1888; it operated until 1902, reopening for a short time in 1905. W.H. Whiting Jr. was the principal and instructor for this all-boys boarding school, which charged $250 (the equivalent of almost $6,000 today) for the nine-month school year. (CCHA.)

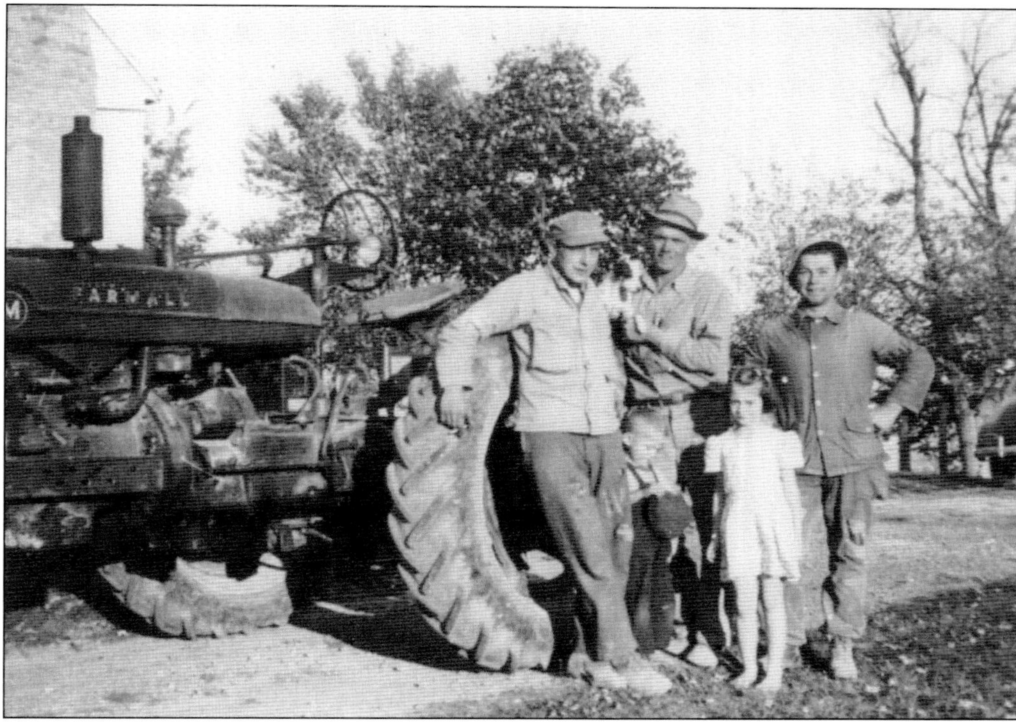

A World War II German prisoner-of-war camp in Winchester provided day laborers to several farmers and businesses in Clarke County. Pictured around 1944 are, from left to right, Erhard Hahn, Monroe Buckley, Buckley's children Sammy and Jane, and Gerhard Kaul. Buckley hired the two men to help with chores at his farm, Edgewood, located near White Post. They stayed in touch even after the POWs were sent back to Germany. (CCHA.)

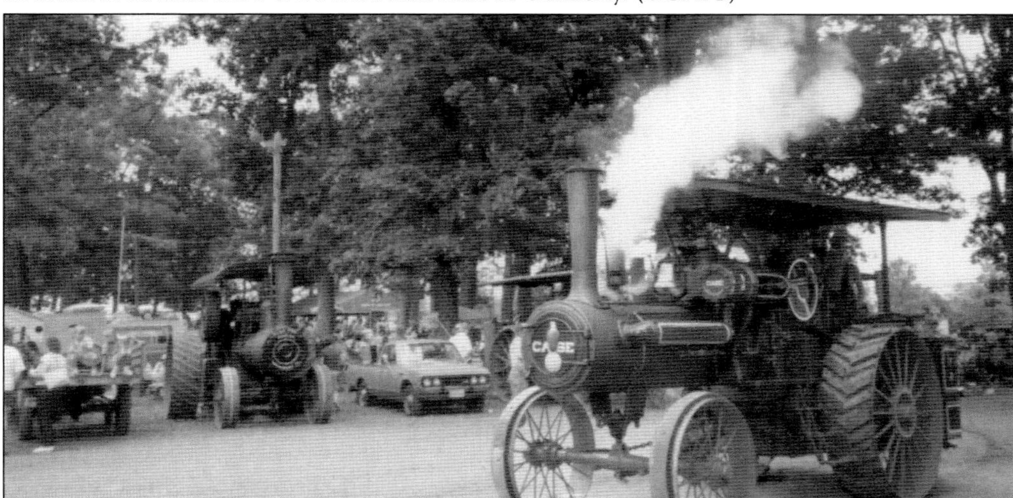

The Shenandoah Valley Steam and Gas Engine Association has staged its annual steam and gas engine show at the Clarke County Ruritan grounds since 1968. Held on the last full weekend in July and drawing large crowds, the affair features antique steam and gas engines mostly associated with farm-related machinery. The picture above was taken at the 1990 show. (CCHA.)

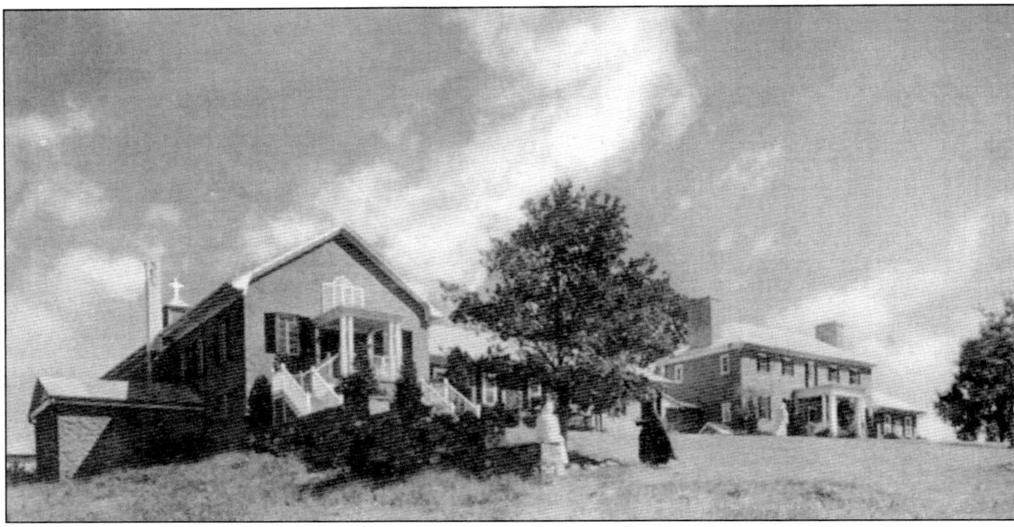

In 1950, the Cistercian Abbey of the Strict Observance, Inc., purchased Cool Spring Farm and several adjoining tracts, totaling nearly 1,000 acres, to establish a monastery. The postcard above shows changes made to the late-18th-century, Georgian-style stone mansion to accommodate the abbey's needs, including the addition of a chapel. Located along the Shenandoah River, the property was the site of the Battle of Cool Spring. Since purchasing the land, Holy Cross Abbey has continued to farm it, and it was placed under protective easement in 2009. In addition to operating a retreat center, Holy Cross has a gift shop that sells books, religious items, and products manufactured by the abbey and other Cisterian-Trappist monasteries. Brother James, who has collected prehistoric and Civil War–era artifacts from the property, is shown helping a customer in the gift shop. (Top, Betty Meade Stuart; bottom, Bonnie Jacobs.)

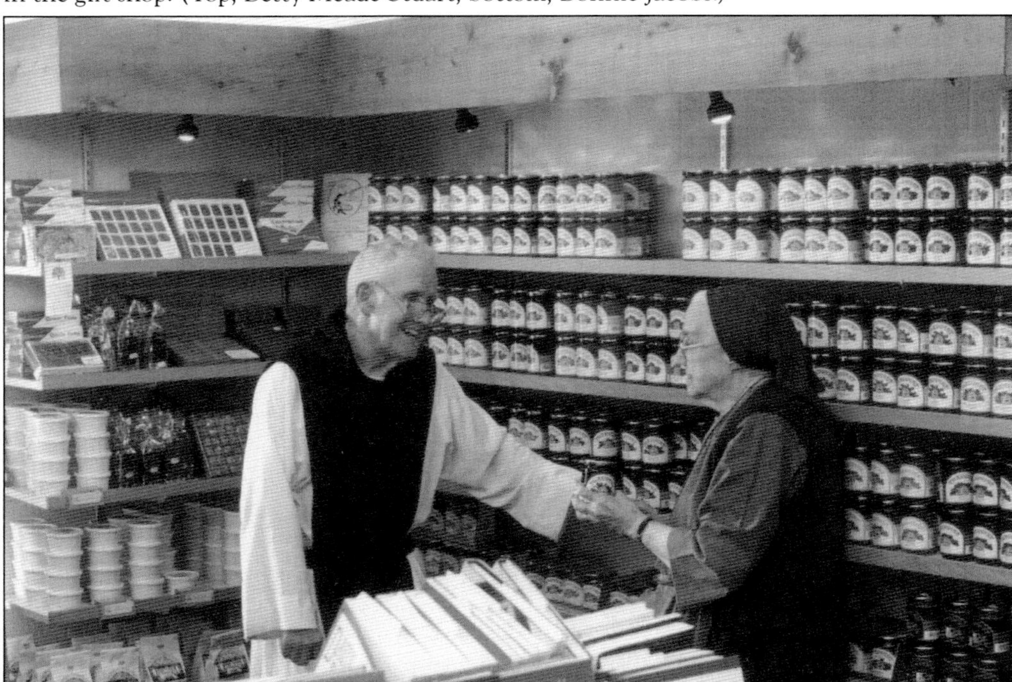

This was a typical 1965 scene in Potter's Barbershop in Berryville. To the left, owner George Potter cuts Iden Mallory's hair, while co-owner John works on an unidentified customer to the right. Their father, George Washington Potter, started the barbershop in the early 1900s. He had seven children, several of whom worked at the shop with him. Although no longer owned by the Potter family, the name of the business was retained. (CCHA.)

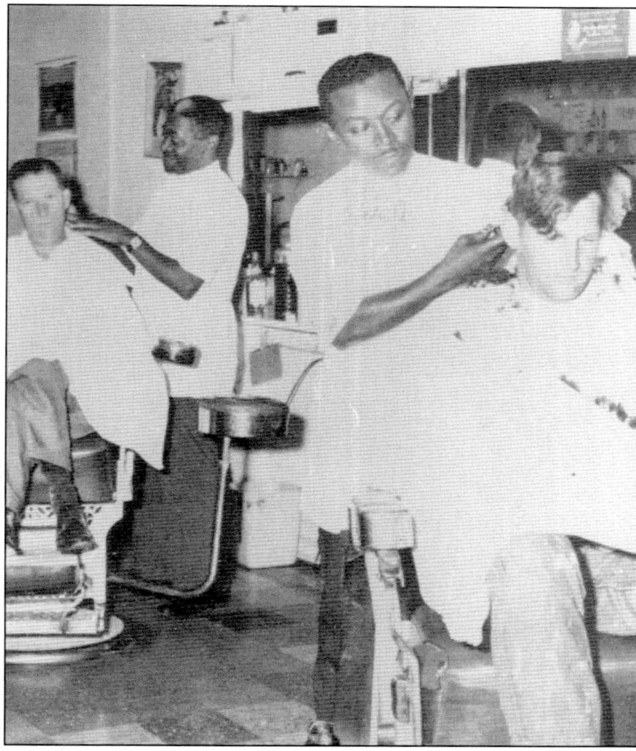

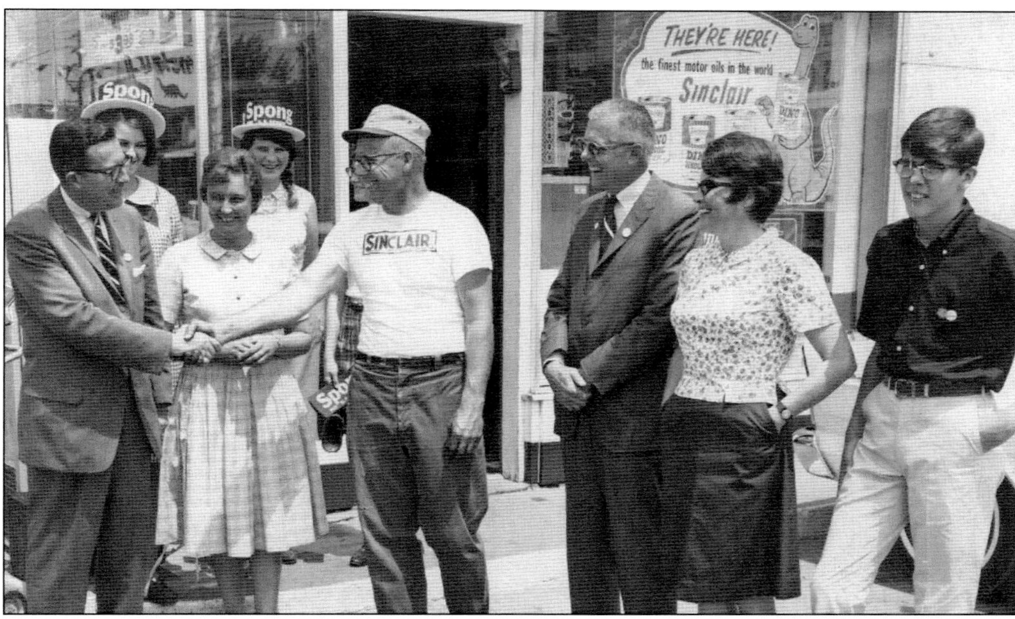

During a 1966 campaign stop, William Spong, Democratic candidate from Virginia for the US Senate, shakes hands with Phillip Kirk in front of Kirk's Servicenter at the northeast corner of Main and Buckmarsh Streets in Berryville. Frances Kirk stands between them, while an unidentified girl (left) and Ann Brown (right) stand behind them. On the right, businessman and community leader John R. Friant, his wife, Nancy, and their son John look on. (CCHA.)

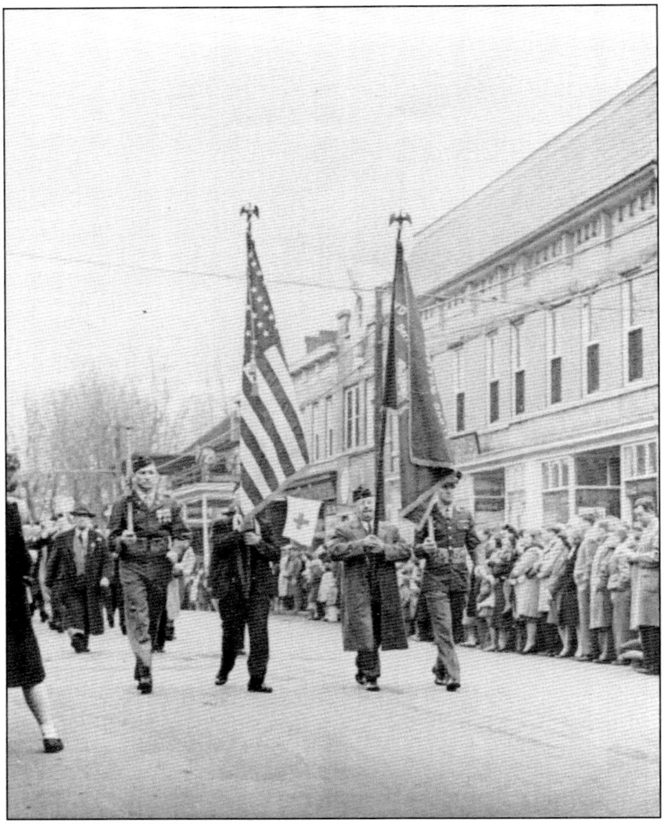

Even today, Berryville's Main Street is an ideal backdrop for old-fashioned community parades. Shown at left is a World War II Victory Loan Parade that occurred on November 11, 1945. The Veteran's Color Guard leads the parade. From left to right are Bill O'Brian, Jim Crim, Herbert Duke Sr., and Pete Reid. On the far right, *Clarke Courier* reporter Kenneth Levi is taking notes. Below is a scene from the US Bicentennial Wagon Train, which passed through Berryville on June 15, 1976. The caravan of wagons had left Texas in January, traveling to Philadelphia for the Fourth of July celebrations. They camped for one night in the Ruritan Fairgrounds at the western edge of town. (Both, CCHA.)

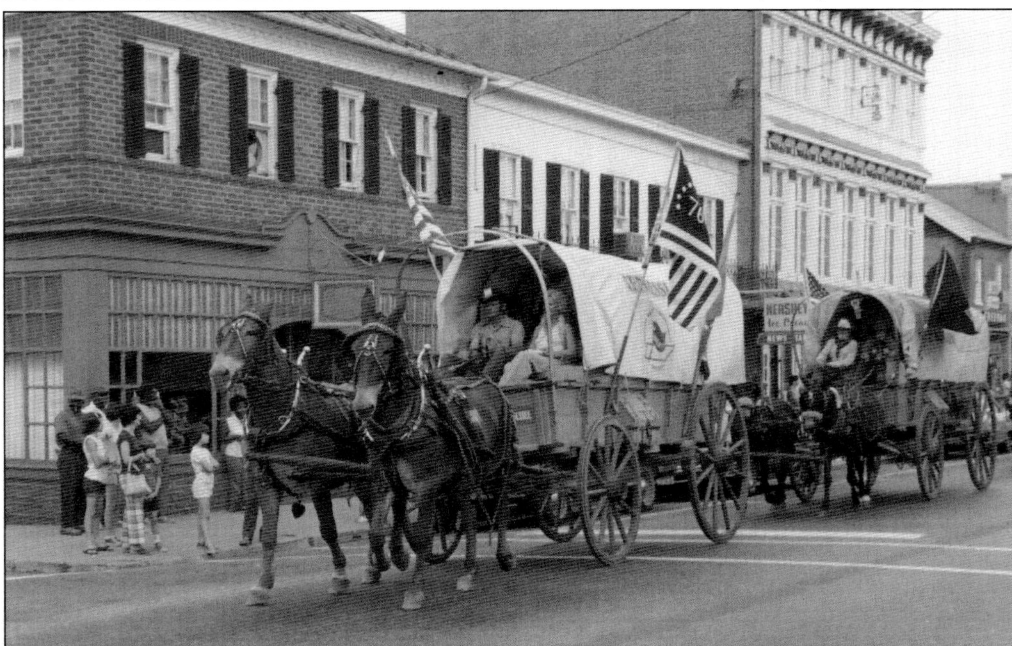

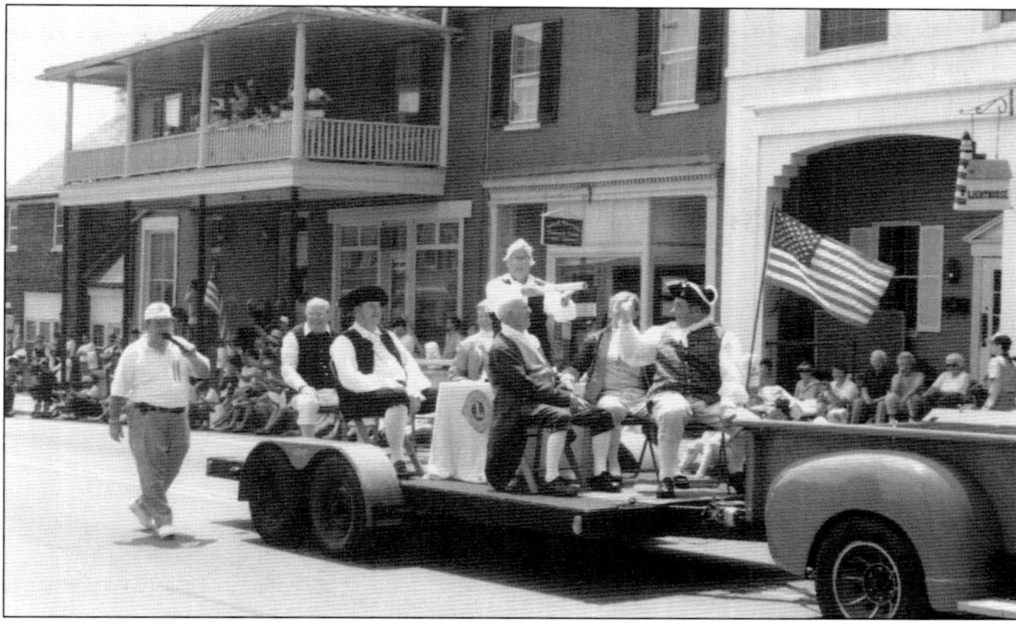

On May 30, 1998, Berryville celebrated the 200th anniversary of its founding. Shown above are men portraying the original Berryville Town Trustees. Announcer Ken Riley stands on the left. Shown in costume are, from left to right, Harold Taylor, Herman Lloyd, John Milleson, Jim Church (standing), Bev Whiting, Fred Curtis, and George McLain. The scene below was taken on the opening day of the yearlong 1986 sesquicentennial celebration of Clarke County's formation. Chairman Billy Thompson and volunteers organized monthly activities at various locations around the county, including parades, tours of historic sites, publications, commissioned art work, and a large celebration at White Post. The banner on the roof of the Goat House, one of the oldest dwellings in the county, reads, "Happy Birthday Clarke County." (Top, *Clarke Courier*; bottom, Bonnie Jacobs.)

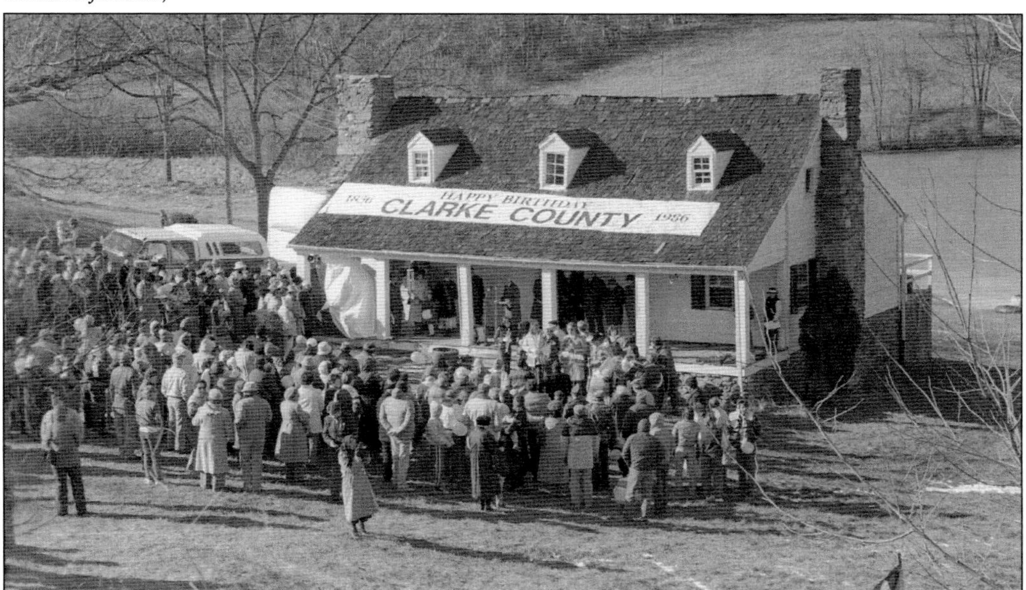

Selected Bibliography

Brown, Stuart Jr. *Annals of Clarke County Virginia: Old Homes, Families, Etcetera of the Southern (South of U.S. Route 50) Section*. Vol. 1. Berryville, VA: Virginia Book Company, 1983.

Brown, Stuart Jr., and Lorraine F. Myers. *Annals of Clarke County Virginia*. Vol. 4. Berryville, VA: Virginia Book Company, 2002.

Farland, Mary Gray, and Beverly Bigelow Byrd. *In the Shadow of the Blue Ridge, Clarke County, 1732–1952*. Richmond: William Byrd Press, 1978.

Gold, Thomas D. *History of Clarke County Virginia, and Its Connection with the War Between the States, with Illustrations of Colonial Homes and of Confederate Officers, with Sketches by H.C. Sommerville, George H. Burwell, George B. Harrison, A. Moore Jr., and M.W. Jones*. Berryville, VA: C.R. Hughes, 1914.

Hofstra, Warren. *A Separate Place. The Formation of Clarke County, Virginia*. White Post, VA: Clarke County Sesquicentennial Committee, 1986.

Kalbian, Maral S. and Leila O. Boyer. *Final Report: African-American Historic Context Clarke County, VA*. Berryville, VA: County of Clarke, 2002.

Kercheval, Samuel. *A History of the Valley of Virginia*. 3rd ed. Woodstock, VA: W.N. Grabill, 1902.

Lloyd, Herman B., ed. *Berryville Celebrates! 1798-1998*. Berryville, VA: Clarke County Historical Association, 1998.

Loth, Calder, ed. *The Virginia Landmarks Register*. 4th ed. Charlottesville: University Press of Virginia, 1999.

Maloy, Deena. *Voices Linger at Old Audley*. Berryville, VA: self-published, 2008.

McKay, Simon B. *Civil War Battle Monuments Clarke County, Virginia*. Berryville, VA: County of Clarke, 2006.

Mitchell, Robert D. *Commercialism and Frontier: Perspectives on the Early Shenandoah Valley*. Charlottesville: University Press of Virginia, 1977.

Myers, Lorraine F., Stuart E. Brown Jr., and Eileen N. Chappel. *Annals of Clarke County, Virginia: Biographical and Genealogical Record of Persons Buried at Old Chapel*. Vol. 2. Berryville, VA: Virginia Book Company, 1987.

———. *Some Old Families of Clarke County, Virginia*. Berryville, VA: Virginia Book Company, 1994.

Norris, J.E., ed. *History of the Lower Shenandoah Valley*. Chicago: A. Warner & Co., 1890.

O'Dell, Cecil. *Pioneers of Old Frederick County, Virginia*. Marceline, MO: Walsworth Publishing Company, 1995.

Proceedings of the Clarke County Historical Association. 25 vols. Berryville, VA: Clarke County Historical Association, 1941–2003.

The Subscribers and Friends of the Blue Ridge Hunt. *Blue Ridge Hunt: The First Hundred Years*. Berryville, VA: The Blue Ridge Press, Inc., 1988.

Taylor, James E. *With Sheridan Up the Shenandoah Valley in 1864*. Cleveland: Western Reserve Historical Society, 1989.
US Department of the Interior National Park Service. National Register of Historic Places Registration Form. Bear's Den Rural Historic District. VDHR file no. 021-5010. Prepared by Maral S. Kalbian and Margaret T. Peters, 2008.
———. National Register of Historic Places Registration Form. Bethel Memorial Church. VDHR file no. 021-0035. Prepared by Maral S. Kalbian, 1989.
———. National Register of Historic Places Registration Form. Blandy Experimental Farm Historic District. VDHR file no. 021-0550. Prepared by Maral S. Kalbian, 1992.
———. National Register of Historic Places Registration Form. Boyce Historic District. VDHR file no. 172-0001. Prepared by Maral S. Kalbian, 2003.
———. National Register of Historic Places Registration Form. Chapel Hill. VDHR file no. 021-0014. Prepared by Maral S. Kalbian and Margaret T. Peters, 2004.
———. National Register of Historic Places Registration Form. Greenway Rural Historic District VDHR file no. 021-0963. Prepared by Maral S. Kalbian, 1993.
———. National Register of Historic Places Registration Form. Josephine City School. VDHR file no. 021-168-5027. Prepared by Maral S. Kalbian, 1994.
———. National Register of Historic Places Registration Form. Long Marsh Run Rural Historic District. VDHR file no. 021-0967. Prepared by Maral S. Kalbian and Daniel Pezzoni, 1996.
———. National Register of Historic Places Registration Form. Millwood Colored School. VDHR file no. 021-0192-0008. Prepared by Maral S. Kalbian, 2000.
———. National Register of Historic Places Registration Form. Millwood Commercial Historic District. VDHR file no. 0021-5009. Prepared by Maral S. Kalbian and Margaret T. Peters, 2005.
———. National Register of Historic Places Registration Form. Springsbury and Lands End. VDHR file nos. 021-0074 and 021-0444. Prepared by Maral S. Kalbian and Margaret T. Peters, 2010.
———. National Register of Historic Places Registration Form. White Post Historic District. VDHR file no. 021-0066. Prepared by Virginia Historic Landmarks Commission Staff, 1983.
Varle, Charles. *Topographic Description of the Counties of Frederick, Berkeley, and Jefferson Situated in the State of Virginia*. Winchester, VA: W. Heiskell Company, 1810.

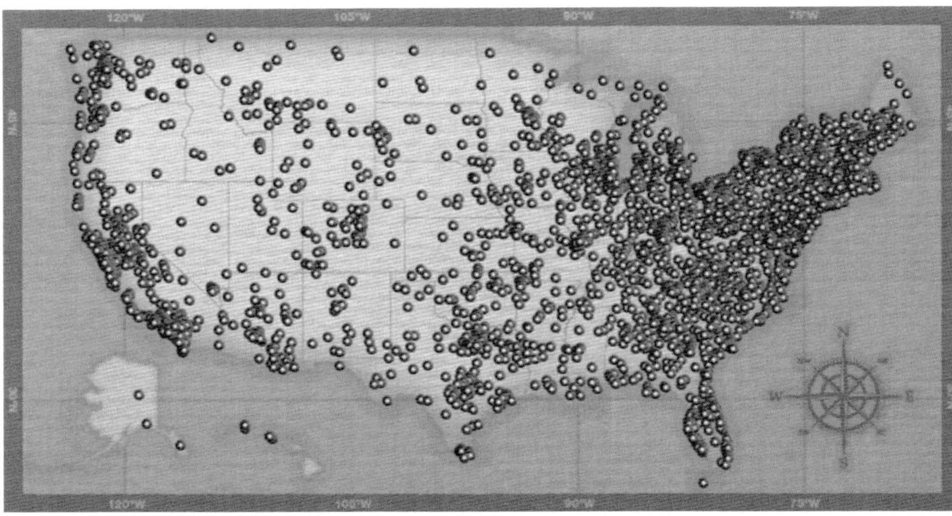